Nov. 1987 7—

THE CHURCH
IN THE
TWENTIETH CENTURY

THE CHURCH IN THE TWENTIETH CENTURY

270.82
Pr 18

ELECT FROM EVERY NATION

PAIDEIA PRESS
St. Catharines, Ontario, Canada

First published in Dutch as *De kerk van alle tijden* by T. Wever of Franeker.
Translated by the author.

ISBN 0-88815-041-5
Printed in the United States of America.

Contents

Introduction

The way

"Show me thy ways," prays Moses at Mount Sinai, "that I may know thee" (Ex. 33:13). And in the New Testament, Christians were briefly referred to as the people of "the way" (Acts 9:2).

What were—and are—the ways of the Lord in the twentieth century? From my study on the ninth floor of an apartment building, I have a good view of a long road and I can clearly see all the traffic and the traffic lights. However, if I come down from my perch and stand right on the street, I become part of the traffic and then I can only see a few fragments of the whirl in which I am immersed. I run the risk of losing my perspective altogether.

The twentieth century, to which we will devote our attention in this volume, is *our* century—imperfect present tense. We walk in its streets, and we see many things that fascinate and frighten us in turn. Who is able to give us an overview of the whole situation, the proper perspective we need in order to understand? Who will give us genuine insight? We need Moses' prayer at every step along the path.

A basic question we should ask is this: Exactly when did our time, which stands out so clearly in contrast to the nineteenth century, begin? Many people point to the year 1914 in answering this question. When the guns of 1914 began to roar, a world full of ideals collapsed. The way of both the church and the world changed so completely that the generation born after 1914 simply could not imagine what life had been like in the pre-war period.

After 1945 we again find people talking about the "pre-war period." Once again there was a distressing crack in the world of human experience. Homesickness or nostalgia was all but gone. "We live in a different world." "That pre-war time will never come back." These were the sort of statements people made to each other constantly. The way of the twentieth century seems to have been broken up repeatedly, almost undermined. It really has been a shocking time, with one apocalyptic scene following the other.

By the year 1900 there was already a general awareness of change.

On January 22, 1901, Queen Victoria of England passed away after a reign which had covered the better part of the nineteenth century (1837-1901). She had been respected, admired and adored;[1] her name had become a symbol—the symbol of the Victorian age.

The English church historian J. R. H. Moorman tells us that during this victorian age the average Englishman paid attention to sermons and Bible reading because it was by such means that a man learned his duty. Duty counted for a great deal in Victorian life and thought, and it was always to be placed before pleasure, which so often led to danger and temptation. Although the standards of decency and respectability began to be challenged toward the end of Queen Victoria's life, a more or less Puritanical style of life was sustained, a style that manifested itself most clearly in the character of the English Sunday.

"With the death of Queen Victoria," writes Moorman, "a new age began. Restraints, taboos and conventions that had been maintained by her strong influence now began to disappear, and life looked very different under the leadership of a man who mixed a good deal with the fast set and enjoyed the pleasures of life.* Yet old habits die slowly, and if there were some who exploited the greater freedom which had been given to them, there were still many of the more conservative temperament who clung to the old ways of life."[2]

Victorianism! In the literature of the twentieth century, we repeatedly come across this expression, usually as a term standing for a mixture of conservatism and Phariseeism. Although this value judgment has been exposed long ago as superficial and inadequate, many people still have the feeling that we can breathe much more easily in the twentieth century, that we live in a more liberal atmosphere. It has been noted by scholars that the church and Christianity suddenly seem to be absent in the novels written at the beginning of the twentieth century,[3] which would seem to indicate the end of one era and the beginning of another. It is the end of the way of the nineteenth century,

---

*This is a reference to Victoria's son and successor, Edward VII (1901-1910).

marked by a greater emphasis on man and machine and on nature and evolution than on Creator and creation or sin and grace. And it is the beginning of the way of the twentieth century, in which some men would finally begin to speak openly of the absence of God.

Initially, however, an optimistic mood prevailed. In the winter of 1899-1900, Adolf von Harnack delivered his lectures in Berlin on the essence of Christianity.[4] He talked about the Christianity of the undogmatic cultural man of his time; the supernatural was gone, to be replaced by the expectation of a kingdom in which God was the Father of all men and all men were brothers. In America, too, a similar expectation of the kingdom gained the upper hand in the preaching of the so-called social gospel. Missionaries in India and China talked more about a Christ who would change the cultural structures of society than a Christ who was crucified for our sins. In spite of the many unmitigated needs, the beginning of the twentieth century seemed to be the gateway to a coming realm of peace, freedom and justice, which is exactly how many people conceived of it.

Shattered illusions

It was an ironic state of affairs; at the same time that a congress of Christian socialists was meeting in Basel to discuss "Christianity and universal peace," the city of Paris found itself under the fire of German guns after a rapid advance by the German troops (August 1914). No "right-minded" man had counted on such a thing. What were people to think of those "right-minded" men from then on?

Over the next four years, 1565 million of the 1700 million inhabitants of our planet were drawn into the great conflict. The war was waged in a horrible manner. Warplanes, submarines, tanks and poison gas all began to play their part, and after the war came hunger and pestilence. In 1918, 22 million people died of the Spanish flu, which claimed more victims than all the battlefields put together.[5]

The problem of war was placed on the agenda of many meetings. In any discussion, it became the problem of man, for it was man who was responsible for the great war.

In 1918 one could hear such slogans as "Never again!" and "No more war!" Many people showed their aversion to militarism by wearing the insignia of the broken rifle. Even so, these efforts could not prevent the continued pulverizing of the image of man erected in the nineteenth century. There were unheard-of atrocities in both Communist Russia and Nazi Germany. The Western world increasingly exemplified what happens to men in "times of stress"; they become "lovers of pleasure rather than lovers of God" (II Tim. 3).

The second world war, in which some 22 million people perished (not including the six million Jews killed in Hitler's concentration camps and gas ovens), surpassed the first one in extent and horror. The ensuing "cold war" was a period of ever-present danger. Because of the continuing possibility of a new conflict, the word *Armageddon* was used repeatedly. What could one expect from even the most highly esteemed of men as they met in the League of Nations and later in the United Nations? Was the apostle Paul right after all in quoting the words of the Old Testament: "No one does good, not even one"?

The rejection of idealism

Even before the catastrophic events of the twentieth century, the idealism of the nineteenth century had been attacked unsparingly.* This idealism had built up enormous systems and had led people to dream exalted dreams; at the same time, it had often removed them a long, long way from concrete reality. The accusation made by Brillenburg Wurth is worth noting: "Is it not shocking that in the heyday of German idealism, the immeasurable misery of the working-class proletariat that resulted from the 'industrial revolution' was not noticed by the great leading minds of those days?"[6]

Theologically speaking, the idealism of the nineteenth century had never recognized, with fear and trembling, the reality of the living God. It had never experienced man's essential human need in his guilt against the Holy One.

At the end of the nineteenth century, the man who tried to terminate the supremacy of intellectual order and moral harmony was the German philosopher *Friedrich Nietzsche* (1844-1900). In no uncertain terms, Nietzsche broke away from both liberal and orthodox Christianity, claiming that the gods of the philosophers were dead, as was the God of the Christians. Instead Nietzsche said yes to a life that recognizes neither sense nor principles. Nietzsche's philosophy is a

---

*I am not using the term *idealism* in the everyday sense of an attitude to life, the attitude of a cheerful man who likes to be guided by higher ideals or glad expectations. I am using it in a more narrowly philosophical sense. Idealism is the philosophy that claims man is not related in the first place to the empirical, objectively existing world but to the world of thought as imagined and ordered by himself. The philosopher Kant and the theologian Schleiermacher both represented and promoted the idealist way of thinking, each in his own way.

philosophy of *life*, the instinctive, irrational, exuberant life that submerges the dikes of the Christian slave morality and opens the way for the antichrist, the blond beast of the future.

Nietzsche wrote no systematic works but spoke in aphorisms and in the language of a violent prophet. He had only a small influence during his own life, but his influence grew as the twentieth century progressed. It has been said that during the first world war, thousands of German soldiers had two books in their knapsack: the New Testament and Nietzsche's *Also sprach Zarathustra*.[7]

In a less revolutionary manner, the refined French philosopher *Henri Bergson* (1859-1941) opposed the supreme power of human reason. He became the father of *vitalism*, the philosophy that maintains we will never be able to penetrate to the essential nature of things by logical analysis and reasoning. Instead, *intuition*, our immediate insight and perception must show us the way.

Bergson exercised a great influence on the culture, art and literature of his time, as well as an indirect influence on theology. Theology was influenced much more decisively by certain other philosophers who wholeheartedly opposed the carefully-constructed systems of the nineteenth century. These were the *existentialists*. Prominent among them were the German thinker *Martin Heidegger* and the French thinker *Jean-Paul Sartre*. These philosophers could almost be called the most consistent pessimists of the twentieth century—almost, but not quite. Their thought takes an unexpected twist when they introduce the element of heroism, of proud personal affirmation of man's fateful existence. The existence of man, they tell us, is a being-thrown-into, a being doomed to an anxious and disconsolate existence. The man who lives existentially accepts this existence; he does not color it with fantasies of his own devising but stands straight on his feet.

S. J. Popma writes: "The existentialistic view of life regards man as wandering aimlessly across the dark crust of the earth under a dark heaven. He knows that he has been thrown there, but he refuses to kneel. He is too proud to look for protection and safety, too sober to devise illusions, and too aristocratic to perish in despair. The passion of life moves through his veins; danger and risk is the climate in which he lives."[8]

Surprisingly, there have also been *Christian existentialists*. The French thinker *Gabriel Marcel*, who became a Roman Catholic in the course of his career as a philosopher, comes to mind. Marcel was an existentialist because in contrast to Descartes, he adopted *being* rather than *thinking* as his starting point. In contrast with the atheistic existentialists (e.g. Heidegger and Sartre), he viewed man's total existence as related to God; God willed such an existence for man. Despite all mystery, we should retain our confidence in Him. The symbol of true human freedom is not the pride of a titan but the humility of a child.

Until the first world war, there was a theological idealism in Europe that amounted to little more than a humanism with a Christian coloring. New thinkers conceived and born in this existentialistic way of thinking now opposed this theological idealism. These thinkers became known as theologians of *crisis* or *dialectical* theologians. The most prominent among them was *Karl Barth*. Also worthy of mention are *Eduard Thurneysen* and *Emil Brunner*; in the Netherlands, *K.H. Miskotte* and *G. C. van Niftrik*; and in America, *Reinhold Niebuhr*. All these theologians, along with many others, played a part in the great changes of the twentieth century. I will discuss their theology more fully later in the book.

For the present I will point out only that this theology is in agreement with the vitalists and existentialists mentioned earlier; God and the divine cannot be caught in our rational and systematic net. God is the Wholly Other, and any contact with Him throws man and the world into a crisis, into judgment. Revelation is a human impossibility; we can never possess revelation or have it at our disposal. Jesus did the impossible when He revealed the hidden God. Exactly for that reason, the gospel is a stumbling block and a folly.

This theology did battle with the shallow, optimistic liberalism that had been fashionable in many quarters. Therefore it was considered by many to represent a return to the old orthodox position. But this conclusion was repudiated by such men as *G. C. Berkouwer* and *Klaas Schilder* in the Netherlands, and *Cornelius Van Til* in America.

A sustained antithesis

An invisible line of partition ran through all the churches. I am not referring to the old antagonism between the Roman Catholic Church (which can here be grouped with the Eastern Orthodox churches) on the one side and the Protestant churches on the other. Rather, the gap I have in mind is the continuing gap between so-called old Protestantism and new Protestantism, or between orthodoxy and liberalism.

In the twentieth century, there were more churches or communities calling themselves churches than ever before. In his "Religious Holland" ("Godsdienstig Nederland") of 1928, L. Knappert mentioned the Roman Catholic Church, the Old Catholic Church and the Free Catholic Church. In 1973 a booklet entitled *Tien keer gereformeerd* (Ten Times Reformed) was published in the Netherlands, in which ministers representing different patterns of thought and various denominations of Reformed origin explained their positions.

Anyone who is looking for the Presbyterian church in the United States must keep his eyes wide open, for he must choose between the "Presbyterian Church in the U.S.A.," the "Presbyterian Church in the United States," the "United Presbyterian Church," the "Orthodox Presbyterian Church," and the "Bible Presbyterian Church," to mention only a few. Similar observations could be made concerning all the major denominational groups—Baptists, Methodists, Lutherans and so forth. In a detailed work on the small sects in America we come across the staggering news that there are some 400 different religious denominations in the United States.[9]

Different points of view have been voiced with regard to this multitude of churches and church-like communities. Until recent times the Roman Catholic Church considered the Reformation a revolution, and the Mennonites in Switzerland still do not have the official status of a church.

Albert Barnes, a Presbyterian minister and the author of a widely used Bible commentary, expresses a contrasting point of view: "The spirit of this land is, that the Church of Christ is not under the Episcopal form, or the Baptist, the Methodist, the Presbyterian, or the Congregational form exclusively; all are, to all intents and purposes, to be recognized as parts of the one holy catholic church."[10] This opinion, which was stimulated by the regular interdenominational revivals, was distinctively American, although it was not shared by the millions of Roman Catholics and Lutherans who immigrated to the United States in the course of the nineteenth and twentieth centuries.

Another view that has been voiced is one of *moderate pluriformity*, the idea that the plurality of churches could be explained by the creation of unique nations, each with its own character and way of life molded in the course of history, and also by the disturbing and devastating influence of sin.[11] Finally, in the twentieth century we come across the very widely accepted idea that the various divisions of the churches are nothing more or less than stumbling blocks—a scandal, a sin. I will have more to say about this point of view in the next section.

All these considerations could not alter two basic facts, however. In the first place, there was the undeniable plurality of churches. In the second place, there was the line of partition running through many of these churches, the antithesis between Biblical, theocentric, Christ-believing Christianity on the one hand and critical, humanistic, horizontalistic Christianity on the other.*

There is mutual recognition evident here. A liberal in one church thinks and speaks in much the same way as a liberal in another church. Evangelical Christians of different ecclesiastical origins are likewise aware that they are united in confessing their Lord as put to death for their trespasses and raised for their justification.

People in the Dutch Reformed *(Hervormd)* Church knew very well how to distinguish between orthodox and liberal preaching. Members of many American churches knew just what they were doing when they chose between "Fundamentalism" and "liberalism." Even in the Roman Catholic Church there was a parting of the ways—at least in the first half of the century—in connection with the papal condemnation of "modernism."

Although all the main points of Christian doctrine, even the total apostolic creed, were at stake, the real bone of contention was always something basic. The real issue was whether or not to accept the Scriptures without reservation as the revealed Word of God.

The historical-critical approach of the nineteenth century might be replaced by form-criticism, and this might in turn be succeeded by the demythologizing of the Bible. The heart of the matter, however, was that modern man, for various reasons, was convinced that he could no longer accept the contents of divine revelation as they were written down. Therefore he tried to bring them up to date in a scientific manner, adding to them or taking away from them (see Rev. 22:18-19).

I might add that the so-called evangelical liberals (Dutch: *rechtsmodernen*), disenchanted by the coldness of old modernism, drew

---

*Here I am using the term *Christianity* in its broadest sense, that is, as applying to all who call themselves Christians.

closer to orthodoxy. On the other hand, the so-called neo-orthodox theologians accepted criticism of Scripture either in part or totally.*

The drive for unity

Our age has often been called the ecumenical era. Early in our century the term *ecumenical* still needed explanation; now, however, it is widely understood because it has come into frequent use.

In the eyes of many, this term is directly associated with the World Council of Churches. The World Council has a long pedigree (about which I will say more later). It first saw the light of life, with much acclaim, in Amsterdam on August 23, 1948. There were delegates from 147 churches, representing 44 countries. The following statement was accepted as the Council's basis: "The World Council of Churches is a fellowship of churches which accept our Lord Jesus Christ as God and Savior."

This basis, however, should not be interpreted or applied as a confessional standard. In an official document we read: "The basis is no confession, no more than the World Council is a church."[12] When the "Remonstrantse Broederschap" (Arminian Brotherhood) in the Netherlands objected to the use of the word *God* in the basis and proposed to substitute the word *Lord*, it was told that the Council left the interpretation of the words in the basis to the participating churches.[13]

A basis is liable to diverse interpretations, and it could hardly be otherwise. What, then, was the *Leitmotiv*, the leading theme of the World Council of Churches?

In essence ecclesiastical disunity is sin, and we may not acquiesce in this sin for even one day or hour. Therefore unity between all the churches should be promoted by all possible means.

Repeatedly the prayer of Christ was quoted: "That they may all be one . . . so that the world may believe that thou hast sent me" (John 17:21). In missionary areas in particular, people had experienced the fragmentation of the churches, sometimes characterized by competition, as something shameful, an outright scandal. It seemed that the time had come for all Christians to join hands and live in accordance with the prayer of Christ. In the twentieth century predica-

---

*Here I would point to the attitudes of Barth and Brunner with regard to the virgin birth. Barth accepts it because he regards it as a sign of the sovereign grace of God, while Brunner rejects it because he considers it a degradation of human sexuality. Both base their stand on their own value judgments.

ment, it was unthinkable to allow human confessions or doctrines to stand in the way of a new unity.

When the basis of the World Council of Churches was changed at a later date, the new wording did not alter this *Leitmotiv*.* This is the reason why some observers began to speak of the *relativism* of the World Council. Not all the churches participated, and in time some other ecumenical organizations of a more clearly confessional nature came into being. Among them were the *National Association of Evangelicals* (founded in 1941 in the United States) and the *International Council of Christian Churches* (founded in Amsterdam in 1948).[14]

Since 1961 the Russian Orthodox Church has been a member of the World Council. The members of the World Council take a common approach as far as the question of a relationship to the Roman Catholic Church is concerned. Thus far, however, the "primacy of Peter" has proved an insuperable obstacle to total participation on the part of the Roman Catholic Church.

Persecution of the church

It is not without reason that the twentieth century has been called the age of the church's heaviest persecutions.[15] I use the plural because there were all kinds of persecutions occurring on almost all the continents. For the present I will simply pass on some relevant facts.

The persecutions were not, as in various other ages, directed against some special group of Christians (e.g. Waldensians, Protestants, Mennonites). Rather, they were directed against Christianity in general and therefore struck Roman Catholics, Protestants and Eastern Orthodox believers.

These persecutions often took place on a large scale. Millions of Christians have been killed. Yet, so many were liquidated behind a screen, as it were, that very few names of the martyrs are known. As a result, there has not been enough prayer raised for those who were persecuted for Christ's sake.

We are reminded of Paul's words concerning the "rulers of this present darkness" (Eph. 6:12), for it seemed as though the demonic powers had descended in a previously unheard-of way to realize as-

---

*In New Delhi (1961), the following basis formula was accepted: "The World Council of Churches is a fellowship of churches which confess the Lord Jesus Christ as God and Savior according to the Scriptures, and therefore seek to fulfill together their common call to the glory of the one God, Father, Son and Holy Spirit."

tounding successes. Totalitarian powers tried to dominate all of life and all expressions of life, strangling Christianity in the process. In Germany the disastrous time arrived shortly after the new regime took power. In Russia the years drag by very slowly for the many Christians trapped in the Gulag Archipelago. There are Christians in that country who are convinced that they live in the land of the antichrist, "to whom it was allowed to make war on the saints and to conquer them" (Rev. 13:7).[16] After the revolution in Russia, one persecution followed another. The church in that country is truly a church under the cross, right to this day. And in the countries occupied by Russia, especially the Baltic States, the Christians have been persecuted in a bloody way. The Roman Catholic Church in Poland already had a very hard time under the Nazis. There are dark shadows across all the Communist countries of the East, of central Europe and the Balkans.

The pressure on the churches of Nazi Germany increased year by year. Yet the number of victims, relatively speaking, was small. When Norway, Denmark and the Netherlands were occupied, Christians in those countries were also killed.

The Greek and Armenians suffered from heavy Turkish persecution during the first world war. In Mexico the Roman Catholic Church was persecuted from 1926 to 1938.

After the Communist revolution in China, the Christians of that country suffered incredible persecution. The oppression was so severe that all traces of the organized church seem to have disappeared.

Christians in various African countries have also had a very difficult time. Thus we need hardly turn the yellowed pages of some ancient book to read about the suffering of the martyrs. In our age new chapters have been added to the book of the martyrs, chapters written in blood.

The way of Israel

Does it make any sense to include a special chapter on Israel in a history of the church in the twentieth century? For several reasons, I believe it does. We must form a clear idea of the enigmatic phenomenon of *anti-Semitism*, which has gained a foothold not only in Christian countries but also in Israel. We should make it our business to know how the various churches reacted during the time of the Hitler regime, when hatred of the Jews reached demonic proportions and a planned extermination of this people (a genocide) was undertaken with considerable success. We should pay careful attention to the miraculous survival of this people, and also to the return of the Jews from many parts of the world to Palestine, just as though they were guided by an invisible hand. We should note the growth of the new state and its preservation in the face of many great dangers. And we should look into the church's relationship to Israel.

As we observe all these things, we cannot help but be reminded of the prophecy of Jesus: "Jerusalem will be trodden down by the Gentiles, until the times of the Gentiles are fulfilled" (Luke 21:24). In the twentieth century we have begun to manipulate the word *eschatological* (which is derived from *eschata*, the last things). There are some theologians who seem to be completely at a loss when it comes to the original meaning of this term. They use it to indicate only that all our days and deeds are related to eternity. I am convinced that this is a mistake, for I believe that the "shadows of tomorrow"[17] loom too large and the "signs of the time" are too clear for us to do away with the usual meaning of the term *eschatological*. Indeed, I am inclined to declare that we live in apocalyptic times.

This does not mean, however, that we can simply use the Bible as a yardstick for measuring the shape and significance of various events of our time. Here I must repeat my earlier warning about the danger of losing historical perspective when we stand in the middle of the road, surrounded by the whirl of life.

We must keep the Bible in our hands when we examine the history of the church in our times. And we must not forget to pray for light.

1

The Calm
before the Storm

Upward

At the end of the nineteenth century we find a certain degree of fatigue and decadence, which I characterized earlier by means of the French term *fin de siècle*. At the beginning of the twentieth century, on the other hand, we are struck by a strong faith in the future, an expectation of better things to come, a feeling pointedly expressed in the German term *Fortschritt*. The new era was symbolized by the opening of the Peace Palace in The Hague in 1913. From then on international disputes would be settled by means of mediation and arbitration.

Scientific progress coupled with a remarkable growth in technical skill was a conspicuous feature of the new age. To give you some indication of what this means, I should first of all mention the bicycle, which became a common instrument of transportation, especially in Europe. The bicycle had been invented in the nineteenth century, and then certain improvements were made as far as its usefulness is concerned. Still, it was not until the early twentieth century that the common man began to reap the benefits. The broadening in contact and fellowship with others first made possible by the bicycle should not be underestimated.

Similar comments could be made about the telephone, which was invented in 1876. In the course of time it became an indispensable means of communication. And then there was wireless telegraphy (Marconi, 1896) and the airplane (the Wright Brothers, 1903).

From the Lumière Brothers came yet another highly important invention—motion pictures, or movies, as we call them today. The news of a daily changing world was presented to the astonished eyes of an inquisitive audience. At the beginning of our century, newsreels already showed these scenes:

> The ship in which Scott hoped to reach the South Pole in the year 1902. The airship of Santos Dumont that had been wrecked in the Bay of Monaco not long before. A visit to London, The Hague, Berlin, and Paris made by three Boer generals. The launching of battle cruisers built for the Japanese at an English shipyard. The big new station for wireless telegraphy at Podhu in Cornwall. Marconi, looking youthful in his checked suit, directing the erection of the mast. The opening of a railway through Uganda. The connection with Victoria Nianza. Equally imposing: the completion of a weir in Assuan [Aswan], a heavy stone structure 40 meters high and two kilometers long.[1]

Science was serving man. The discovery of X-rays was a major breakthrough in medical science, along with the discovery of radium by Pierre and Marie Curie in 1898. With cities better lighted at night than ever before, people who enjoyed good incomes could move about much more freely. Families became smaller because of the increase in the use of contraceptives.*

It seemed that the rise of an ideal society was inevitable and would not be long in coming. A moderate socialism, which deviated from orthodox Marxism and was therefore called revisionistic or reform socialism, attracted many of the laborers in western Europe. Their aim was no longer violent revolution but a gradual improvement of social relations which would usher in the ideal state of the future.

In this era the "Social Gospel" found many adherents in America. Although there were definite nuances to be distinguished within the Social Gospel camp, the overriding mood was an optimistic expectation that the Kingdom of God was about to come, especially through the radical application of social measures.

---

*See Religion in Britain since 1900, ed. G. S. Spikes (1952). In England during this period, the average size of a family dropped from 7-8 children to 2-3 children (p. 31). Birth control was not allowed at that time in orthodox Protestant families or Roman Catholic families.

Cultural Protestantism

In those days theologians began to take on the role of cultural prophets.* Their message, it appeared, had more to do with the value of culture for Christianity and of Christianity for culture than with the redemption of the sinner through the grace of Christ and the gratitude for that redemption which the Holy Spirit grants.

In Germany an "Association of Friends of the Christian World" was founded in 1903. The theologian *Martin Rade* was prominent in this association. Beginning in 1888, the ideas of such leaders of liberal theology as Ritschl, Harnack and Herrmann were popularized in a periodical entitled *The Christian World*.

Rade, who died in 1940, was a remarkable man. In his old age he stood up for the Jews, who were then being persecuted in Hitler's Germany. At the beginning of our century he enlisted the cooperation of young *Karl Barth*, who was later to break radically with cultural Protestantism. What did Rade want, and what did the "Friends of the Christian World" have in mind? Their aim was to "bring the cause of the Gospel to the attention of cultivated people of all classes and to place all areas of culture and society under the light of the Gospel."

But what did they mean by "the cause of the Gospel"? Ritschl had emphasized the ideal of the coming Kingdom of God, in which Christians would be present as the moral leaders of the world. He rejected the doctrines of original sin and redemption by the sacrifice of Christ. As for Harnack, he had reduced the Gospel to a bare minimum—the imitation of the historical Jesus. Rade followed in their footsteps by accepting completely the radical criticism of the Scriptures. He wanted a Christian religion that would share joyfully in all the good and beautiful things of the world and enthusiastically correct the faults and defects of society. It goes without saying that his ideals were in line with the spirit of his time. And there were others who expressed similar thoughts on these matters.

As long as we are dealing with Germany, the name of *Ernst Troeltsch* (1865-1923) must also be mentioned. Troeltsch was a very talented man who drew a distinction between the new Protestantism that was born in the eighteenth-century Enlightenment era and the old Protestantism of the Reformers. The confessional standards of the

---

*I use the term *culture* here to mean both the domination of nature and the products of human civilization.

new Protestantism were "God, liberty and immortality" and "a regeneration of a higher kind that would unite culture with God."[2]

In England during this time, an effort was made to form a Church Socialist League under the slogan: "Christianity is the religion of which Socialism is the practice." This effort never amounted to much.[3] A resolution of the Lambeth Conference of 1908 met with a better response. The resolution contained the statement: ". . . this Conference recognizes the ideals of brotherhood which underlie the democratic movement of this century, and . . . calls upon the Church to show sympathy with the movement in so far as it strives to procure just treatment for all and a real opportunity for living a true human life."

The twentieth century in England also witnessed the growth of Scriptural criticism, and consequently criticism of Scripture's super-natural contents as well. As the century progressed, such criticism penetrated ever more deeply. In 1907 the Congregationalist preacher *R. J. Campbell* published a book entitled *The New Theology*,* in which he suggested that Christ's divinity meant that He differed from other men in degree rather than in kind. Two years later he wrote: "Christhood is manhood at its highest power."[4]

As we turn to America, I must mention the name of the historian *Preserved Smith*, who was the son of a theological professor. Smith maintained a special interest in church history viewed as part of the history of civilization. He was a very able writer and produced a biography of Luther as well as a two-volume history of modern culture in which he agreed with Troeltsch's thesis that the new era was ushered in not by the Reformation (and the Renaissance) but by the Enlightenment of the eighteenth century. In the course of time Smith refused to call himself a Christian; he wanted to be no more and no less than a humanist. He preferred Voltaire to John Wesley, and in his books he paid more attention to scientific, philosophical, political, economic and artistic developments than to religious matters.[5] In Smith's case we really cannot even speak of "cultural *Protestantism*"; the interest in culture had devoured the interest in Protestantism.

In Canada at about this time, Young Pierre van Paassen made his appearance as a colorful speaker. He was an immigrant from the Netherlands who had originally belonged to the Free Reformed Churches *(Afgescheiden Kerken)*. Van Paassen studied at Victoria

---

*An expression used repeatedly in the twentieth century, much like the cliché *the younger generation*.

College in Toronto, a Methodist institution, and about 1914 served as a chaplain among the miners in northern Ontario. There were many Scandinavians among the miners. He delivered lectures to them on many cultural subjects, ranging from Marx's *Kapital* to Ibsen's Nora, from Andersen's fairy tales to Multatuli's Max Havelaar.

When Van Paassen was asked how he preached during those days, he replied that he believed he had been called just as the prophet Isaiah was called. In his autobiography we find the following fragment of a sermon which he delivered when a strike in the mines was threatening:

> Two great currents of new life are coursing through our world today: the religious and the social. Like two parallel streams of water running to the same sea, these two seek each other. In the hearts of those who are seized with the religious ideal, a certitude is growing that God has sent them to build a bridge toward those brothers who, while perhaps denying God's existence, are, nevertheless, athirst for justice and righteousness. Our hope and desire is to walk and to work together with them.
>
> Jesus walks amongst us right here in the Porcupine* area announcing the kingdom of God, the era of co-operation and comradeship when cut-throat competition and poverty and hunger and war shall be no more . . . We do not see Him as one enveloped in the mystery of the Holy Trinity . . . We see Him as a helper, as a brother, as a fellow worker, as the banner bearer in the workers' cause . . . If it comes to a strike, we shall walk together behind His banner, the scarlet banner of the cross . . .[6]

That Van Paassen was not the only one with such convictions soon became evident. A listener had made a stenographical report of the sermon and sent it to the superintendent of the Methodist Church in Toronto, accusing Van Paassen of sedition. The superintendent then sent Van Paassen the following telegram: "Say it again and again and again! You are on the right track."[7]

Neo-Calvinism

Should the Dutch Calvinists who organized themselves in various areas of life at the beginning of the twentieth century also be numbered among the cultural Protestants? There are some writers who think that they should. They point particularly to *Abraham*

---

*The area of gold mines in the neighborhood of Timmins.

Abraham Kuyper

Kuyper, who was the founder of the Free University and the leader of the Antirevolutionary Party.*

Kuyper was the man who stimulated interest in Christian activities of various sorts by means of the slogan: "There is not an inch of ground on which Christ, the Sovereign of all does not lay His hand and say, 'This is Mine.' " It has been said of Kuyper, in particular, that his thinking represents a *neo*-Calvinism, and that it deviates very substantially from the original Calvinism. Kuyper, we are told, was more concerned about the building of a kingdom in this world than the expectation of the Kingdom that is to come from above; he expected more from a common grace reaching out to all men than from a special grace given to the elect only for Christ's sake.[8]

As we seek to evaluate this criticism, we must realize what the actual situation was. At that time there were various associations and organizations in the Netherlands that were devoted to Christian action. As their motto many of them used the phrase "Pro Rege" (For the King). Such organized Christian action signified a marked contrast with the picture that prevailed in a slightly earlier period when liberal, modern Christians dominated the scene. At that time believers in Christ confessed His name in church, school and personal witness but hardly at all through organized Christian action.

Under the inspiring leadership of Kuyper, the situation was changing and would continue to change. Moreover, Kuyper found able fellow workers in the great dogmatician *Herman Bavinck*, the philosophical classicist *J. Woltjer* and the jurist *D. P. D. Fabius*. In social affairs Kuyper was assisted particularly by the Reformed minister *A. S. Talsma* and his Free Reformed colleague *J. C. Sikkel*.

---

*The Christian political party in the Netherlands founded in the nineteenth century by Guillaume Groen van Prinsterer.

A Christian social conference that met in 1905 came to this important conclusion:

Herman Bavinck

> The purpose of a trade union is to help the workers in their struggle for improved legal status within their trade and in their related struggle for an organization of their situation as workers that will enable them to carry out their God-given calling to develop their personal power and talents and to use them in a proper way on behalf of family and trade, state and church. The trade union exists because a satisfactory arrangement of labor relations is only achieved if the parties can act with sufficient independence after the contract is signed. In the course of time the trade union also serves the social interests of the employer . . . It should occupy itself with good legislation for the people as well as the direct moral edification of the workers.

In 1909 the Christian National Trade Union was founded in the Netherlands with the following basis: "The Christian National Trade Union accepts the Christian principles as its basis and therefore rejects the class struggle."

A description of the many activities of this association and of the many other Christian organizations, especially in the area of education, lies outside the scope of this book. However, against the background of what we have learned to this point, we are now in a better position to answer the question whether these new efforts represent *neo*-Calvinism in the sense of a departure from the original Calvinism. Along with many other writers, I would answer this question negatively,[9] although I do recognize that the Christian action of that era was fashioned somewhat by the circumstances and stamped by the unique personal insight of Kuyper.

First of all, the *historical situation was different*. Whereas in the sixteenth century one could still speak of the "Corpus Christianum," i.e. the Christian society, in the twentieth century there was only a part of society that could be called Christian. That Christian sector was separated from the unbelieving sector by a deep gulf (the antithesis). Therefore public life could only be organized by means of common, organized action. Only by such a route could the fullness of life be claimed for Christ as King, to use Kuyper's language.

Secondly, *Kuyper's unique personal insights* must be borne in mind. Complementing his stress on the antithesis was his distinction between special and general* grace. In his influential weekly *De Heraut* (The Herald), he wrote a series of articles in which he tried to imbue his readers with the knowledge of faith of the Reformed fathers. He started with the topic of special grace. But he could not and would not close his eyes to the gifts God has granted to *all* His creatures. He saw that sin and the curse have been checked in their course, and also that unbelievers participate in the development of the possibilities present in the creation of God. Hence he expected that things would go downhill as far as "higher culture" was concerned (i.e. recognition of God, respect for the good, the true and the beautiful), but he expected things to improve in the area of technical culture (i.e. the increasing mastery of the powers of nature).[10]

It is not correct, therefore, to characterize Kuyper as a cultural optimist. He repeatedly spoke about the "small beginnings" of the new obedience,[11] and he expected that apostasy would increase in twentieth-century Europe, culminating finally in the appearance of the antichrist, an incarnation of sin and the herald of the end of our age.[12]

Calvin also taught a doctrine of "common grace,"[13] but Douma is right in stating that this doctrine assumed only a modest place in his preaching and teaching. The Genevan Reformer placed more emphasis on the theme that believers travel through this world as pilgrims.[14] S. J. Ridderbos observes that common grace has a purpose of its own in Kuyper's view (i.e. the development of the potentials of creation), whereas Calvin always connected it to special grace; through common grace, all excuses are taken away from the unbelievers.

---

*Kuyper preferred to speak of "*common* grace," in order to avoid the impression that all men are saved by the grace of Jesus Christ. Many of his most important works are concerned with this topic.

Roman Catholic Modernism

It was not a movement, because there was no trace of an organization. Nevertheless, it happened spontaneously and almost simultaneously in both England and France, and to a lesser degree in Germany and Italy. This shows us that there was definitely something in the air; similar causes and circumstances were having identical effects. I am speaking of Roman Catholic Modernism, in which the spirit of the times was knocking on the door—the spirit of a time of progress, a time of criticism of what was old and an eager expectation of what was new.[15] The names of George Tyrrell and Alfred Loisy are associated with this way of thinking.

George Tyrrell (1861-1909) was of Irish birth, and in his youth he belonged to the Anglican Church of Ireland. He was a gentle boy who literally could not hurt a fly and could never eat a fish which he had seen being caught. In early years his ear had been hurt by an unfortunate fall, and the ensuing surgery left him with a weak constitution. Tyrrell was a sensitive person, yet he was not always caught by the right sounds: he was attracted by the Roman Catholic Church, which was not well thought of in Irish-Anglican circles and therefore enjoyed the aura of the "underdog." At the age of 18 Tyrrell became a Roman Catholic, and he became a Jesuit one year later. He believed he had found something sensitively true and mystically beautiful, and not even at the hour of his death was he willing to concede that he had been mistaken. In fact he was not a traditional Roman Catholic at all —and certainly not a Jesuit. But when the time of conflict came, and even when he was excommunicated, Tyrrell, with a stubbornness which he himself ascribed to his Irish temperament, still considered himself one of the best sons of the church.[16]

What, then, did Tyrrell want and expect? If we look at him from a distance, he is reminiscent of another well-known Anglican who became a Roman Catholic—John Henry Newman. But Newman eventually became a cardinal, whereas Tyrrell's body was denied a burial in consecrated soil.

Newman had developed a theory of the *development* of the church's doctrine. Just as the plant and flower unfold from the bud, the total development of Roman Catholic doctrine was already present in germinal form in the theology of the original church (see Volume VI, Chap.8). Tyrrell also believed with all his heart in development—but in a totally different way. He wanted to preserve the old terms as the wrappings of a precious treasure. But that treasure was what really counted, not the wrappings, which should be thrown away once they had served their purpose. He believed this had been irrefutably demonstrated by historical criticism, the criticism of Scripture in the nineteenth century.

Tyrrell's friend Baron von Hügel,* among others, had urged him to read the critical works of various German theologians. Through this reading Tyrrell was confronted with the great dilemma that would continue to haunt the twentieth century: How could one remain a faithful son of the church while at the same time honoring the so-called results of Biblical criticism?

The *tour de force* he performed in this area is evident from this quotation:

> No definition of the *historicity* of the Virgin Birth could *mean* more than that the Virgin Birth was part of revelation. Because and so long as the denial of its historicity seems to destroy its religious value, she will and must affirm its historicity in order to affirm those values. In the implicit affirmation she is right of necessity; in the explicit protective affirmation she may be quite wrong.[17]

Bookkeeping by double entry! The church should know very well that no honest theologian could believe in the virgin birth any longer; at the same time she had to go on speaking to the common people about the virgin birth for the sake of the religious value that was somehow bound up with it.

Similar remarks could be made about *Alfred Loisy* (1857-1949), of whom Herman Bavinck said that he "used the infallibility of the church in a clever way to unite the modern conceptions of the teaching of Jesus with Roman Catholic orthodoxy."[18] Loisy had learned some lessons from Renan (see Volume VI, Chap. 5), whom he admired. As early as 1902 Loisy proposed ideas that would later come to be known as "form-criticism," especially among Protestant scholars.[19] We get to know Jesus only by means of the tradition of the early church, and therefore we must learn to sift through that tradition carefully.

Loisy also wanted to retain the old formulations of the church, while at the same time reinterpreting them. Take, for example, the expressions "He descended into hell" and "He ascended into heaven." For a long time people had believed actual places were referred to, but

---

*Friedrich von Hügel joined the Roman Catholic Church in his younger years and settled down in England. He was in favor of a combination of critical thinking, the modern conception of culture and Roman Catholicism. Many considered him to be an authority. Tyrrell and Loisy were his friends.

Loisy was convinced that no educated man could believe such a thing any longer. Still, he did not propose to do away with such language. Instead he maintained that the church should create room for a rich spectrum of opinion.

The Roman Catholic Church at the beginning of the twentieth century had not yet reached the point where it could allow such tremendous latitude. "Modernism" was condemned in the syllabus *Lamentabili* and also in the encyclical *Pascendi Dominicae Gregis*, which followed in 1907.

In the syllabus a number of modern heresies were summed up and condemned, including the following:

> 11. Divine inspiration cannot be applied to the entire Holy Scripture to such an extent that it guards against all error in all its parts and in each section.
>
> 18. John claims to have been an eyewitness of Christ; in fact, however, he was only an eminent witness of the life of Christ in the Church at the end of the first century.
>
> 35. Christ was not always aware of His Messianic dignity.
>
> 52. Christ never meant to establish a church that would continue to exist through a long series of ages; on the contrary, Christ's idea was that the Kingdom of heaven would arrive well-nigh immediately, at the same time as the end of the world.

The encyclical was to a large extent a commentary on the syllabus. Also condemned were certain distinctions made between the Christ of history and the Christ of faith, between the Church of history and the Church of faith, and between the sacraments of history and the sacraments of faith. Finally, in 1910 all the priests had to swear the so-called anti-Modernist oath, in which all the errors mentioned in the encyclical and the syllabus were expressly rejected.

Three students

The distinction between the Christ of history and the Christ of faith, which usually turned into a separation, was condemned by the papal encyclical. Because this distinction was applied, the historical Jesus was criticized in many different ways. Paul Althaus wrote the following commentary about this period: "In the New Testament lecture halls of that time, numerous young theologians lost the faith of their parental home and of their church."[20]

It would be instructive to look briefly at three gifted theological students in Germany who were exposed to such influences at that time. Each of them was to play a significant role later in his life.

Otto Dibelius was born in 1880 and studied from 1899 to 1903 in Berlin. In his autobiography he characterizes this early period of his life by saying: "Ein Christ ist immer in Dienst" (A Christian is always in service). A little later in his life he appeared to be a faithful evangelical minister of moderate convictions, but in the struggle against National Socialism he very clearly showed his colors. Later, in East Germany, he became a leader in the struggle against the equally totalitarian Communist regime that was established there.

In his student years Dibelius was unmistakably influenced by cultural Protestantism. He had a deep respect for Harnack, one of his teachers, and also for Hermann Gunkel, his Old Testament professor, whom I will discuss later. Characteristic of Dibelius as a student is this anecdote:

> I remember once sitting with Wilhelm Schneemilcher in his apartment. (He subsequently became Secretary-General of the Evangelical Congress on Social Problems.) He read me something of Goethe's with great enthusiasm and said that once the pietistic orthodoxy of the older generation had finally been set aside, a new generation of pastors could speak to the educated with Goethe in one hand and the Bible in the other, and a new age would dawn for our church. I was not altogether convinced. But something of this optimism reigned in all our hearts.[21]

In 1900 Dibelius became a member of the German Student Association. Typical again is the information he gives us about the aims of this association: it was intended to "combat free thinking, Marxism, and the Jewish influence in public life, and to inculcate patriotism among students." Bismarck was regarded as Germany's greatest hero, and the ideal was a greater Germany. That was how many young theologians of the time thought and dreamed until the great disenchantment arrived.

Karl Barth, who was born in 1886, was also a theological student during those days. He came from an orthodox Reformed Swiss milieu. His father was appointed a New Testament professor at Bern in 1891, and in his paternal home a stable and cheerful atmosphere prevailed.[22]

During his years as a student, Barth became a liberal in religious matters and a socialist in politics. He was an eager reader and listener and was irresistibly drawn to the great theologians of his time: Harnack, Gunkel, Herrmann and Kaftan. He viewed them as men standing in the midst of life in that era, raising their voices with prophetic power. Harnack, who was later to feel deeply disappointed in this promising pupil, fascinated Barth because of his versatility, historical sense and cultural refinement. Barth was later to compare him to Origen.

Barth drew some conclusions from his academic experiences when he entered the ministry in 1909 as an assistant pastor in Geneva. He expressed these conclusions in an article which he published under the title "Modern Theology and the Work for the Kingdom of God."[23] He had lost much and received little in return: "Both tables of Moses have slipped away from us . . . What do we still have? . . . A more or less accurate knowledge of the Christian past, which, as we all know, is a relative matter scientifically speaking, and our own religious life—at least, if we do indeed have something of the kind." Before that he had already expressed himself clearly: "As far as science is concerned there are no absolutes, neither in the world of nature nor in that of the spirit." With these empty hands he entered the manse. It should not surprise us to hear that for years he was vexed by the "predicament of preaching."

Finally we should look at an American student who studied in Germany in those days—*John Gresham Machen*, who was born in 1881. Machen was a Presbyterian who had studied theology at Princeton and visited Europe repeatedly. In 1905 he attended lectures at the University of Marburg, and in 1906 at the University of Göttingen.

It is evident from Machen's letters how much he enjoyed his contacts with German students.[24] He was fascinated particularly by the teachings of Herrmann, and as a result he hesitated for a long time before accepting the responsibility of becoming a minister in his own church.

Herrmann was a man with a warm heart. He took the position that it is possible to accept historical criticism in its totality, including the rejection of the virgin birth and the physical resurrection of Jesus, while retaining and defending faith in the true Jesus, the moral Jesus. He spoke of the love of Jesus with great tenderness and even called Him God, although he denied the orthodox doctrine of the two natures, divine and human. Herrmann was willing to speak of Jesus as God because in Him we meet a perfectly moral (ethical) human person.

For some time Machen was profoundly unsettled by Herrmann's ideas. He could not agree with them, but they were presented with such authority and conviction that he felt entirely unable to refute them. He thought about his situation day and night and suffered from it. He even decided to quit his theological studies.

Then Machen went to Göttingen, where he attended the lectures of more leading German theologians, including *W. Bousset*. He was a proponent of the "religionsgeschichtliche Methode,"* which considered the Jewish and Christian religions to be products of the history of humanity's evolution, just as the other religions were. Machen became critical of this method, as is apparent from what he wrote in a letter to his brother Arthur: "What Bousset has left after he has stripped off the form is certainly well worth keeping; but whether it is the Christian faith that has been found to overcome the world is very doubtful."[25]

To keep his spiritual balance, Machen visited a Baptist church in Göttingen. His German friends in the student club "Germania" considered this to be beneath his social position and therefore urged him not to wear the club's colors while visiting the church. On that occasion Machen wrote to his mother: "The Germans are very tolerant about little questions like the person of Christ, but when it comes to the outward form of religion, they are more intolerant than the most bigoted of the orthodox."[26]

It would later become evident from Machen's justly praised apologetic writings just how profitable this period of his life had been. Machen had looked into the heart of modern theology.

Church attendance

There are two things that should be said about church attendance in this period. First, the cultural Protestants were excellent pulpit orators. Second, there were more and more church members who no longer attended any services.

As far as the pulpit oratory of the cultural Protestants is concerned, it is interesting to read Machen's judgment concerning some of the sermons he heard in New York. In a letter to his mother dated November 14, 1914, he wrote:

> Last Sunday I heard Dr. Parkhurst on Madison Square. The interior of the church building is characterized by a certain rich and magnificent simplicity, and the music seemed to me the finest church music that I have ever heard. The whole service was possessed of perfect unity . . . the sermon was exceedingly stimulating. There was not a touch of Christianity in it . . .

---

*The method of the history of religions. Gunkel applied the same method to the Old Testament.

On a later occasion (March 14, 1916), he wrote:

> In the afternoon I heard Harry Emerson Fosdick. Fosdick has great
> vogue—especially, I believe, among college men. And he is dreadful!
> Just the pitiful modern stuff about an undogmatic Christianity. I can
> listen to liberals like Dr. Parkhurst—powerful, earnest seekers after
> God—without becoming impatient. But this kind of stuff makes me
> somewhat tired . . . I should hate to think that Christianity were re-
> duced to such insignificant dimensions.[27]

It is rather remarkable that Otto Dibelius, proceeding from a different outlook, arrived at much the same conclusion. Looking back
upon the days of his youth, he tells us that the "famous pulpit orators
were the worst." In the 1880s Berlin had more brilliant preachers than
ever before or since. "But it was exactly during this period that parish
life decayed and Berlin became a worldly city." Dibelius then offers
the following example.

One Sunday about 1900, a detachment of soldiers appeared in
one of the big churches in Germany's capital. They were led by a
young officer. Pastor Kraatz, a very liberal minister, preached that
day, and his sermon was interspersed with comments critical of the
Gospel. Finally the officer, who came from a strict religious family,
could stand it no longer. He signaled to his men, and they all left the
church together. Their departure was not completely noiseless. The
church council protested because a public worship service had been
disturbed. When the case was brought to court, the judge asked the
minister to state what he considered the purpose of a sermon to be.
The answer was: "To discuss religious questions."[28]

Such discussion, however, was not what most churchgoers were
looking for when they came to church. As a result, more and more of
the members began to stay away from the services. It should also be
noted that, in general, the lowest-paid workers did not show much interest in the church anymore. Many of them accepted the new gospel
of Marxism, or perhaps a more moderate socialism, and turned their
backs on the church.

About 1900, the labor movement in England was more tinged
with Marxism than ever before. It has been estimated that about one-
third of the population of England and Scotland no longer attended
church, except for baptisms, confirmations, marriages and funerals.[29]
In London the statistics are much more startling; the number of
churchgoers was rated at about 16 percent.[30]

The figures for Germany are still more spectacular. According to

Kupisch, there were still some oases of piety in the old Pietistic revival areas on the eve of the first world war, but when the population as a whole was considered, only about four percent still attended church. Of course there were still a considerable number of "Christians-on-wheels," i.e. people who came to church only in a baby carriage, a wedding car or a hearse.[31]

The official figures being circulated by the churches those days are much higher, of course.* The main reason is that in various countries all citizens were considered members of the established church. It should also be remembered that people were generally reluctant to say they did not belong to any church at all.

On the other hand, the free churches and the orthodox groups within the larger churches increased in numbers—and therefore also in church attendance. This is true of the Reformed *(Gereformeerd)* Churches in the Netherlands, and also of the Reformed Fellowship within the Dutch Reformed *(Hervormd)* Church. It also applies to the Christian Reformed Church in North America and the various churches of Reformed origin in South Africa, as well as the churches that came together in Scotland in 1900 to form the United Free Church of Scotland. In the United States we see the same pattern in the confessional Lutheran churches and the Bible-believing Southern Baptists. All this time there was a hunger for the Word of God and a desire to proclaim the Gospel.

On the eve of the catastrophe

The outbreak of the first world war did not come as a complete surprise to the people of Europe. On the other hand, it cannot be said that people were totally prepared for it.

Because of a series of agreements and alliances between the major powers, Europe had been divided into two camps. Both sides were building up their armaments. The spirit of nationalism was on the rise, and there was economic mistrust in the air. The dynamite lay ready for someone to light the fuse.

Still, people were not actually expecting it and counting on it. Not one of the major powers really wanted war.[32] Men of culture dreamed of never-ending progress. Neither the workers nor the men of the

---

*The statistics for the unchurched in the Netherlands are as follows: 2.26% in 1899, 4.97% in 1909, 14.43% in 1930, 17.04% in 1947. In Germany as of 1950, only 3.5% were officially unchurched. In Sweden 95% of the people belong officially to the established church, and in Denmark 98%.

middle classes could imagine the terrors of a modern war. Still, there are two exceptions to be noted.

The name of *Friedrich Nietzsche* was already mentioned earlier. Nietzsche glorified the "will to power" and predicted in one of his last works: "Such wars will come as the world has never seen . . . Soon Europe will be shrouded in darkness . . . Our heart is overflowing with thankfulness."[33] Nietzsche's influence grew, and it would continue to grow between the two world wars.

A comparable influence was exerted by the sociologists *Georges Sorel* (1847-1922) and *Vilfredo Pareto* (1848-1923), who both prepared the way for postwar Fascism. Sorel was the founder of *syndicalism*, the doctrine of the continuous revolutionary agitation of the workers; he favored a permanently hostile attitude that would be conducive to the creation of a new society.

As for Pareto, he was an *elitist*, like Nietzsche. He believed that the parliamentary system should be replaced by a government of the elite. The elite is entitled to seize power if it finds itself excluded from power.

Both Sorel and Pareto glorified violence. Mussolini listened to them as he wandered about outside his own country, and he borrowed many of his ideas from them. Thus, brute force found its defenders.

The frightening arms race continued unchecked as general staffs made their secret plans. But the great mass of the people simply didn't believe it.

We find this reflected in what happened at the famous World Missionary Conference in Edinburgh in 1910. The chairman of this conference was the energetic American, John R. Mott, who had written a book entitled *The Evangelization of the World in This Generation*. Great plans were made, and the enthusiasm certainly deserves our admiration. Messages were received from the German emperor, Wilhelm II, and Theodore Roosevelt, the President of the United States. The messages were applauded. But as we read through the extensive reports of this conference, we cannot find "any indication of what the English people and the whole world were about to experience, or in which way the service of God would be able to restore faith."[34]

We find a comparable naiveté in a certain article written in a Magdeburg newspaper to mark the occasion of the silver jubilee of the government of Wilhelm II. The author of the article was no one less than Abraham Kuyper. Kuyper did not write without certain reservations; yet we do find him saying:

The serious element in our people honors in the German emperor the many talents for which he is renowned; it sympathizes with him in his ethical-religious tendencies; and on his anniversary it offers him the sincere wish that he may reign for a long time, and that our God and his may grant a peace that will never be disturbed as a ripe fruit of his noble endeavors.[35]

In the Netherlands, the centennial of the country's liberation from Napoleon was celebrated with great joy in 1913. The children sang cheerfully:

'Tis everybody's duty
to give for the defense
of his beloved fatherland
the best of all his strength.

In that same era we find the "Wandervögel" (birds of passage) roaming through Germany—young people who, in great simplicity, sought to escape culture in order to enjoy nature in true Romantic fashion. On their first Free German Day of Youth in 1913, they issued a message in which they proclaimed that they wanted to be honest with themselves by taking the responsibility for shaping their lives in accordance with their own decisions.

That was indeed high-sounding language. It is unlikely many of them realized that within a year they would have to put this Meiszner formula (named after the place where the vow was made) into practice on the field of battle. Approximately 12,000 leaders of the "Wandervögel" went to war, most of them as volunteers. Only 5000 returned alive.[36]

2

The Great Upheaval (1914-1918)

August 1914

Everything seemed to be normal. As usual, the month of July opened the holiday season—for the middle classes of England, Germany and France, at any rate. Then came August, as many Europeans enjoyed their vacations at the beaches, in the forests, on the mountains, just as though they didn't have a care in the world.

Everything may have seemed all right, but something had happened. In Sarajevo a Bosnian student named Princip had shot Archduke Franz Ferdinand and his wife. The Archduke was the heir to Austria's throne, and so his death created some severe international tensions.

Still, what right-minded man would have dreamed of war? There simply *had* to be a peaceful solution.

Then the incredible, irrevocable chain of events was unleashed: the Austrian ultimatum to Serbia (July 23), the German ultimatum to Belgium (August 2), the general mobilization in Russia (July 30), Germany's declaration of war on France (August 3), England's declaration of war on Germany (August 4).

Large military forces, armed with the latest weapons, were about to attack each other. But at that time there was no one who really

39

understood what this would mean. The general idea was that the whole business would be settled by Christmas.*

The widespread enthusiasm for the war was most remarkable. As early as July 25, there were great demonstrations in Vienna. The multitudes sang lustily: "God save the emperor Franz." In St. Petersburg "everyone was wildly excited, as though what had arrived was not a war but their own long-awaited happiness." The troops assembled from various parts of Russia: ". . . the Russian leave-taking was almost a joyous affair, with the reservists dancing away to balalaika music and raising the dust on the trampled earth of the trackside. They would call out in obviously drunken voices while their relatives made the sign of the cross over them and wept as they drew away."[1]

In France an author expected that the war would be "amusing." Another wrote that it would be an opportunity to "picnic on the grass."[2] The same kind of attitude was prevalent in Germany and England. Princess Blücher wrote about "an endless procession of trains filled with soldiers, enthusiastic cries, waving of handkerchiefs . . . girls in white and ladies having the Red Cross bands on their arms who gave the thirsty men something to eat and to drink. It all looked like a great national feast . . ."[3] In London big parties were organized at the outbreak of the war. People waved the Union Jack, sang patriotic songs and behaved exultantly.[4]

The English were convinced that they were fighting a chivalrous war for honor and justice. The French were still looking for revenge for their defeat of 1870. The Germans were fighting for their fatherland and for the right to exist. As for the Russians, they were fighting for their holy native soil. The various ideals were as high as they were unreal.

Uprooted trees

The tornado of the war uprooted even the strongest trees. Things that had seemed unassailable had collapsed like sand castles before the waves.

Western culture! How proud it had been of its impartiality, and of the objectivity of science! Truth reigned supreme, despite national and political controversies.

---

*One of the slogans of the English soldiers was: "Home by Christmas." See J. Williams, *The Home Fronts: Britain, France and Germany, 1914-1918* (1972), p. 13.

But the imagined excellence of science already received a deadly blow in 1914 when the famous Sigmund Freud declared in Vienna: "All my libido is given to Austria-Hungary."[5] Sir Walter Raleigh, a famous professor of English literature at Oxford, declared that same year: "The air we breathe is better than it has ever been for years."[6] H. G. Wells, together with J. W. Headlam, the well-known biographer of Bismarck, was in charge of the anti-German propaganda in England. Wells declared that "this was [is] the greatest of all, not merely another war, — it is the last war."[7]

Such statements were certainly not inspired by scientific honesty. And the scholars who fared the worst were the men of science who had so long been proud of their impartiality—the historians. In 1914, several of the governments involved in the war published "official documents," with the help of the historians. After the war an abundance of source material was published in Austria, Germany, Russia and England. It then became apparent that the original set of "official documents" included a host of falsifications and omissions.[8]

In Germany the great historian Eduard Meyer suspended his work on his monumental history of antiquity to publish a sharp attack on the British empire. Ernest Lavisse, the leading French historian, did something even worse. In 1915 he denounced a neutral proposal designed to promote a discussion of the issues in the war and the conditions for peace, a discussion that would bring together intellectuals from the countries at war. In an address at the Sorbonne, Lavisse denounced Germany as "the greatest poisoner on earth." In the United States the historian Roscoe Thayer was one of the fiercest war propagandists. Yet, during the war years he was twice elected president of the American Historical Association.

The attitude of the historians was disappointing, and the same was true of the socialists. Right up to the outbreak of the war they went on singing the Internationale, but then nature overcame nurture. In their respective parliaments they voted in favor of war budgets. The German socialists feared the designs of the Russian Tsar, while the French socialists feared German militarism. The French socialist leader Jean Jaurès, who had pleaded for peace, was murdered on the eve of the war.

What about the theologians, the great men of optimistic cultural Protestantism? On the day war broke out, Ernst von Dryander, Berlin's court chaplain, preached for the members of the *Reichstag* on the text: "If God is for us, who is against us?" Adolf von Harnack drafted the emperor's call to war,[9] and his colleague Reinhold Seeberg wrote a declaration on behalf of Germany's professors, in which he stated that there was no difference between the spirit of German science and the spirit of Prussian militarism. "Both are one, and we also belong." No fewer than 500 intellectuals signed this declaration, including many theologians.

In England we find a similar situation. There was no compulsory military service there; the army consisted wholly of volunteers. Winnington-Ingram, the bishop of London, became one of England's most successful recruiting officers.[10] The archbishop of York declared that every man with a conscience "should take his place until the war is over."[11]

In France the church historian A. Baudrillart played an important role. He led a Roman Catholic elite in a hateful propaganda campaign against Germany. Germany was solely responsible for the war and was the worst enemy of the Roman Catholic Church.[12]

I should add, however, that Pope Benedict XV (1914-1922) called the war the "suicide of civilized Europe" and incessantly urged peace negotiations. There were other voices with the same message. In England an effort was made in 1916 to organize a "National Call to Repentance and Hope." If there was repentance, the light of hope might begin to shine.

But this movement had no chance; it came to nothing. The war mood was prevalent. But as time slipped by, that mood was accompanied more and more by feelings of despondency and aversion.

Demoralization

J. S. Engall, an English second lieutenant serving at the front at Somme, wrote to his parents in 1916 that he had taken communion the previous day with dozens of other soldiers, and that he had never attended a more impressive service:

> I placed my soul and body in God's keeping, and I am going into battle with His name on my lips, full of confidence and trusting implicitly in Him. I have a strong feeling that I shall come through safely; but nevertheless should it be God's holy will to call me away, I am quite prepared to go; and . . . I could not wish for a finer death; and you, dear Mother and Dad, will know that I died doing my duty to God, my Country and my King. I ask that you should look upon it as an honor that you have given a son for the sake of King and Country.[13]

A. Marwick, who quotes these words in a book entitled *The Deluge*, is of the opinion that there were only *some* who believed this way. "Those early volunteers who had a simple old-world religious faith were probably most immune to the numbing influence of trench-life; but they and their faith were extinguished in the Battle of the Somme."[14] I believe Marwick is exaggerating; there were many men on both sides who managed to hang on to their faith. Still, there is no denying that a great demoralization took place.

When ideals vanished, as was the case in higher circles, and when age-old values seemed to be shattered—was there any difference then between good and evil? The soldiers were allowed to go home on furlough, but they were given contraceptives beforehand.[15] The general idea was: "Give the boys a good time." That good time consisted to a large extent of consuming alcohol and enjoying sex.[16] According to Bishop Ward, many soldiers who went to the front witnessed for the first time in their lives the sight of long rows of men waiting at the doors of brothels, as though waiting to get into a movie theater.

A short campaign had been anticipated, but it turned into a long war in the trenches. What this meant for the men themselves has been vividly depicted for us in such books as E. M. Remarque's *Im Westen nichts neues* (English translation entitled: *All Quiet on the Western Front*). It seemed that the only moral value left was comradeship.

As far as the home front was concerned, family life had been uprooted. Church life also suffered as a consequence. The men were at the front, and that meant women and children were at work on the farms and in the factories—busy with work of all kinds, both weekdays and Sundays. There was a great deal of theft and violence; order and discipline receded.

Herman Bavinck wrote in 1920: "Because of this war and its manifold miseries, thousands upon thousands have fallen prey to skepticism, materialism and atheism."[17] As far as the neutral countries were concerned, H. Algra has summed up what went wrong: "The nation has become materialistic during the war years; it manifested an egoistic spirit in many ways. Often the nation felt like a spectator in this bloody war, experiencing the sensation from afar—but in the meantime profiting, and profiting again. Often the nation showed no more pity for all the misery than is expressed in the sigh: 'If only we can stay out of it!' "[18]

The end of the war did not bring about repentance. Neither did the Treaty of Versailles bring about real peace, in spite of the League of Nations of which it spoke.

In America the armistice was greeted with ecstasy. The air in New

York was filled with noises made by every conceivable object. "In Harlem, the Negro district, the street dancing started. The barrooms were crowded . . . Eight hundred Barnard college girls performed a folk dance . . . An artist drew a protrait of Germany's emperor Wilhelm on the sidewalk and invited everyone to trample on it."[19] This was the beginning of the "Roaring Twenties," followed in the 1930s by the Great Depression.

In Russia the revolution had started in 1917. Its effect on the position of the church will be discussed in another chapter.

In Germany's November revolution, the emperor and all the princes lost their thrones, and therefore also their influence in the church. The Weimar Constitution of 1919 decreed: "Each religious community arranges and administers its own affairs within the boundaries of public law. It appoints its office-bearers without the cooperation of the state or of civic municipalities." In this way the various churches received the freedom to arrange their own affairs. In some of the states of Germany, the government of the churches was entrusted to a "Konsistorium" (an ecclesiastical committee) or to a bishop. In 1922 the German Evangelical Alliance of Churches (D.E.K.) was founded in Wittenburg, the site of Luther's tomb.

Armenia

Nearly hidden behind the curtain of European events, a horrible event took place in Turkey. The Armenians in that country were almost all massacred during the first world war.

The Turkish Armenians had already been persecuted fearfully in the nineteenth century (see Volume VI, Chap. 13). After that a period of relative quiet followed. Then, in 1909, some 20,000 Armenians were killed in Cilicia and northern Syria.

When Turkey sided with the "central powers" (Germany and Austria) in November of 1914, it did not trust its Armenian subjects. In spite of solemn promises of allegiance, the Turks feared that the Armenians would support the Russians if there was an invasion. The Ottoman government therefore decided to transport the entire Armenian population of 1.75 million people to Syria and Mesopotamia (except for the Armenians living in Constantinople, Smyrna and Kütayha).

The Armenians, for all practical intents, were defenseless. In some areas they surrendered voluntarily. Only in the town of Van were they saved by the arrival of the Russian army.

What this so-called transport was really all about is apparent from the fact that some 600,000 Armenians were killed immediately or murdered along the way. Their possessions were confiscated. Their real crime, it appears, was religious; the surviving women and children were forced to accept the Islamic faith.[20]

Decline of the West?

What were the prospects for Europe and for the Western world in general in 1918 when a peace was made that really was not a peace? A great many ideals had been shot to pieces on the battlefields. Many people believed that the temper of the times was expressed in a massive two-volume work written by a German named *Oswald Spengler* (1880-1936). This work, which was published some months before the capitulation of Germany, was entitled *Der Untergang des Abendlandes* (English translation entitled: *The Decline of the West*). The book became a bestseller, and within eight years some 100,000 copies had been sold. In America it was much read after 1929, when the Great Depression struck.[21]

Psychologically speaking, the book's success was due to a misunderstanding. Many people took it for granted that the book had been written to defend the thesis that the decline of the German empire was a sign that pointed to the decline of Western civilization as a whole. In 1921 Spengler protested with all his heart against this misrepresentation by publishing an essay which he entitled "Pessimism?"

Spengler had already been at work on his *magnum opus* in 1914. During the war years he not only hoped for but counted on a German victory. Still, in view of what he saw happening in Germany and in Western civilization as a whole, he gathered and organized materials aimed at demonstrating that the Occident or the Western world was heading into an unavoidable decline.

An *unavoidable* decline! Spengler did not write history in the traditional vein, a history of the different peoples of the world in their relationships to each other, a history that moved from antiquity to the middle ages, and from the middle ages to the modern period. To him such divisions were simply banal and short-sighted. He did not discuss peoples, nationalities and races, but *cultures*—cultures that followed one upon the other, each one dying off after completing its own round of existence. Each culture led its own life, comparable to the life of a man or a biological organism: first there was spring, then summer and fall, and finally death in a winter from which no culture was able to escape.

Spengler's range of vision was very comprehensive. Even China and Mexico came under his purview. He distinguished an *Apollinian* culture comprising Greco-Roman antiquity, a *Magian* or *Arabian* culture to which the Babylonians, Egyptians, Arabians and Jews belonged, and a *Faustian* culture which has embraced the Western world since about the tenth century.*

This is not the place to describe the different cultures as Spengler viewed them and compared them with each other. Yet it should be pointed out that although Spengler's knowledge of historical facts was formidable, he deliberately rejected the traditional historical method, which aims at objectivity. Spengler instead emphasized the gift of intuition, of insight, of flashes of illumination. Armed with this gift he even devised predictions and played the role of a *cultural prophet*. It was this prophetic role that fascinated people, for Spengler seemed to speak with indisputable authority. The hands of the clock of "Schiksal" or fate pointed unmistakably to the end of the Faustian culture in all of the Western world.

Spengler claimed he had discovered a permanent law, that of the transition of an overripe culture into a *civilization*, which was the transition from autumn to winter. To become a civilization, he maintained, was the "unavoidable destiny of a culture."[22] He used the comparison of a withered tree which in time is uprooted by a storm.

A culture on its way to destruction—this was civilization in Spengler's view. On the outside it still bears the marks of vital power and luxury, but it is vegetating, pining away, declining.

A culture is creative; it always opens new perspectives. A civilization, however, is sterile; it analyzes what it finds at hand and wants to maintain its prosperity at all costs. A culture thrives in rural areas, while a civilization looks to the corrupt metropolis as its center. A culture is marked by a sense of artistic style, while a civilization is characterized by the breakdown of style and form. A culture continues from the freshness of spring to the beauties of summer, while a civilization shows the faded colors of autumn.[23]

Spengler dates the Faustian civilization as beginning about 1800

---

*The term *Apollinian* is derived from the Greek god Apollo, who was the god of music, singing and art, and the symbol of harmonious balance. The term *Faustian* reminds us of Goethe's Faust, who symbolizes the universal man of the Renaissance in his striving after liberty and happiness.

and ending in the year 2000, when the decline of the West will be complete. He points to the critical situation of the years in which he lives—the degeneration in the arts, the growth of the big cities, the drawbacks of democracy, the rise of the fourth estate.

Spengler believes the crisis is demonstrable in materialism, socialism, parliamentarism and religion. There are problems of property and of marriage. Moreover, both materialism and the class struggle go their unrelenting way. A new caesarism appears on the scene, now taking the form of dictatorship.* Catastrophes occur with distressing regularity. Europe is subject to continuous shifts in the balance of power. The predominance of the white peoples of the earth is coming to an end.

Spengler points to the decline of the old Roman empire and writes: "The vulgar theater, expressionism, boxing matches, Negro dances, gambling, and races—one can find all of this back in Rome." Then he adds:

> The high birthrate of the original populations is a natural phenomenon to which nobody turns his mind . . . Now, however, we meet the Ibsen woman,** the female comrade, the heroine of a comprehensive world-city literature, from modern drama to the Paris novel. Instead of children these ladies have soul-conflicts; marriage is a professional job, and the point is that "the one understands the other." It makes no difference whether an American lady does not want to have children because she does not want to miss a "season," or a Parisian lady because she is afraid her lover will desert her, or an Ibsen heroine because she wants to be her own boss. They are all their own bosses, and they are all sterile.[24]

What makes the reading of Spengler so distressing is that he indicated no way out. Everything is subject to "Schiksal" or destiny.

Arnold Toynbee, who was born in 1889, forms quite a contrast to Spengler. In his ten-volume *Study of History*, this great historian mentioned a number of consecutive civilizations—no fewer than 21 in all. Toynbee emphasized the challenge contained in the crumbling of each civilization, and the possibility of responding to that challenge. He believed he was witnessing the dawning of a new world religion, a

---

*The ideas of Spengler doubtless promoted the rise of National Socialism. Still, Spengler was no friend of Hitler, whom he attacked in 1932 in the preface to his collected works; he called him not a hero but a "heroic tenor"—in other words, an actor.

**In his dramas the Norwegian playwright Hendrik Ibsen (1828-1906) criticized society, including "bourgeois" marriage.

religion that included the "elements of truth" contained in the world's four "higher" religions, i.e. Christianity, Islam, Hinduism, and Buddhism. Toynbee has on occasion been called a Christian, but his syncretism leaves no room for the absolute uniqueness of Christianity.

As far as the crisis of the Western world of his own time was concerned, Toynbee believed it had already started about 1500 and would last some 400 years. (This was his theory concerning all cultures.) Signs of disintegration were to be found everywhere, for a new culture cycle was about to succeed the old one. It was Toynbee's belief that the end of the universal state of the Western cultural cycle had arrived. When the second world war started in 1939, he assumed the victor might well be the founder of the new universal (police) state.[25]

Right up to the time of his death, Toynbee was considered by many to be an authoritative voice. Although many of his ideas have been criticized by other historians,[26] it is undeniable that he was a brilliant thinker who demonstrated remarkable insight into the events and cultural developments of history.

Spengler and Toynbee were not the only thinkers who issued warnings to the West after 1918. We should also take a brief look at Johan Huizinga and P. A. Sorokin.

Johan Huizinga (1872-1945) was a famous and highly perceptive historian at the University of Leiden. In his last two works, *In de schaduwen van morgen* (In the Shadows of Tomorrow, 1935) and *Geschonden wereld* (Damaged World, 1945), he expressed his apprehensions about the symptoms of decadence clearly visible in the culture of his time.

In his 1935 book Huizinga refers directly to Spengler and calls his work an "alarm signal for numerous people in the whole world." He criticizes Spengler, however, for speaking of man as an animal of prey who is therefore to be classified among the higher creatures. He writes: "All such thinking which looks attractive and passes for realism whets the appetite of teenagers."

Among the great ills of his time Huizinga points to the continuous immaturity, which he speaks of as "puerilism." He also mentions superstition and insincerity.

> Man lives in his wonderland literally like a child, even like a child in a fairy tale. He can travel by plane, speak with another hemisphere, eat a snack from a slot-machine, get a continent in his house by means of the radio. He presses a button, and there is life. Will he come of age by this kind of life? The opposite is the case. The world has become his toy. Who can be amazed when he behaves like a child?

When he talks about superstition, Huizinga first mentions the practice of finding out "what the stars foretell" and similar things, but he then goes on to emphasize man's confidence in modern arms:

> The continuing confidence in the effectiveness of war is almost literally a superstition, a remnant from times past. How is it possible that a man like Oswald Spengler in his [book] *Jahre der Entscheidung* [1933] can still indulge in those superstitious fancies? How utterly unfounded and romantic is that illusion—his caesars with their heroic professional soldiers! As if the modern world, in case of necessity, would still be able to restrict the use of its powers and means.[27]

In his book *Geschonden wereld*, which was written ten years later, Huizinga expressed essentially the same point of view. It was a dismal book written in a very dismal time. He appealed to the necessity of an increase in love and humanity, but in the same breath he added: "Just now this war [the second world war, 1939-45] has again sown everywhere its fatal seed of hatred and vengefulness, more than any war before it. How is it possible for the highest of all Christian virtues to gain ground now?"

Huizinga spoke appreciatively of the values of Christianity, but he immediately raised a question about them: "Can one really believe that in the time that is now approaching, the average intelligent man will again live with such conceptions as crucifixion, resurrection, predestination, and judgment?" As for Huizinga himself, his hope was in *real* (not vulgar) humanism, in men of good will.[28] One might well ask, however, whether Huizinga, who was the personification of humanism at its best, was able to comfort many hearts with such affirmations.

Finally, we should look at the criticism leveled at Western civilization by P. A. Sorokin, who was also born in 1889. Sorokin was a Russian who left his homeland in 1923 and became an American citizen in 1930. Shortly thereafter, he was appointed professor of sociology at Harvard University.

In *The Crisis of Our Age*, Sorokin compares the destruction caused by some 967 wars waged between 500 B.C. and A.D. 1925. He concludes that the first century A.D. was the most peaceful one of all, and that the first 25 years of the twentieth century have left us with more wartime destruction than any full century before, with the exception of the situation in Italy in the third century B.C. And if we take account of the second quarter of our century, even that third century B.C. looks rather peaceful.

Sorokin speaks of the breakdown of family life as one of the most serious phenomena of his time. Here he describes its effects: "The result is a surging juvenile delinquency, an increasing number of people without moral integrity multiplying the number of criminals . . . from ordinary killers to the bodyguards of dictators." He goes on to speak of the steadily increasing suicide rate, of all the mental illness, of the dishonesty of diplomats, and writes: "There is almost no government in whatever Western country that has never broken the most solemnly sworn oaths to its subjects—that did not change the fundamental laws (be it constitutions or certain regulations) or refused to acknowledge its obligations concerning the gold standard, securities and loans, the inviolability of judicial pronouncements and numerous other matters."[29]

I realize that in quoting these authors I have gone beyond the bounds of the period to be dealt with in this chapter, but the demoralization of the era during and after the first world war occupied people's minds for a long time. In the next chapter we shall see how it also evoked some different answers.

3

Theology of Crisis

Out of the depths

Earlier we encountered *Karl Barth* as a student influenced by modern theology and as a young minister weighed down by the "predicament of preaching." Although he spent the years of World War I on neutral ground in the Swiss village of Safenwill, he could feel the war rushing by at close hand. When he saw Western culture being broken to pieces in the trenches, what message was there left for him to preach—if he ever had a message? ("Both tables of Moses have slipped away from us," he had written.)

Liberalism provided no answers. It is pathetic to sense the pathos and grief felt by the Swiss liberal church historian Walter Nigg as he describes the situation of his fellow liberals and what was left of their way of thinking in the decades immediately following the first world war: "Their decline reminds one of the last act of a Shakespearean drama, in which we often also find the heroes lying prostrate on the ground."[1]

By his own testimony, Barth experienced a *dies ater*[2] when a good number of German theologians, his former teachers among them, signed a manifesto in which they justified the German contribution to the war. For years he had been attracted by religious socialism, and in

51

1915 he became a social democrat. But after the war he realized as never before that no salvation could be expected from this movement. But where could he find it instead, and what could he preach?

In 1919 he answered this question in a most remarkable way in a commentary he wrote on one of the books of the Bible. It was the book that had so often aroused human consciences—the Letter to the Romans. The commentary made an impact, especially when it was reprinted in 1922; it struck the theological world like a bombshell.*

What was so striking about this commentary? Why did people find it both refreshing and frightening? It was not that the book was unscholarly, although Barth's teacher von Harnack expressed himself rather derogatorily on this point in 1923 when he wrote: "You have changed the theological chair into a pulpit."[3] Barth had in fact written the book in the traditional scholarly way, surrounded by a lot of other books. He was very well informed.

Still, there were two things that stood out. In the first place, Barth's exegesis of this book of the Bible did not consist exclusively of detailed historical criticism—although Barth did not reject the historical-critical method as such—but emphasized the timeliness of the apostolic message for man, for the church of today. Secondly, he applied his message in the form of a sharp attack on the whole spirit of nineteenth-century liberalism, faith in human progress, cultural optimism—in short, on all the things that had been considered to be of the highest value.

A divine judgment had just struck the earth in the events of the first world war, but Barth went on to ask: Is there not a permanent judgment, a *crisis* of God, over the whole world and all men? With the Letter to the Romans in his hand, Barth called on the people of his time to consider that judgment of God. His slogan was: "God is in heaven, man is on earth." And God is the Holy One, the one who is Totally Other! There is an infinite qualitative gulf between time and eternity, between man and God. All talk about God, all theology and all preaching, should therefore bear an *eschatalogical* character. By this term *eschatalogical* Barth did not mean to refer to the coming end of all things but to the permanent relatedness to God, whom we can never know directly from human *experience* or from the course of

---

*The second printing was a new edition involving such extensive revisions that Barth could honestly say that he had "left no stone unturned." He was struggling to find his way.

history but only when it pleases the Lord to reveal Himself in a moment of time, as the tangent touches the circle.

The central theme of the Letter to the Romans is the resurrection gospel. The resurrection, moreover, is much more than historical fact; it represents the intersection of time and eternity. In the resurrection we see the absolute antithesis between the justice of God and the justice of man. All human righteousness falls under the judgment of God and is subject to the crisis—human sensuality and greed, human science and morals, human religion and even the Christian religion.

In his sharp condemnation of Christian religion, Barth was in agreement with *Kierkegaard*, whom he greatly admired in those years. Kierkegaard had sharply attacked the secularized, established church of his days. Barth was also influenced by *Dostoevski*, for whom the blindness and hardness of autonomous religious man is embodied in the figure of the Grand Inquisitor.[4] Barth compared the "religious" man to the Prometheus figure of Greek mythology; Prometheus stole the fire of the gods for his own use. But Barth argued that if we condemn the church in this way, we should also show solidarity toward her and condemn ourselves—and if we condemn ourselves, in that very act the hope of resurrection begins to dawn.

In Barth's commentary on Romans, we hear a cry from the depths. Because it was so genuine, it won a wide hearing. Barth himself declared later that he was like a man "who, ascending the dark staircase of a church tower and trying to steady himself, reached for the banister, but got hold of the bell rope instead. To his horror, he then had to listen to what the great bell sounded over him, and not over him alone."[5]

Neo-orthodoxy

After his commentary on Romans, Barth's influence increased steadily. Within his own lifetime he was hailed as the greatest theologian of his time, the most important Protestant theologian after Schleiermacher, and a man who could be placed on the same level as Augustine, Anselm, Aquinas, Luther and Calvin.[6] This may sound rather high-flown, but it does indicate how much and how widely Barth was respected, not only by Protestants but also by Roman Catholics. He was revered not only in Switzerland and Germany but also in the Netherlands, Scotland and America. In England, however, his influence was never very extensive.

In 1921 Barth was appointed to a chair of Reformed theology

established at Göttingen. Four years later he moved on to Münster, where he taught dogmatics. Barth continued his work from 1930 to 1935 in Bonn, but he was finally dismissed because of his participation in the struggle of the "Confessing Church" against the totalitarian claims of the Hitler regime. (I will say more on that subject later.) Barth was then appointed professor of dogmatics at Basel, where he continued to teach until 1962 and to work until his death in 1968. Students from various countries crowded his classroom as he talked with them from his chair or exchanged ideas with them in discussion.

As the years went by, his major work, the *Church Dogmatics*, grew, one impressive volume following another. When 12 white volumes finally stood in a row on the shelf, he spoke of them together as "the lady with the crinoline."[7] But a final volume still remained unwritten. In 1967 he issued a volume on the doctrine of baptism, in which we read the following revolutionary words: "How will the church be a mature church, or become a mature church anew, as long as it stubbornly, and against its better knowledge and conscience, continues to waste the water of baptism in such an irreverent way as it has been doing for more than a thousand years?"[8] A year later he was dead.

Karl Barth

When Barth's theology is characterized as "neo-orthodox." the prefix "neo-" should be stressed, for it is in fact different from the old orthodoxy. We should not forget, however, that Barth's theology was experienced in the first place as an orthodox appeal, and it has influenced a great many people as such. Back in 1937, the liberal Walter Nigg wrote with dismay about the construction of an "orthodox doctrine influenced by the theology of Calvin."[9] A much more moderate evaluation is presented by G. W. Bromiley, the American translator of Barth's *Church*

Dogmatics, who speaks of "an attempt to write a biblical and evangelical dogmatics which cuts across established orthodoxy at many points."[10] Bromiley appreciates especially Barth's acceptance of the doctrine of the Trinity, his acceptance of the virgin birth, his acceptance of the place and significance of the Holy Spirit, his fundamental conviction that dogmatics should not be founded on human psychology or philosophy but on the self-revelation of the triune God, his rejection of any natural theology and his continuing emphasis on Christology.[11]

We should indeed pay attention to these things, and we should not forget that Barth sounded his trumpet in a critical period against the spirit of the age. But to say this, is not to say enough—for more than one reason.

In the first place, it should be noted that Barth's argumentation repeatedly moves between two poles, between yes and no, between accepting with the one hand and giving back with the other. In other words, he uses a *dialectical method*. His use of this method is closely bound up with his conviction that God is in heaven while man is on the earth. It is impossible for man to ever speak directly about God; he can only talk about God indirectly or paradoxically.

In the second place, we must bear in mind that despite his radical criticism of cultural Protestantism, Barth remains a child of the nineteenth century in several respects. This becomes very evident when we look at his *doctrine of Scripture*. On the one hand he does not hesitate to speak of the Bible as the Word of God as far as its form and content are concerned, and in his *Church Dogmatics* he engages in enormous exegetical expositions in which criticism of Scripture, generally speaking, plays no role. On the other hand, he never breaks with the historical-critical approach to Scripture, which he values greatly. Some comments he wrote back in 1923 in his commentary on Romans are very revealing on this point: "As for the relativity of all human words, including those of Paul, I share the opinion of Bultmann and of all intelligent people."[12] It is noteworthy that Barth presents Bultmann and himself as "intelligent people," i.e. critical people, people who are even able to criticize the letters of Paul. Also unmistakably clear are certain words in his *Church Dogmatics*: "The prophets and apostles as such, even in their function of witnesses, even when writing down their witness, were real historical men as we are, and therefore sinful in their actions and indeed guilty of error in the spoken and written word."[13]

There is only one answer to the question of how it is possible for

Barth to identify the word of Scripture with the Word of God to such a degree, while at the same time qualifying the word of Scripture as a totally human word. That answer is to be found in Barth's fundamental principle of the high and holy God who never abdicates His power, even though He speaks through the fallible human word whenever it pleases Him to do so. We should also bear in mind the influence of *Martin Kähler*, who distinguished between the "history" of the historical Jesus and the "witness" of the suprahistorical Christ. I will have more to say about Kähler when I discuss the position of Rudolf Bultmann, who was Barth's early friend.

It becomes obvious, however, that when the principle of the total authority of Scripture is abandoned, there are some serious consequences, for it is impossible to criticize the *form* without at the same time criticizing the *contents*. This becomes evident, for example, in Barth's doctrine of *creation*.

What we find in the first chapters of the Bible, according to Barth, is a *saga*. A saga is something quite different from a myth. A myth is a story devised by pagans, a story about gods and divine matters, as they fantasized about the gods and wound up identifying the gods with the world. In a saga we find the fantasy of a witness to revelation, a witness who believes in a God as separate from this world. Although the Biblical stories about creation and the fall into sin are fantasies, they do bear witness to the living God and His world.

The inadequacy of this distinction between two kinds of fantasy soon becomes clear. For one thing, questions concerning the historicity of creation, of the fall into sin, and of the state of innocence remain unanswered. In fact, these questions lose their importance in Barth's way of thinking as soon as he applies his distinction between "history" *(Historie)* and "Geschichte."

"History," for Barth, is the human story of what actually happened. That story as such is subject to human criticism. History represents what really happened, but it is not yet divine revelation. "Geschichte," which Barth also speaks of as "urgeschichte," is the acting of God in time. The resurrection of Christ belongs to the domain of "Geschichte," but it need not therefore be part of "history" as well. "Geschichte" can only be experienced by an act of God as He discloses Himself and makes us contemporaries of what we observe.

All of this is rather confusing and almost looks like a play on words. It sometimes appears as if a part of the nineteenth-century heritage that has been dismissed at the front door comes sneaking into the back door again.

I do not have adequate space in this context to summarize the entire theology of Karl Barth. In conclusion I will simply draw your attention to several points in connection with the doctrines of election and infant baptism.

Barth emphatically rejects Calvin's doctrine of predestination; he denies that God knew and loved His own from eternity while passing other people by. This doctrine, which has long been a stumbling block, was also an offense to Barth, who maintained that, in Christ, God has said yes to all men. Christ was the great Elect, and at the same time He was the great Reprobate. In Christ all men are called to believe in the condemnation of their sins. Unbelief is therefore "an objective, real and ontological impossibility. Faith has become an objective, real and ontological [i.e. essential, belonging to the essence] possibility for everyone."[14]

Such talk raises an unavoidable question: Was Barth a universalist then? Did he believe in the universal salvation of humankind? He refused to give an answer to this question.

As far as infant baptism is concerned, Barth did not join the ranks of the Baptists, but he did defend one of their fundamental convictions in a powerful way; he claimed there is no Scriptural proof for this kind of baptism. Barth argued that the essential element, i.e. the believing reception of the sacrament, is lacking in the case of infant baptism. Consequently he characterized infant baptism as "an execution without a victim."[15]

Now, the comparison between baptism and an execution is not a very good one. But a more important consideration is the argument advanced against the position defended by Barth, namely, that in the New Testament, children of believers are regarded as members of the church to whom the salvation of the Lord is promised (see Acts 2:39: I Cor. 7:14).

Finally, we must never forget how Barth witnessed incessantly to the surprising wonder of God's grace. One day this became apparent in a touching way when Barth was discussing the pope and the office of Peter in the church with the Roman Catholic theologian Hans Küng. The two theologians did not agree, but Küng said at last: "All right, I believe at any rate that you are speaking in good faith." Barth replied: "Do you really believe that? I don't believe it. When the day comes that I must appear before my Lord, I will not come with all my works, with my *Dogmatics* on my back. All the angels would laugh at me! Neither will I say: 'I've always had good intentions; I've always acted in good faith.' No, at that moment I will only say: 'Lord, be merciful to me, a sinner.' "[16]

Emil Brunner

The life of Barth has been marked by various conflicts. In the first place, he did battle with the theologians of religious experience and of culture by whom he had been fascinated during his student years. Harnack was their spokesman when he called Barth a "despiser of scientific theology." Barth also became involved in controversies with representatives of Dutch Reformed theology, especially with *Klaas Schilder* and *G. C. Berkouwer*, who were young theologians at the time, and *Cornelius Van Til* in America. Finally, he became embroiled in conflicts with a number of theologians who had supported him at first but who later, for various reasons, turned their backs on him. Here *Friedrich Gogarten, Rudolf Bultmann* and *Emil Brunner* should be mentioned.

It is remarkable that a clear "No" has twice been expressed as far as the relationship between Barth and Brunner is concerned. The first time it came from Barth, and the second time from Brunner.

In 1932 Barth addressed a sharp "No" to his friend and supporter Brunner when he began to teach ever more clearly that there was still a point of contact in "fallen"* man for the working of the Word of God. In Barth's opinion, the outlines of a new "natural" theology were taking shape here. He even warned Brunner against moving in the direction of Rome. In his answer, Brunner declared to his regret that Barth had forced a rupture in their "faithful collaboration in the struggle," but they still agreed on the main points as far as he was concerned.[17]

The second "No" was heard in 1961 when Brunner wrote an article in the *Neue Züricher Zeitung* in which he sharply rejected Barth's conciliatory attitude toward Communism. Barth had written an open letter to the Christians of eastern Europe in which he said: "One can, after all, preach Christianity, believe Christianity and live Christianity under a Communistic regime." Brunner replied: "And so the poison which paralyses the will to resist—is becoming virulent. Thus the church, without at all being Communist, is unwittingly doing the work of Communism."[18]

Brunner, who was born in 1889, was a somewhat younger contemporary of Barth. Like Barth, he was a Swiss who had parted company with his liberal theological teachers. He was deeply impressed

---

*I have placed this term between quotation marks because neither Barth nor Brunner believed in a historical fall into sin.

with Barth's commentary on Romans; in *Die Mystiek und das Wort* (Mysticism and the Word, 1924), he definitely turned away from the man-centered theology of Schleiermacher which had dominated the nineteenth century.

At first Barth thought very highly of Brunner and praised him for his "outstanding abilities." He commended him because, like Barth, he "saw in the Word of God and in His revelation the first condition of all real knowledge."[19] Yet there was that great conflict in 1932. Was it only a misunderstanding? Despite the ongoing agreement, a fundamental conflict between the two theologians had arisen.

Brunner remained an apologist all through his life. His theology

Emil Brunner

has been called a *missionary* theology.[20] He felt the need of a common basis of discussion, and he found it in the remnants of the image of God which are still present in every man. Man is still accountable in his knowledge and conscience; there is still a general revelation.

Barth denied any general revelation and argued instead that there is only one revelation in Jesus Christ, who will Himself take care of the point of contact.[21] Brunner, however, continued to speak of a revelation in creation, which leaves man without an excuse. There is still a creation-order recognizable in marriage, the family and the state. This creation-order is the point of departure for social ethics, which only comes into its own in personal relationships governed by the Biblical command of love.

From Brunner's point of view, many perspectives open up for which a Biblical Christian can only be thankful.[22] However, it would be a serious mistake to deduce from this that Brunner's theology is indeed a Biblical theology.

When Brunner speaks of the image of God, he reminds us of what we read in the Heidelberg Catechism about the creation of our first parents, Adam and Eve, in Paradise. However, he does not believe, any more than Barth does, that those first parents actually existed. "There was not some human being that lived ages ago in prehistoric times and could be identified as Adam created in the image of God; Adam is you and me and everyone."[23] Brunner recognizes only the empirical man of today. He does not even leave room for the man who will come to be; in essence, he does not believe in the resurrection of the body.[24]

What does Brunner make of Scripture, then? He regards Scripture very highly as the first-ranking witness of the revelation, but this revelation only becomes a reality in personal encounters. Therefore we must abandon all ideas about a verbal inspiration, which is only legalism anyway. If anyone cares to appeal to II Timothy 3:16, where we read that "all scripture is inspired by God," Brunner would tell him II Timothy was not written by Paul but was written in the second century and wrongly attributed to Paul. The letter contains both Jewish formalism with regard to Scripture and the legalistic structure of an organized church under the leadership of a bishop.[25]

Brunner's influence has been greater than Barth's in Anglo-Saxon countries and in Japan. In 1913 Brunner taught in Leeds, and in 1919-20 he studied at Union Seminary in New York. He sympathized with the (twentieth-century) Oxford movement at the beginning of the thirties. Brunner was also a guest professor at Princeton in 1938-39 and at the Christian University of Japan from 1953 through 1955. His main function, meanwhile, was teaching dogmatics at Zurich.

The rather practical-humanistic trend[26] of Brunner's dialectical thinking afforded him easier access to the not-so-speculative Englishmen and the pragmatic Americans. Most of his works have been translated into English.

Rudolf Bultmann

Barth was once characterized as a "troubler of Israel" because of his angry condemnation of the theology prevalent thus far. Rudolf Bultmann, who was originally one of his collaborators, has been called the "disturber of the peace of neo-orthodoxy."[27]

At first Bultmann was attracted by dialectical theology. He was at that time a young and promising New Testament professor at Marburg who had already written an important work entitled *Geschichte der synoptischen Tradition* (1921). He agreed with Barth about the relevance of the living Word of the living God, and he also agreed with him on his conception of Scripture; that is to say, Bultmann regarded Scripture as a fallible human word subject to historical-critical investigation, while truly witnessing to God all the same. But in the course of time they parted company exactly on this point. Barth's Biblical criticism did not play a dominant role in his own thought. Bultmann, however, engaged in Biblical criticism in such an extraordinarily consistent way and to such an extent that Barth felt it necessary to refute it.[28]

What was so special or different about Bultmann's Biblical criticism? In the first place, it was "form-criticism." Form-criticism is an approach to Scripture that took many Old and New Testament scholars almost by storm in the twentieth century.

Form-criticism had already begun with the teaching of *Herman Gunkel*, who suggested there were different forms of literature present in the background to the Old Testament, including myths, fairy tales and sagas. This idea was applied to the New Testament by *K. L. Schmidt* in 1919 when he published his book *Der Rahmen der Geschichte Jesus* (The Framework of the History of Jesus). Schmidt says we do not find a biography of Jesus in the gospels; what we find instead is a collection of testimonies of the faith of the early church. These ideas were carried through by Bultmann in his book on the history of the synoptic tradition* (1921) and also in his later works. In his opinion he had shown them to be correct.

We can take it for granted, according to Bultmann, that we meet with *second-hand information* in the gospel stories. What we find in the gospels is a collection of traditions concerning Jesus, traditions that took shape over the course of time and then were written down.

---

*Matthew, Mark and Luke are often called the synoptic evangelists because they each offer a synopsis or general view of the life of Jesus.

Each gospel is a *congregational book* in a double sense; it contains the congregational theology or the theological conceptions of the early church, and it has to provide for the growing educational and liturgical needs of the young church.

Because of this alleged state of affairs, Bultmann believes these gospel stories bear a thoroughly mythological character; they give expression to the thought-world of people who were imbued with mythical ideas. Bultmann introduces these mythical ideas as follows:

> The earth is viewed as a three-storied structure, with the earth in the center, the heaven above, and the underworld beneath. Heaven is the abode of God and of celestial beings—the angels. The underworld is hell, the place of torment . . . . The earth is the scene of the supernatural activity of God and his angels on the one hand, and of Satan and his demons on the other . . . . This aeon is held in bondage by Satan, sin and death (for "powers" is precisely what they are), and hastens toward its end. The end will come very soon, and will take the form of a cosmic catastrophe . . . "In the fullness of time" God sent forth his Son, a pre-existent divine Being, who appears on earth as a man. He dies the death of a sinner on the cross and makes atonement for the sins of men. His resurrection marks the beginning of the cosmic catastrophe. Death, the consequence of Adam's fall, is abolished, and the demonic forces are deprived of their power. The risen Christ is exalted at the right hand of God in heaven and made "Lord and King." He will come again on the clouds of heaven to complete the work of redemption, and the resurrection and judgment of men will follow. Sin, suffering, and death will then be finally abolished. All this is to happen very soon; indeed, Paul thinks that he himself will live to see it.[29]

I don't propose to discuss the question of whether these words of Bultmann accurately describe the world view of the people of the New Testament times. The point is that he maintains that such a world view is absolutely unacceptable to modern man since it would require a "sacrifice of the intellect," a renunciation of thinking. Today we are acquainted with unchangeable laws of nature which exclude any and all miracles. We know there is an omnipresent causality that leaves no room for an alleged hand of God, and we also know sickness is caused by microbes—not by demons.

What is Bultmann's intention, then? Does he propose to remove all those myths from the Bible? That would be to follow the route already taken by D. F. Strauss (see Volume VI, Chap. 5) and all the negative critics in the nineteenth century. No, what Bultmann has in mind first of all is to "interpret" those myths. He wants to read them in the light of the Jewish-apocalyptic milieu* in which the gospels originated (in his opinion), according to the influence of pre-Christian Gnosticism** and of the miraculous faith of the first disciples. More important, however, is the effort to bring out the deeper meaning of those myths. This, according to Bultmann, is the task of Christian preaching.

What is the message, the "kerugma,"† of the New Testament, the collection of writings that are entirely unacceptable from a scientific standpoint? It is that we are straightforwardly confronted with our own selves, with decisions we must make, with our authentic existence.††

Let's listen to what Bultmann tells us about the meaning of the cross, for example:

Rudolf Bultmann

To believe in the cross of Jesus does not mean to concern ourselves with a mythical process wrought outside of us and our world, but rather to make the cross of Christ our own, to undergo crucifixion with him. As far as its meaning, that is, its meaning for faith, is concerned, it is an ever-present reality.[30]

He talks about the resurrection in similar fashion. On the one hand it cannot be regarded as a historical

---

fact; it took place only in the visions of the disciples. On the other hand, it has a personal meaning because it points to *my* resurrection to a new life. This is the recurring theme in Bultmann's "demythologizing." G. E. Ladd therefore writes: "If salvation is correctly understood in terms of authentic existence; if authenticity means complete independence of all external securities, including objective acts of God in history and objectifying theological statements about God, man and salvation; then it is difficult to see how anyone prior to the emergence of existentialism can properly be called Christian."[31]

The influence of Bultmann's theology has been great. However, his disciples (G. Bornkamm, H. Conzelmann, E. Fuchs, and E. Käsemann in Germany; J. M. Robinson and S. M. Ogden in America) have no ready answer to the question of *how much* the gospel stories can still be considered genuinely historical. Generally speaking, there is a quest for a basis of more historical reality than Bultmann wished to concede. Still, if the Scripture that cannot be broken (John 10:35) is not received in all its parts as the authoritative Word of God, this quest will remain a searching and groping for uncertain things.

Reinhold Niebuhr

Like Bultmann, Reinhold Niebuhr (born in 1896) was the son of a Lutheran minister. Like Barth, he was initially attracted by socialism. Yet he was unlike both men insofar as he was an American who took his stand against both a superficial American faith in human progress and the kind of orthodoxy that tolerates social abuses.

Earlier I wrote about the American faith in progress (see Volume VI, Chap. 6), and later I will have more to say on this subject (see Chapter 13 below). That faith fostered great confidence in the inborn goodness of man and in the expected coming of a kingdom of God in which peace and love would reign through a joint effort of all men.

Orthodoxy, according to Niebuhr, sings its psalms on Sunday but neglects to practice what it preaches on the other days of the week. Because of its pessimistic doctrine of man, it makes no serious effort to improve the world.

When Niebuhr was a young pastor in Detroit, the city of Ford, he saw the poverty of many workmen at close quarters. He did not shrink from taking their side. At that time (1915-1928) he was a socialist and a pacifist. As the faithful pastor of his congregation, he was not just sitting in his study hurling some big words and mighty slogans at the world.

The old Lutheran faith, the paternal heritage, did not depart from him. He himself says the following about his Lutheran heritage:

> I relearned the essentials of the Christian faith at the bedside of a nice old soul. I was conscious of the nobility which was the fruit of the simple faith of a simple woman; and that was not the only time in parish duties in which I learned the meaning of Christ's prayer: "I thank thee, Father, that thou hast withheld these things from the wise and prudent and revealed them unto babes."[32]

This did not mean, however, that Niebuhr had become orthodox. As he continued to theologize and philosophize he did use orthodox terms to an increasing degree. Still, he attached a *neo-orthodox* meaning to them.

From 1928 until his retirement in 1960, Niebuhr was a professor at Union Theological Seminary in New York. He was involved in an amazing number of activities as a teacher, author, writer of many articles and books, and an advisor to many. Just as Barth's commentary on Romans upset European theological thinking, Niebuhr's *The Nature and Destiny of Man* (1941) changed the theological climate in America.

What were Niebuhr's ideas? He wanted to be a *realistic* theologian—a man speaking to man in his actual situation. And what is man, according to Niebuhr? He is a sinner. The human situation is marked not by good but by evil.

As far as sin is concerned, Niebuhr does not speak of a *chronological* order in which we have first a good creation and then disobedience to God, followed by an unhappy existence for man. Niebuhr characterizes sin instead in terms of the *vertical* order of existential philosophy. There are several strata of consciousness to man as he is and always has been. Man is at the same time a piece of nature and a free personality, and this dualism always marks his existence. He wants to go up, but he is pulled down. The result is a situation of anxiety. In that anxiety man is completely (existentially) aware of himself. He looks for security and protection for his selfhood and tries to exert power.

Niebuhr is a master in describing how power is used and abused in modern life. He speaks of social injustice, discrimination and exploitation and mentions atomic power, which can both enrich life and destroy it. In other words, the history of so-called human progress is at the same time the history of inevitable imperfection.

The light of the cross shines above all this as a magnificent symbol of what is impossible with men. Christ dies denying Himself. He has the power to deliver Himself, but He does not make use of that power.

The grace of God makes us share in the cross of Christ. One of Niebuhr's beloved texts is Galatians 2:20: "I have been crucified with Christ; it is no longer I who live, but Christ who lives in me."[33] Since he is justified by his faith in the Crucified One, the Christian leads a life which, although imperfect, aims daily at the practice of *agapé*, of Christian love—not just in his personal life but also in his social relations.

Undoubtably, some Biblical themes come through here. Still, we should listen to G. Brillenburg Wurth who, after drawing this conclusion, immediately goes on to say: "Meanwhile, our serious objection has not been disproved, namely, that Niebuhr's overall presentation of the cross and the resurrection in the spirit of existentialism looks more like a revelation about the deepest existential relation between God and man than a Biblical depiction of the true history of salvation, the history in which God, in Christ, performs His saving historical acts, for us as human beings and apart from our contribution."[34]

Essentially Niebuhr does not believe in a historical beginning, a historical middle (the Incarnation is a "myth"), and a historical end (there are only eschatalogical symbols). His theological thinking is dominated by his philosophical premises.

In this chapter on the theology of crisis, there are various other neo-orthodox theologians who could be mentioned, such as *T. Haitjema, G. F. van Niftrik*, and *K. H. Miskotte* in the Netherlands. Just as in the case of nineteenth-century "Vermittlungstheologie," we can speak of right-wing and left-wing currents among them, depending on their attitude toward Biblical criticism.

Reinhold Niebuhr

4

Back to the Sources

Necessary reflection

When I talk about "sources" in this chapter, it will be in a very careful, limited manner. I do not mean to talk about the sources from which we draw our faith-knowledge. If that were my topic, I would arrive at the *Sola Scriptura* of the Reformation. I would also have to deal with the many hermeneutical* questions raised in our century. On the other hand, I cannot completely avoid mentioning those ultimate sources, for I must deal with some of the ideas of the Reformers concerning the authority of Scripture.

Neither do I mean to deal with the sources from which we draw our knowledge of the history of the church—the writings of the apostolic fathers and the church fathers, the acts of the councils and of the synods, the lives of the saints, the works of the scholastics and mystics, the chronicles of the monasteries and the works and biographies of the Reformers. There are so many sources for the church's history that they can hardly all be mentioned.

Many of those sources had been published in the course of the nineteenth century. Both in history in general and in church history,

---

*Pertaining to the science of interpretation.

much was achieved. We continue to be filled with respect when we examine the books containing sources published in that century.

I think, for example, of the so-called Weimar edition of the works of Luther (1883-1909). In the "Corpus Reformatorum" there were editions of the works of Melanchthon (1834-1860), Calvin (1863-1900) and Zwingli (1905-1968, not yet completed). There was the publication of the correspondence of the Reformers in French by A. L. Herminjard (1866-1897). From 1840 on, the English Parker Society put out editions of the works of English theologians from the Reformation era. Kuyper published an edition of the works of Johannes à Lasco. In 1882 Kuyper and some others established the *Bibliotheca Reformata*, and we should also note the *Bibliotheca Reformata Neerlandica*, edited by S. Cramer and F. Pijper (1903-1910), and other such ventures. As for the Roman Catholics, they republished the works of Thomas Aquinas between 1882 and 1904.

All these publications and sources were composed and printed with the greatest accuracy. But when all the work was done, some questions were still unanswered. Who was the real Luther? What was the authentic concern of Zwingli? What about Calvin? How is Thomas Aquinas to be interpreted? What place and meaning should be assigned to the Anabaptists and Mennonites?

In the preceding chapter I talked about *neo-orthodoxy*, a term that immediately raises questions about similarities to orthodoxy. Comparable questions could be raised about such terms as neo-Lutheranism, neo-Calvinism, and neo-Thomism. Earlier I talked about the Zwingli problem (see Volume III, Chap. 2). Moreover, *Neo-Protestantism* has been advanced as a topic for discussion by Ernst Troeltsch (see p. 23 above) and others.[1] The self-confidence expressed in this term clearly meant an abolition of the original Protestantism, which had been so badly mauled in the crisis of World War I.

A new quest was underway for some authority other than the authority of one's own conscience, a stronger authority than one's own power of thinking. Was it possible the Reformers might still have a message for the church of the twentieth century? Some reflection was necessary and unavoidable.

A Luther renaissance

The term "Luther renaissance" is often used to refer to the renewed interest in the *real* Luther and his significance for the church of today. That interest has increased especially since 1917, the fourth centennial observation of the year in which Luther nailed his 95 Theses to the door of the Castle Church in Wittenberg.

Karl Holl (1866-1926), a Luther scholar of the first rank, delivered a speech in 1917 on the topic "What did Luther understand by religion?" It was such a good speech that Harnack, who was certainly not of one mind with Holl, felt compelled to observe: "Both theological science and the Protestant church have arrived at a new stage in their understanding of the Reformer Luther since the appearance of Holl's book about him, a book that represents Holl's greatest achievement."[2]

What was the significance of Holl's work? Above all, he elucidated Luther's life and work in a strictly scientific manner and made him appear before our eyes as a living human being. And Holl refrained from adding that while all of this might appear very fascinating and interesting, it is not relevant to our time anymore. Such a disclaimer would be the approach adopted by the historicist school.* That was how the great men of cultural Protestantism usually dissociated themselves from Luther.

Holl recognized the significance of Luther *for the present*. He described his distressed conscience and his continuous afflictions— but not as fascinating psychological phenomena or as starting points for a nineteenth-century theology of experience. Rather, he pointed to Luther's encounter with the living God who touched his conscience, who frightened him but also comforted him with the assurance of His grace.

Holl pictured both Luther and Calvin as men who had a message relevant to the confusion of their time. By their decree that all things should be done to the honor of God and the welfare of one's neighbor, they had influenced the culture of their own time, along with its political science, economic thinking and art. Only a similar religious theory and practice, Holl believed, would be sufficient to revive and restore the world of the twentieth century.[3]

Holl was only able to write as he did because of his deep knowledge of the works of Luther. Through his work Holl stimulated a renewed, intense study of the sources. In 1918 a Luther Association was founded in Germany, of which Holl served as chairman for some years. In 1932 a Luther Academy was established. Since 1925, a year-

---

*Historicism is the idea of the time-relatedness of all historical persons and events, the idea that they can therefore have only a relative value. Ernst Troeltsch has been called an important representative of historicism.

book published by a Luther Association has surveyed the ever-growing Luther literature.

There are a number of other important thinkers who could be mentioned with Holl. For the present I will note only *Werner Elert* (1885-1954) and Paul Althaus.

In his "morphology of Lutheranism,"* Elert tried to draw an overall picture of Luther's influence in all areas of life. He believed that the confession of justification by faith could have far-reaching consequences for the life of the nation and the state, for law and politics. When put together with the Lutheran doctrine of "calling," it could also have great implications for the daily work of the Christian.

In his major work on the last things, *Paul Althaus* tried to apply Luther's principle of Scripture[4] in a modern way. As he wrote about the future of Christ, he felt unable to accept the relevant Scripture passages at face value, for in his opinion they are time-bound and contradict each other on more than one point. He therefore applied a standard he believed was found *in* the written Word of God, but which also transcended it, i.e. went beyond it. He defined this standard as "the promise which is Jesus Christ, the Crucified and Risen One, Himself."[5]

This was and remained the Achilles heel of many of the newer studies of Luther—the critical approach to the Scriptures which, in its subjectivism, did not disallow the position of the nineteenth century. This applies particularly to the Luther renaissance in Sweden, which is usually connected with such names as Aulén, Nygren and Wingren (the so-called school of Lund).

Although both *G. Aulén* and *A. Nygren* have often written splendid things and did not want to return to the modern theology of the nineteenth century, they stuck to their critical views of Scripture to such a degree that the liberal Swedish theologian J. Lindskog could make this declaration concerning Aulén's theology:

> If I were an African Negro I could certainly say about David Livingstone what Aulén says about Christ. His love was God's own love, nothing less. He did God's own work . . . and a devout Hindu could certainly claim for Gandhi what here is said about Livingstone.[6]

---

*The term *morphology* was used often by Oswald Spengler to refer to the method by which he compared the characteristics of the different cultures. Elert uses it to describe the structure of Lutheranism.

Aulén in fact denied the virgin birth of Christ, His physical resurrection and even His divinity. The works of Wingren, including a study of Luther's doctrine of calling (1942), bore more of an orthodox Lutheran character.

In America, too, important studies of Luther appeared. A translation of Luther's works in six volumes was published between 1915 and 1932. A large-scale new translation based on the Weimar edition has been published in part since 1955; eventually it will finally include 55 volumes. R. H. Bainton wrote a very popular Luther biography entitled *Here I Stand* (1950). J. H. Grimm wrote a fine history of the Reformation (1954). Also important are the studies of the liberal W. Pauck, which have been published together in his book *The Heritage of the Reformation* (1961).

Intense study of Calvin

The well-known German church historian Gustav Krüger wrote in 1929: "Apparently we have not yet found the basis for a systematic exposition [of Calvin's ideas], and every attempt to do so must meet with special difficulties, given Calvin's method and manner of working."[7] In the same year, the Dutch theologian Klaas Schilder spoke of "an encouraging interest in Calvin, which is [yet] not at all a product of an understanding of Calvin." He characterized his own era as a "time in which many who hardly want to follow Calvin—or not at all—appeal to him all the same."[8]

Two remarkable statements! And they both relate to the same problem: What was it that Calvin really stood for? Krüger attributes this problem to alleged inconsistencies in Calvin himself, while Schilder attributes it to a failure on the part of the research workers.*

Since the beginning of our century, a significant number of Calvin studies have been published. A 59-volume edition of his *Opera* was completed in 1900, a scholarly achievement of the first rank. Also noteworthy were Abraham Kuyper's impressive lectures on Calvinism, delivered in Princeton in 1898 and published in both English and Dutch in 1899. We should remember the Calvin biography published by Williston Walker in America in 1906, A. Lang's biography published in Germany in 1909, and Emile Doumergue's monumental biography, published in France (7 volumes, 1899-1927). Moreover, a number of special studies have ap-

---

*Schilder discussed the position of Prof. T. L. Haitjema, i.e. that of dialectical theology.

peared, such as Prof. Bohatec's studies on Calvin's doctrine of providence and on the special character of his theology (both 1909), and S. P. Dee's study on Calvin's conception of faith (1918). There are many other such studies which could be mentioned. Still, there was such a lack of unanimity that Hermann Baucke, a young German theologian could write a brilliant study in 1922 (shortly before his own death) on the problems of the theology of Calvin. What were those problems?

The scholars disagreed on the relationship between Luther and Calvin. A. Ritschl had maintained that Calvin was only a partisan of Luther, a kind of pocket-sized Luther. This was denied by Ernst Troeltsch, who had in turn placed both Reformers under the heading of the middle ages. Modern thinking, he believed, began with the Socinians and the Anabaptists.

There was also a disagreement on Calvin's starting point, the dominating principle of his thought. Ever since the days of Schleiermacher, who had based his work on man's feeling of absolute dependence, each new theological system was dominated by its own unique, fundamental conviction. Was it true that Calvin had done the same thing, that he had built up a system founded on his doctrine of predestination or on the sovereignty of God? And was it true that this system had some rationalistic overtones?

There was also disagreement on newly discovered details of Calvin's doctrines. Martin Schultze, for example, wrote a monograph in 1901 on a small but important chapter of the *Institutes*, the one on "De meditatione futurae vita" (Meditation about the future life). He concluded Calvin was basically a medieval man who defended asceticism and despised the world. If this was true, what was left of the significance of Calvin and Calvinism for cultural life, and of the calling, which is so highly rated by many, to serve God "in all areas of life"?[9]

Other such problems were also discussed, often taking on a special slant because of the rise of dialectical theology, which at first almost seemed Calvinistic. It would carry me too far from my purpose to also outline the ingenious "solution" Baucke offered for the problems that were raised. I will only quote his conclusion:

> Calvin is the brilliant theologian and founder of churches, the powerful hero of piety. He does not represent a new type of religion; but that he fashioned the new form of religion reared by Luther into an independent and peculiar form, both in theology and in the church, is proven

by the living witness of the church founded by him, the theology living and working in it and its living piety.[10]

After Baucke's initial work, several other studies appeared in which efforts were made to characterize Calvin's theology. In his survey of these studies, Wilhelm Niesel drew the following conclusion in 1938: "The decisive contribution made by all these theologians in the light of current points of view is that the problems of Calvin's theology are not the result of structure or contents but of the fact that it makes a serious effort to be a real *theology*."[11]

This is essentially a simple conclusion. At one time Melanchthon characterized Calvin as "*the* theologian." What he really wanted was to speak of God in *all* his theological work—with his hand on the Bible, in the service of the church, and for the welfare of the world. It took many years to discover this position because it was considered obsolete in academic circles. The liberal, modern theology had not produced theologians worthy of the name!

I could mention the names of a great many more scholars who are important for their Calvin research in the first half of our century, research that still continues year after year.[12] One such scholar who definitely deserves mention is the remarkable theologian *A. Lecerf*. Originally a political leftist, he was converted through the reading of the *Institutes* and had himself baptized against the will of his parents when he was 17 years old. In 1938 he became a professor of dogmatics at the theological faculty of Paris. He was also the founder of the Société Calviniste de France (Calvinistic Society of France).

Earlier I mentioned *J. Bohatec*. A Czech by origin, he was a thorough student of Calvin and became a personal friend of Herman Dooyeweerd, a law professor at the Free University of Amsterdam. Bohatec became co-editor of the periodical *Philosophia Reformata*, in which Dooyeweerd, the author of *A New Critique of Theoretical Thought* (Dutch first edition entitled *De wijsbegeerte der wetsidee*), set forth his Calvinistic philosophical ideas. Bohatec's fellow workers included D. H. T. Vollenhoven, S. U. Zuidema and Hendrik Van Riessen.

Finally, we should take note of the fact that translations of the *Institutes* were published in various languages. In 1931 there was a Dutch translation by A. Sizoo, a Japanese translation in 1934 by Masaki Nakayama, a German translation in 1955 by O. Weber, and a French translation in 1955-58 by J. Cadier.

Reformed isolation

This expression was coined by G. C. Berkouwer. It has to do with the unconditional acceptance of the authority of Scripture in accordance with the position of Calvin.[13]

Calvin's own position, for that matter, has been much in discussion in the first half of the twentieth century. We must speak of two groups of Calvin researchers. The first group asserts that Calvin was one of the first—if not the very first—to distinguish between Scripture and the Word of God. Calvin, we are told, fearlessly criticized the Scriptures. The second group maintains that Calvin did call Scripture the Word of God. He recommended textual criticism, but under no condition did he permit criticism of Scripture itself.

It is exactly in this area that the difficulty of making a truly historical judgment becomes apparent. Many theologians had been drenched by the steady rain of criticism on the Bible; they could only understand certain expressions used by Calvin in his exegetical works in a way that is critical of Scripture. Even Doumergue had expressed himself in such manner.[14] Niesel claimed we cannot draw from Calvin's commentaries a doctrine of graphical inspiration,[15] while the Dutchman J. A. Cramer wrote a book in 1926 in which Calvin is presented as believing in the inspiration not of the *matter* but of the *form* of the Gospel.[16] In his thesis *Calvijn's opvatting over de inspiratie van de H. Schrift* (Calvin's Conception of the Inspiration of Holy Scripture), D. J. de Groot dealt extensively with the alleged evidence. He showed anew what had always been known, namely, that Calvin taught the verbal inspiration of the whole Bible. After him the German W. Krusche and the American K. S. Kantzer affirmed the same point with profound erudition.[17]

This is not merely a theoretical discussion; it affects people who love the Word of God. Such people are upset and deeply shocked when they read such statements as those made by J. A. Cramer, a professor of ethical-Reformed persuasion:

> It has been proven by science that death and corruption held sway before there was any human "sin." It has been proven by science that the Biblical conception of the world with a heaven above and an earth beneath is untenable. It has been proven by science that all kinds of ancient Semetic materials have been brought together to form the Old Testament, that tribal histories have been made personal histories and have become the histories of the patriarchs, and that the first five books of the Old Testament could not possibly have been written by Moses.[18]

Prof. Cramer wrote these words in a booklet in which he sharply criticized Biblical instruction as it was given in the Christian schools, the so-called schools-with-the-Bible. Clearly we are moving in the same sphere here as in the case of Bultmann's ideas. Many people considered Cramer's viewpoint to be an assault on Scripture.

Against such a background, we should view certain decisions made by the synods of the Reformed *(Gereformeerd)* Churches in the Netherlands, which led to the use of the phrase "the isolation of the Reformed conception of Scripture." Those decisions included the one made in 1920 concerning Rev. J. B. Netelenbos, a decision in 1926 concerning Dr. J. G. Geelkerken and the one in 1933 concerning Dr. J. G. Ubbink. The Geelkerken case in particular stirred the feelings of many people who wanted to make fun of the Reformed congregations for trying to force a minister to believe in a talking serpent.

Only through shortsightedness, however, can the conflict be reduced to such minimal proportions. At the time, Berkouwer (among others) showed that the question under discussion was whether "science" (natural science or historical science with all its branches) should be given priority over the word of the Bible itself in the interpretation of Scripture.[19] He was right when he spoke of a phase in "the great struggle of the last hundred years about the authority of Holy Scripture."[20]

Neo-Thomism

In Roman Catholic circles, too, old sources were brought to light again and studied with care. After Leo XIII published his encyclical "Aeterni Patris" (Of the Eternal Father, 1879), the cry was heard: Back to Thomas! The Pope emphatically recommended "the precious wisdom of St. Thomas" as a medicine against the religious and social abuses of his time. He also wanted to see the old wine put into fresh wineskins, and therefore he used the expression "vetera novis augere." What was old should be enriched by what was new. For this reason the term "*neo*-Thomism" seemed well-chosen.

Among those who spared no efforts in seeking to promote the revival and study of the great thinker of the middle ages was the Belgian cardinal *Mercier* (1851-1926). From 1906 on, Mercier was Archbishop of Malines. He founded the Louvain Higher Institute for Philosophy, opposed the Modernism of the Roman Catholic Tyrrell (see p. 29 above), founded the *Revue Néoscholastique de*

*Philosophie,** and tried to demonstrate the significance of the teaching of Thomas as distinct from the philosophical currents of the time. Earlier we saw that at about this time the works of Aquinas were republished.

Mercier was followed by a series of scholars from different countries. There is little point in mentioning all their names. I will restrict my comments to two of them, the Frenchman *Jacques Maritain* and the Englishman *G. K. Chesterton*, who were both fascinating and eloquent figures, each in his own way.

The life of Maritain reflects the history of his times. He was born in Paris in 1882 as the son of a Roman Catholic father and a Reformed mother. Baptized in the French Reformed Church, Maritain received his catechetical instruction from the liberal minister Réville. Later he studied at the Sorbonne, where he came under the influence of Bergson's vitalism. Maritain married a Jewish Russian émigré named Raissa Oumansoff, who remained his faithful companion and fellow worker until her death in 1960. Together they were converted to a sincerely confessed Roman Catholicism, as a result of their friendship with Léon Bloy, a militant Roman Catholic novelist who did battle against injustice of all sorts.

The reading of Thomas's *Summa Theologica* was a revelation to Maritain. He discovered how the Christian faith and natural philosophy need not be at variance, and that a synthesis could be constructed. Hadn't Thomas, in his days, devised such a synthesis between the doctrine of the church in his time and the philosophy of Aristotle? From that point onward, whether he was teaching, writing or conversing with friends, Maritain only served one ideal: "Vae mihi si non thomistizavero."[21]

Beginning in 1914, Maritain taught in Paris. He spent the years of the second world war in America, and from 1948 to 1953 he taught at Princeton University. At the end of his life he was honored by Pope Paul VI at the closing session of the second Vatican Council. He died in 1973.

It is impossible to indicate the fullness of Maritain's ideas even by way of summary. We can only gather some impressions. He made sharp attacks on the thinkers who, in his opinion, caused the degeneration of the once-Christian civilization: the anti-intellectual Luther, who so angrily denounced Aristotle, the rationalist Descartes,

---

*Neo-scholastic Philosophical Review—one of the many periodicals published with the aim of studying and spreading neo-Thomism.

the emotional Rousseau, who taught the natural goodness of man, and Kant, the critic of reason who completed the work of his predecessors.

Over against these teachers of error, Maritain offered the doctrine of Thomas, who showed that although human knowledge is limited, it is still of great value. It is limited because man is wounded by the fall into sin and must therefore have his knowledge supplemented by divine revelation. Yet human knowledge is so great that the existence of God can be proven. Thomas's proofs of the existence of God are merely the development of a natural human intuition raised to the level of scientific certitude. For that reason Maritain calls his system integral humanism, in contrast to the anthropocentric humanism which was destroying the modern world in his time.*

Maritain's humanistic philosophy looks at man in his grandeur and weakness in the full reality of nature, sin and sainthood. Maritain looks at the world in the same manner; the world is good because it is God's creation, but at the same time it is in opposition to Christ as dominated by the lust of the flesh and the eyes.

Precisely because Maritain so keenly observed this double existence, he fulminated sarcastically during the last years of his life against the Roman Catholic "new moderns" (such as Küng and Schillebeeckx). He considered them to be worse than the moderns who had appeared in his church at the beginning of the century. In his last important work, Maritain wrote:

> The point is, people no longer believe in the devil and in the bad angels, nor the good one, naturally. They are only the survivors of some Babylonian imagery.
>
> In such a nice perspective, the objective content to which the faith of our forefathers clung, all *that* is myth (isn't our big job today to get rid of the horrendous guilt complex?), and like the Gospel of the Infancy of Christ, the resurrection of the body, and the creation. And the Christ of history, of course. As for hell, why take the trouble to deny it? It is simply better to forget it, and that's probably what we had also better do with the Incarnation and the Trinity. Frankly, do the mass of our Christians ever *think* of these things, or of the immortal soul and the future life? As for the Cross and the Redemption, ultimate sublimation of ancient and sacrificial rites, we should consider them as the great and stirring symbols, forever inscribed in our imagination, of the labor and collective sacrifices needed to bring nature and

---

*Integral—being an indispensable part of a whole. Anthropocentric—placing man at the center.

humanity to the degree of unification and spiritualization—and of power over matter—where they will be delivered at last from all the old servitudes and will enter into a kind of glory.[22]

Rarely has the new Roman Catholic (and Protestant) theology of the second half of our century been so strongly denounced.

We should also look briefly at *Gilbert Keith Chesterton* (1874-1936). Like Maritain, he was a layman (in Roman Catholic terminology) and a convert from Protestantism. Chesterton was a man of the most disarming humor and the most cheerful affirmation of life. He was the creator of the priest-detective Father Brown who, by his almost naive and matter-of-fact allocation of factual data, unravels the most difficult of problems while at the same time appearing to be an (indirect) apologist of the worldly wisdom of Thomas Aquinas. One of the most remarkable traits of a man like Chesterton is that he represented the thoughts of Thomas in his own way.

This becomes very apparent in his book *Orthodoxy* (1907), in which he defends the "rationality" of the Christian religion. Of this work a Dutch Jesuit wrote: "Any Church Father would have been

proud to have written this book."[23] It is even more evident from his short biography of Thomas, published in 1933 and reprinted for the nineteenth time in 1960. Immediately after its appearance, the learned French Thomist Etienne Gilson wrote: "Chesterton makes one despair. I have been studying St. Thomas all my life and I could never have written such a book." Also: "I consider it as being without possible comparison the best book ever written on St. Thomas."[24] What is so extraordinary about this book is that although it is written in a highly readable way, it penetrates to the very heart of the person and the doctrine of the great scholastic and describes him as the philosopher of "common sense," a man who serenely accepted natural life but saw the radiance of the grace of God everywhere.

Unfortunately, Chesterton did not show any more appreciation than Maritain for the life and work of Luther. Essentially he considered him a pessimist, and also "a bit of a big bully."[25] Chesterton had no insight into the total depravity of man, and therefore no eye for the radical necessity of the grace of God. Yet, he saw everywhere the wonder of God's presence. Perhaps we can best call him the man who saw the wonder of common things, and therefore the commonness of wonder.

5

Totalitarian Powers:
Communism

Rise

It seems proper to open this chapter by raising an obvious question: If we deal with such historical currents as Communism and Fascism, aren't we exceeding the limits of this book, which is intended to deal with the history of the church? Aren't we entering the area of general history, or perhaps political, economic and philosophical history, while losing sight of church history?

An objection could indeed be raised if the intention was to analyze the above-mentioned currents in all their aspects and details. But note that I spoke of *totalitarian* powers. This means that these powers have claimed—and continue to claim—authority in all areas and activities of life, including church and religion. It is important to approach them from this perspective.

Let me begin with some important facts. It is an historical dictum that the Communists have regarded the church as important enough to be worth persecuting ruthlessly. I will focus specifically on that persecution in another chapter. They have relentlessly exposed the weak points of a church that seemed to have outlived itself. (Later I will show the church has by no means done this.)

It should not be forgotten either that the Communists have changed the worship of God into an extreme idolatry by establishing a special *state cult*. What we find here is a remarkable continuation of Greek Byzantinism as it made its impact on Russia (see Volume I, Chap. 15 and Volume VI, Chap. 12). Communism clearly requires our attention both in its relation to religion and as a pseudo-religion.

We are struck in the first place by the phenomenal *growth* of Communism. It has been said (with a certain degree of exaggeration) that Lenin started in 1903 with 17 adherents, and conquered Russia in 1917 with a party of 40,000 members; by 1959 Communism had conquered one billion people.[1] This looks like a meteoric development, and it is most unlikely as far as Russia was concerned. Hadn't Karl Marx prophesied that the great revolution (which would inevitably come) would take place in the most developed industrial countries of Europe, i.e. England, France and Germany, while semi-medieval Russia would lag far behind?

Although there were indeed some reasons behind the revolution, the term *inevitable* should be used sparingly in the writing of history.

Looking back, certain things stand out. In the first place, there was a great contrast between classes in Russia, which gave rise to repeated peasant revolts in the nineteenth century and a narrowly suppressed revolution in 1905. In the second place there were the two wars lost by Russia, first against Japan (1904-05) and then the first world war (1914-17). Both had ended in shameful defeats. The Russian losses in the latter war had been immense. Many of the people felt deceived and longed for a new order. In the third place, there was the presence of the revolutionary elite. In the nineteenth century Russia had produced quite a number of extremists, leftist socialists, anarchists and nihilists. In the twentieth century a number of revolutionaries of extraordinary quality appeared on the scene—men who dared to seize power and hold on to it.

The leader among them was Vladimir Ilich Ulyanov (1870-1924), commonly known as *Lenin*. He was a fascinating, inspiring man, and he became an idol. The mausoleum on Red Square in Moscow containing Lenin's mummy is Russia's central sanctuary until the present day. Hedrick Smith, an American who lived in Russia for several years, has the following to say about it:

> Lenin is an ubiquitous ikon. The veneration of his bodily remains is reminiscent of the worship of the relics of saints in Christendom and Islam. The effort to perpetuate the illusion of immortality by preserving his remains in the Mausoleum is another obvious parallel with

religion. Secular shrines to Lenin, modest or gigantic, are omnipresent in Soviet life, sown like seeds from on high across the full length and breadth of this enormous country. The main square of every city is dominated by a statue of Lenin leading, exhorting, declaiming, gesticulating or striding boldly into the bright future . . . Banners in Leningrad proclaim: "Lenin lived. Lenin lives. Lenin will live."[2]

Why this boundless idolization of Lenin? Why the parallel incredible homage paid to Stalin, especially after the second world war? Why the acceptance of the words of Mao, the party leader in Communist China, as gospel? Why the enthusiasm with which the bearded face of Castro is saluted in Cuba and other countries? I will have something to say about these questions in connection with the *ideology* of Communism.

Ideology

The literal meaning of the term *ideology* is something like "doctrine of an idea" or "doctrine of ideas." It has been widely used in Communist circles ever since Marx wrote his book on "the German ideology." It is loaded with revolutionary content. Taken in the broadest sense, it is taken to mean "a blueprint of the society of the future made by a special group or elite and the planning of special strategies and methods aimed at the actualization of the blueprint, or at any rate an attempted actualization."[3]

What is involved here is not just classroom theory but also practice out in the street—literally. Lenin's writings furnish clear proof of this. I will mention only two of them here.

In the first place there is his booklet *What Is To Be Done?* (1902). Lenin expresses himself most clearly here on how to start a revolution and keep it alive. *Not* by means of so-called democratic methods, *not* by means of the trade unions or the workers, and *not* by means of a liberation of the peasants, who would from then on have their own property. The way to start a revolution is by means of an elite group of professional revolutionaries who dedicate their total life to the struggle and use all available means, even deceit and terror, as they work together in secret as a group of conspirators. The new state of affairs should be built, as Lenin himself put it, "from the top to the bottom, not from the bottom to the top."[4] Leon Trotsky, Lenin's great collaborator (although later an exile and one of Stalin's victims), made the following prophecy about this point of view: "The organization of the Party takes the place of the Party itself; the Central Committee takes the place of the organization; and finally the dictator takes the place of the Central Committee."[5]

It was quite clear Marxism had arrived at a turning point. According to Marx, the forthcoming revolution was in the first place a matter for the proletariat, an inescapable result of an economic process. According to Lenin, however, the "intelligentsia," the Red elite, had to be dominant in the first stage. Revolution would be accomplished by a perfectly organized party.

Lenin

I should also mention Lenin's *State and Revolution*, which he wrote in 1917, the year of the revolution. In this work he urges the use of violent means. "The replacement of the bourgeois state by the proletarian state is impossible without a *violent* revolution."[6] Lenin quotes Engels, who had said that in a revolution, "the one part of the people imposes its will on the other part by means of rifles, bayonets and guns."

It is not my task in this book to describe how these rules were applied in all subsequent years up to the present. To substantiate the seriousness of the matter, I only want to clear away a misunderstanding, a widespread assumption still held by many people today. Stalin's "purges," which exterminated the whole of the old guard of Bolshevism, condemned millions of people to death and covered the country with a girdle of concentration camps, were thought to be a deviation from orthodox Leninism.

This is simply not the case, as we can see from a number of considerations, including the rehabilitation of Stalin in recent times.[7] Solzhenitsyn, an insider, writes the following angry words about this misconception:

We may justifiably wonder whether "Stalinism" is in fact a distinctive phenomenon. *Did it ever exist?* Stalin himself never tried to establish any distinctive doctrine, nor any distinctive political system of his own. All Stalin's present-day admirers, champions and professional mourners in our own country as well as his followers in China adamantly insist that he was a faithful Leninist and never in any matter of consequence diverged from Lenin.

Solzhenitsyn then calls some facts to mind. During the revolution the land was given to the peasants, only to be taken into state ownership soon afterward (1922). The factories were promised to the workers, but were brought under central administration in a matter of weeks. The trade unions were not used in the interests of the workers but in the interests of the state. The bordering nations of Transcaucasia, Central Asia and the Baltic States were crushed during Lenin's days by force of arms. Between 1918 and 1921 the concentration camps were already packed with people. The Cheka* started its summary executions. In 1922 the church was persecuted and plundered. Beastial cruelties were perpetrated in Solovki** (1922). Stalin is generally credited with the enforcement of collectivization, but the reprisals that came after the peasant uprisings in Tambov and Siberia in 1920 and 1921, during Lenin's time, were as harsh as anything done later.[8] All these measures fitted only one system—the totalitarian state.

Totalitarianism

When John, on the island of Patmos, sees a beast rising out of the sea, he witnesses the whole earth following the beast with wonder. Then another beast appears, making incomparable propaganda for the first one and "causing all, both great and small, to be marked on the right hand or the forehead, so that no one can buy or sell unless he has the mark, that is, the name of the beast or the number of its name" (Rev. 13).

Here we find a prophecy of totalitarianism *in optima forma*—military, ideological and economic totalitarianism. The outcome is the apotheosis of the state and its leader, who becomes a world leader, taking everything and everyone into his service and forcing all

---

*The Cheka was the Russian secret police, known by that name from 1917-1922.
**On the Solovetsky isles in the White Sea, the first systematic Soviet labor camps were established.

men down on their knees. In the totalitarian states of the twentieth century, we find a beginning of the fulfillment of this prophecy.

Lenin had wanted to place the leadership of the planned revolution in the hands of a small revolutionary elite, which would in turn be unconditionally obedient to him. The revolution was supposed to continue until the promised land of the classless society was reached. The leader lasted, but the promised land disappeared behind the horizon.

The result was a completely centralized state without even the semblance of democracy. The rigorous hand of the leader stayed on, and the leader became invested with divine authority.

The leader was the wise man. The words of Lenin, written down in his collected works, were deemed infallible, like those of Marx in *Das Kapital*. He was the almighty one. In preconceived five-year plans he renewed the order of society. Whenever he took one step backward, it was to take two steps forward. He was omnipresent. His eyes, an immense net of espionage, saw everything, and his ears listened to whispered conversations. He was able to give his people heaven (someday, in the future) and also hell (in the present, by forcing them into the indescribable isolation of the concentration camps). The leader became virtually immortal. Every day people were paying tribute to him on Red Square.

Meanwhile, freedom was gone. The machinery of the state was a bureaucracy of servile officials. Trades and industries were collectivized. The time of an impartial administration of justice was over. Schools and universities served the party. It did not matter that millions of kulaks* perished. Neither did it matter that millions of workers perished.** All that mattered was to achieve the great ends of Communism.

Even terror had a value of its own.

> The concentration camps and extermination camps of totalitarian regimes serve as the laboratories in which the fundamental belief of totalitarianism that everything is possible is being verified. To the totalitarian dictator himself, their very existence is the supreme proof of his omnipotence. At the same time, they offer the great advantage of being so horribly far removed from the experience and understanding of the nontotalitarian world and mentality that even in the face of overwhelming proof the world hesitates to believe in this central institution of the totalitarian power and organization machine.[9]

---

*A kulak was a free farmer with one or two laborers.

**"I would wager that Russia's battle of ferrous metallurgy alone involved more casualties than the battle of the Marne" (L. Kochan, *The Making of Modern Russia*, 1967 edition, p. 291).

The place of the church

As we saw earlier, Marx was a sworn enemy of the church (Volume VI, Chap. 9). He was not reluctant to spread even the grossest slander about Christianity. The rule he set was: "If society produces a product like religion, then it must be changed to such an extent that it produces religion no more."[10]

At the beginning of the twentieth century, socialism and Communism followed in Marx's footsteps by manifesting an explicit aversion to religion and sometimes even requiring an explicit atheism as a condition for membership in the party. Still, they usually upheld the slogan: "Religion is a private matter." Religion, it was argued, belongs to the personal area of the human soul.

For Lenin and his followers, however, such a way of thinking was an impossibility. How can a totalitarian state be squared with personal freedom, or with a God who is higher than all earthly gods? Lenin is full of sarcasm whenever he talks about God and religion. He writes: "Every notion of God, indeed, any flirting with such a notion, is an inexpressible meanness and an infamous infection. Religion is a form of spiritual pressure which is being exerted upon the masses of the people and which is still added to their oppression by labor, care and lonesomeness."[11] He even called religion "a kind of spiritual brandy in which the slaves of capitalism drink down the image of humanity."[12]

He was not only talking about the Russian Orthodox form of religion, which had indeed been accused by others of being an outward display of empty imagery.* Neither was he complaining mainly about the cooperation between the altar and the throne. Because he was a thoroughly materialistic atheist, he objected to any and every form of religion—especially the Christian groups that recognize the social calling of the church and represented a really active Christianity. He considered the Baptists more dangerous than the Orthodox, for example, precisely because they had been persecuted during the tsarist times and might for that reason attract some attention. He declared: "A free-thinking atheist and materialist bourgeoisie[13] is to be preferred to Christians who sympathize with communism; it can be used for the socialist work of construction; it is usually indifferent to the question of a 'general outlook,' whereas the Christian com-

---

*On the other side of the spectrum we find in this church a mystical piety, a striving after the experience of communion with God.

munists make a breach in the integral wholeness of the communist
'world outlook.' "

Now we can see why there was such bitter *persecution* of the
church. We can also see why there was so much *exploitation* of the
church whenever exploitation seemed to be to the state's advantage, as
was the case during the second world war. Finally, we can understand why the delegate of the Reformed Hungarian Church of
America to the World Council of Churches in New Delhi (1961) spoke
as he did when a request to admit the Russian Orthodox Church to
membership was being discussed:

> Our church feels itself to be at one in Christian charity with the great
> Russian Orthodox Church. Thousands of martyrs in the recent
> persecutions bear witness to the glorious Christian belief and the fide-
> lity of the clergy and laity of that great Church. If the official
> delegates who present themselves as nominees of that church do cor-
> rectly represent it, then we agree to its admission. But if the official
> representatives of the Russian Orthodox Church wish to use this
> platform for political ends, contrary to the spirit of the Russian
> Church, and if they mean to make themselves spokesmen of their
> Government's point of view (based on the principles of atheistic materi-
> alism and of the undemocratic system of party dictatorship) then, in
> that case, our Church wants to see its opposition noted in the report
> of the proceeding. In the meanwhile, we will abstain.[14]

The American Hungarians had assessed the situation in a very
penetrating way.

6

Totalitarian Powers: Fascism and National Socialism

Rise

The place is Rome in the 1930s, and the event is a solemn occasion; some young Fascists are taking their oath. The reporter is an English archbishop, an eyewitness to the scene:

> A vast crowd waited patiently long before the hour of the ceremony; as the clock struck eleven Mussolini appeared; at a run, followed by his panting Cabinet, he inspected the serried ranks of the Italian youth, who with thousands of spectators went into a wild delirium of enthusiasm; when he reached the platform he held up his hand; there was at once dead silence, then with one voice the youth took the oath of loyalty to the movement, promising to hate all who were opposed to it. When this was finished, the Dictator kissed two of the representatives of the youth just admitted; this was followed by another hysterical outburst of enthusiasm.[1]

Another place—Nuremburg, 1936. The event of the day is a parade involving no fewer than 140,000 party functionaries in honor of the Führer, Adolf Hitler. The narrator is a reporter for the *Niederelbisches Tageblatt:*

The last banner has been carried into the field. The 140,000 are shrouded in a sea of columns of light, similar to an impenetrable wall of defense; anyone trying to invade it would meet with death. The song containing the oath rises in an endless cone of light. It is sung by the Oldensburg students.* It is sung with great devotion, for that's the reason we are all here—to receive new power. Yes, that is it: the hour of devotion to the Movement occurs here, and it is protected by a sea of light against the darkness from outside. The arms of the men are raised to salute the dead who died for the Movement and in the war. Then the banners are raised again. Dr. Ley** speaks: "We believe in a Lord God who governs and guides us and who has sent you, my Führer, to us." Those are the closing words of the national organization leader, and they are underscored by the applause that rises from the 150,000 spectators and lasts several minutes.[2]

What does all this mean? Twice, a "movement" has been mentioned. What was that "movement" and who set it in motion?

Properly speaking, there was no Fascism or National Socialism before 1918.[3] Still, at several places and in various ways, the first steps down the road had already been taken. It was a road that would eventually lead Europe at a bewildering pace to a cataclysmic upheaval. I will mention only a few of the signs of what was to come.

In connection with the nineteenth century we already had occasion to talk about *Romanticism*, which was a reaction against the rationalism that preceded it. Fascism is comparable in certain respects, for it is an *irrational* movement that began as a protest against intellectualism and scientism at the end of the nineteenth century and the beginning of the twentieth century.

Mussolini and Hitler did not appeal to the intellect but to feelings, to the power of imagination. It was Hitler's conviction, in particular, that intricate arguments did not amount to much; he could gain much more by hammering in slogans that were repeated over and over. In Italy, Mussolini's friend d'Annunzio concisely presented a number of such slogans: "Volunta, volutta, orgoglio, instinto. Quadriga imperiale."[4]

Although Romanticism lovingly delved into history, Fascism and National Socialism collected evidence from history. Mussolini recalled the glories of ancient Rome. Hitler claimed his "Third Reich" would develop to the highest possible degree all that had flourished in the medieval Holy Roman Empire of the German nation and all that the

---

*Students of the elite school where the future Nazi leaders were trained.
**Robert Ley was the leader of the labor front and of the organization of the party.

empire of Bismarck aimed to achieve. I would hasten to add that one can hardly speak of a genuine science of history here: history was repeatedly and shamefully abused when it was used in such a manner.*

We should remember the continuous use of the famous term *Aryan* to refer to the German race, the culture-bearing race, the culture-creating race, the best race in the world. Yet this term, which is properly used in scientific definitions of a certain group of languages, really has nothing to do with human blood and human qualities. We should also remember the glorification of the German people by Alfred Rosenberg, who claimed the German nation was born "nicht erbsündig, sondern erbladig."** Finally, we should not forget the eulogizing of the German people by the medieval German mystic *Eckhart* who, as a truly free German, had been at odds with the Pope. The English scholar Robert Cecil writes: "However much this Dominican may have suffered at the hands of Pope John of Avignon, he has been much more maltreated on the pages of the man who admired him, Alfred Rosenberg."[5] These are examples of a mistaken appeal to history, but at the same time a passionate appeal to the national sense of honor.

What was the situation after the first world war? Both in Italy and Germany, times were tough. Both these countries were almost ungovernable. Morality was in a state of chaos.

In Italy one strike followed another. The factories were occupied by the workers, and gangs ransacked the country. Although the Italians had backed the right horse when they joined the allies and therefore belonged with the victors, they felt deeply disappointed by the result of the war. Poverty was rampant, and there was no leadership.

Germany was offended and humiliated by the Treaty of Versailles. The Treaty required a confession of guilt on Germany's part concerning the origin of the war, it imposed astronomical reparations payments and it left the Rhineland occupied. This led inevitably to a feverish inflation, which disrupted economic life and reduced many

---

*Soviet historians have been guilty of the same type of distortion. This has been demonstrated by W. den Boer, among others, in "Roman History in the Judgment of Soviet Historians," where he speaks of a "phantom that has little to do with history" (in *Tussen kade en schip*, 1957, p. 240).

**Not with original sin, but with original nobility—see *Der Mythus des 20. Jahrhunderts* (1930), p. 71. Rosenberg was the "philosopher" of the Nazis.

people to begging. Unemployment increased. In 1920 a short-lived soviet republic was proclaimed in the German state of Bavaria. (The same thing happened in Hungary.) Any appeal to the national honor, to the desire to create order with a strong hand and ruthless means, met with widespread support.

The actual course of events is well-known and does not need to be spelled out here. In 1922 the Fascists in Italy made their march on Rome, borrowing a slogan from Garibaldi: Rome or death! In 1933 Hitler came to power in Germany and immediately began implementing his coordination *(Gleichschaltung)* of all areas of life and all human activities. The results were visible. Order was restored, and excellent highways were built. In Italy swamps were drained and grand edifices erected. Unemployment vanished.

Yes, but at the same time grand-scale idolatry was committed, as men were proclaimed infallible leaders. Outrageous acts were performed in their names. A keen observer in the Netherlands in 1933 already realized what it all added up to:

> Everywhere in Germany the "coordination" takes place, implemented by the brown special hordes of policemen who shrink from nothing. Opponents are imprisoned or sent to concentration camps, and the courts of law are turned into servile instruments of the men who are in power. The crude displays of power and the often repeated sensational

Hitler shaking hands with "Reichsbischof" Ludwig Müller.

shows have their effect on the masses, who get stunned and dazed by all that browbeating and are passively carried along on the waves of racial hatred and chauvinism. Nobody dares to utter a sound. The press is muzzled, the books of the best authors are burned or brought to the paper mills to be destroyed, newspapers daring to urge moderation are proscribed, and every paper has to be the mouthpiece and propaganda trumpet of the dictatorship. This is hailed as the renewal and liberation of the German people, a nation that has found its way back to itself.[6]

As we consider this situation, we should bear in mind that a large number of both the German and the Italian people had become either totally indifferent as far as the church was concerned or were only members on paper. The number of the non-committed church members in Germany in 1920 has been estimated as three-fourths of the total membership. In 1925 there were already 1.33 million people in Germany who were not members of any sort of church organization at all.[7] In Italy it was—and still is—quite possible to be an ardent Communist while at the same time availing oneself of the means of grace in church. Both Hitler and Mussolini were nominal Roman Catholics. To a large extent people were spiritually disoriented.

Ideology

Does it make sense to speak of an "ideology" of national socialism?* Or should we speak instead, as several authors have done, of an "opportunistic nihilism," an arbitrary reaching out for power and attempts to create opportunities to seize power and hold on to it by means of terror?[8] Or was Jan Romein right when he relegated this entire movement to the economic area, interpreting it as the resistance of the bourgeoisie, the low-income middle classes, to the inevitable rise of socialism? Can we then speak of "capitalism in its stage of decline"?[9]

With these and similar points of view, stressing the predictible or even the unpredictible, we will never quite be certain about this ideology. There certainly was a "blueprint," even if the leaders often acted in accordance with their intuition. All those acts certainly were not predetermined by exclusively economic laws. Under the banner of the Nazis, all sections of society united—not least among them the idealistic youth.

---

*From here on I will speak of National Socialism when referring to the German and Italian brands together; I will speak of Italian Fascism only for purposes of singling it out.

What were Hitler's fixed patterns of thought, the ones that marked his speaking and acting right to the end? I would point in the first place to a way of thinking prevalent since the middle of the nineteenth century, i.e. so-called *social Darwinism.*

Charles Darwin had concluded that fixed biological laws control the evolution of all living beings. He pointed to the struggle for life and the survival of the fittest, the most important specimens and species. Applied to human society, this meant the stronger would inevitably prevail over the weaker. Darwin's German prophet Ernst Haeckel taught: "Thousands of good and beautiful and admirable species of the animal and vegetable world have perished during these 40 million years because they had to make room for other, stronger species . . . The same thing applies to the history of nations."[10]

The young Hitler had read Haeckel,[11] and by 1923 he had already expressed similar ideas: "All nature is a big struggle between power and weakness; it is an eternal victory of the stronger over the weaker. If this were only slightly different, nature would be in a state of decay. The people transgressing the elementary law would rot away."[12] In *Mein Kampf*, the textbook of Nazism, he later wrote with the same clarity: "Those who wish to live should fight, and those who do not wish to fight do not deserve to live."[13] Mussolini wrote in the same vein: "Only war raises all human capacities to their highest tension and enables the nations who have the courage to wage it."[14]

It was only a single step from social Darwinism to the fundamental conviction of National Socialism, namely, the primary value of *race and blood.* Just as strong animal races were the only ones that persevered in the struggle for existence, the best blood *had* to prevail in the competition between human races, and the best blood was to be found in the Aryan race.

The myth of the Aryan race (and it was indeed nothing but a myth, a product of the imagination), which eventually led to the registration of men with stud-book numbers, originated in the ideas of the French count *De Gobineau*. He was the author of a four-volume work entitled *Essai sur l'inégalité des races humaines* (Essay on the Inequality of the Races of Man, 1853-55). Those ideas were then set forth in detail by the Germanized Englishman *H. Stewart Chamberlain* in 1899 in his book on "the foundations of the twentieth century." Those ideas were then pushed to extremes by Alfred Rosenberg, the "philosopher" of the Nazi movement, in his book on "the myth of the twentieth century."

Although Rosenberg was aware the term *Aryan* was of no scientific value, he clung to it stubbornly, using it to refer to what he regarded as the highest form of humanity. He was echoing a mystic feeling already found in Meister Eckhart but also present in the talk about "Aryan India," "Aryan Persia," "Northern Hellas," and "Northern Rome." And then there were the genuine Germans of his own time, of course. In 1934 a student wrote to Rosenberg about a passage in his book that had particularly impressed him. It was the following: "Today a new faith awakens; the myth of the blood, the faith to defend with one's blood the divine essence of humanity."[15]

If we make a comparison, the Communists identify history with the class struggle, while the Nazis were convinced of the inexorable necessity of the race struggle. There is also an analogy in revolutionary method between the two: "The strategy of Lenin is the model of both Mussolini and Hitler."[16] That strategy is decided upon by an elite under the leadership of a man at the top, a Führer or Duce who intuitively knows what is best. The people submit unconditionally to this leader. Of course this meant a new idolatry. The cult of Moscow's Red Square was surpassed by that of the Party days at Nuremberg. The children of the people were sacrificed to the Molech in Germany.

The ideology of Hitler was marked from the start by the rapacity expressed in the term *Lebensraum* (room to live). Hitler's objective was to found a greater German empire by conquering the great open spaces to the east, especially in the Soviet Union. This dream was of overall importance as far as the course of events in the second world

The so-called "Kristallnacht" of November 8 or 9, 1938 was the beginning of the "Final Solution." The next day Jews throughout Germany were harassed by the S.A.

war is concerned, and it eventually caused the defeat of Germany. Mussolini went after more *Lebensraum* in his own way by trying to establish an Italian empire in Africa.

Finally, Hitler's actions (but not those of Mussolini) were marked from the start by a rabid *anti-Semitism*. He never made a secret of his hatred of the Jews. Anyone following him could be aware of the fact that a fierce attack would be launched against the Jews, with all available weapons thrown into the battle.

In this regard Hitler was the heir of a bad tradition. Earlier (in Volume VI) I discussed Russian and French anti-Semitism. In Poland there was also anti-Semitism. *Dmowski*, the leader of the National Democratic Party there (1864-1939) blamed the Jews for all the country's calamities.[17] In the Bohemian part of Austria, anti-Semitism was also prevalent. As for Germany itself, Bismarck received an anti-Semitic petition in 1881 signed by 225,000 people; the petition demanded the prohibition of Jewish immigration from eastern Europe and the removal of all Jews from high offices and positions in the educational system.[18] In Vienna, where the young Hitler received impressions that would be of great importance for his later life, anti-Semitism was especially strong. For years the mayor of the city was Karl Lueger, a man Hitler admired. Lueger was in favor of a *national* socialism, in contrast to an international-Jewish socialism.

Step by step Hitler tried to settle accounts with the Jews, and he was almost successful. He regarded himself as an instrument in the hands of providence: by exterminating the Jews, he would keep the world from being completely dehumanized.[19] Finally he had them killed in his gas ovens—not just by the thousands but by the millions. We still find it mind-boggling that in spite of a growing opposition, he continued to find henchmen to carry out such policies among the citizens of Germany, a people once so proud of their culture.

Totalitarianism

The developments succeed each other with an inexorable logic. After the assumption of power comes the elimination of parliamentary democracy, and then the prohibition of all political parties except that of the leader. A law issued by the German Reichstag on July 14, 1933, decreed: "Anyone who wants to call into being the organization of another political party, or wants to form a new political party, is punishable with arrest to a maximum of three years or imprisonment from six months to three years, unless the act requires a higher punishment by other regulations.''

After the political parties were eliminated, the troublesome members of the ruling party would be removed by means of a "purge." Then concentration camps would be established to house any and all who did not agree with the new regime. After that all the workers would be organized in a labor front. The young people would be forced to join the Hitler youth. Even leisure would be regulated, through the "Power by Joy" movement. The leadership of the army would be placed in the hands of the dictator. A single Protestant church would be created under a national bishop. Any books judged to be dangerous would be burned. All free expression of opinion would be muffled. And all of this would be accompanied by a general espionage and debilitating terror.

The intimidation subsequently experienced in the occupied countries went so far that the Englishman George Orwell wrote these comments in *1984*, his novel about the future: "If you want a picture of the future, imagine a boot trampling on a human face, for ever." All of life was undergoing coordination *(Gleichschaltung)*. What did this mean as far as the church was concerned?

The place of the church

National Socialism and Christianity were incompatible. Perhaps this comes out most clearly in the secret instructions given to all the German district leaders by Martin Bormann, one of Hitler's collaborators:

> National-socialistic and Christian ideas are incompatible. The Christian churches are based on ignorance and try to keep as many people as possible in a state of ignorance. Only in this way are the churches able to maintain their power. National socialism, on the other hand, is based on scientific foundations. Just as the harmful influence of astrologers, fortune-tellers and other swindlers has been crushed and suppressed by the state, every possibility of the church being influential must be thwarted.[20]

The concordats that both Mussolini and Hitler were able to make with the Roman Catholic Church were evidently inspired by self-interest. Under the Lateran Treaty of 1929, the Pope was granted sovereignty over the Vatican City, whereas he in turn recognized the kingdom of Italy with Rome as its capital. In the Concordat that followed, the Roman Catholic faith was accepted as the state religion of Italy. The bishops were allowed complete freedom in the exercise of their office, while Christian marriage and Christian schools and associations were placed under the supervision of the state. Friction soon arose concerning the education of the youth. In 1931 the Church accepted a restriction requiring the education of Roman Catholic youth groups to be concerned only with religious matters.[21]

Hitler, too, concluded a concordat with the Pope (September 10, 1933). The agreement seemed to guarantee complete ecclesiastical freedom. The stipulations of this agreement, however, were not observed. Soon Roman Catholic organizations were forbidden, and in 1939 confessional schools were forbidden by law. All instructors and teachers had to swear an oath of allegiance to the Führer. Much publicity was given to certain lawsuits instituted against clergymen who were accused of financial swindles and immoral acts. Later in this book I will discuss the direct persecution and the energetic resistance of various Roman Catholic clergymen.

As far as the Protestant churches in Germany are concerned, Hitler seemed to have the wind at his back at first. A rather loose federation of some 22 provincial churches had been established in 1922 as the "German Evangelical Church Association." In 1933 this association was turned into a national church *(Reichskirche)*. In the general elections for the synod of that year, the so-called German Christians, assisted by effective government propaganda, gained an overwhelming majority. Who were those "German Christians"?

There was a good deal of variety in their ranks, and many of their members simply wanted to be good Germans and good Christians at the same time. Nevertheless, the leadership, including Rev. Hossenfelder, wanted a streamlined church in which Christianity would be combined and coordinated with National Socialism. It was to be a church with no Jews (not even baptized Jews), in which the race principle and the doctrines of the Führer would set the tone. The eyes of many were opened when a majority at the synod voted to introduce the "Aryan paragraph" into the church order. Afterward, Dr. R. Krause, the leader of the German Christians, declared in a large meeting in the Berlin Sports Palace:

> We must purge ourselves of all that is non-German in liturgy and confession, and of the Old Testament with its Jewish morality of rewards and its stories about cattle-dealers and pimps . . . When we call attention to the parts of the gospel that speak to our German heart, the essential teachings of Jesus, which agree unreservedly with the requirement of National Socialism (and we are proud of that), shine forth

lucidly and brightly. We should be on guard, therefore, against exaggerated pictures of the Crucified One. We have no use for a leader who is a god enthroned far away; what we need is a fearless warrior . . . Hero-worship should become the worship of God.[22]

With such comments being made, many eyes were finally opened. The churches were roused to resist. I will discuss that resistance in a special chapter. For the present I will only state that hundreds of Protestant and Roman Catholic clergymen were transported to concentration camps because of their faith convictions. Many of them died there. The same thing happened to servants of the church in the occupied countries.

A pseudo-religion

Because of the pseudo-messianic character of National Socialism and because of its talk about the providence of God, there were many people—including Christians—who did not immediately discern the demonic character of this movement. In Germany, as we saw earlier, membership in the church was no more than a formality for a great many people. It was widely believed that the cross and the hooked cross (swastika) did not exclude each other. Even in the Netherlands there were ministers who sympathized with National Socialism, although they were few in number.[23] The Roman Catholic Church, judging by the concordats in Italy and Germany, seemed to consider cooperation to be a possibility. The Church was playing it safe.

This was nothing but an illusion, and a very dangerous illusion indeed. Like Communism, National Socialism was really a pseudo-religion. It aimed not only to monopolize political behavior and social institutions but also to take over life in its totality, including thinking and doing, dogma and liturgy, preaching and the ethics of the church. An editorial in a Dutch newspaper on May 11, 1933, shed some light on the situation with the following words:

> The National Socialist revolution in Germany rages victorious through the entirety of the life of the nation. It batters the gates of the Christian church now. Everything must be streamlined *(gelijkgeschakeld)*, because everything has to derive the food of life from the same source . . . No sphere of life has any sovereignty anymore. The church, too, if it wishes to endure, will have to bow before the new state and above all serve the interests of the state. But in that case it must first refuse obedience to its real King.[24]

The term *streamlining* (coordination, *Gleichschaltung*) used here was very common during the Nazi era. The press was streamlined, education and instruction were streamlined, and the administration of justice was streamlined. Even the church was subject to the inexorable law of being streamlined in accordance with the ideological model of the almighty state. The church was to be streamlined in the machine of the idolatry of the state, which in fact meant its subsequent elimination.

The most important function of the church—prophetic witnessing—was doomed. Again we cannot avoid a comparison with the situation of the churches behind the Iron Curtain. Just as a pseudo-religion began to develop in the countries under the hammer and sickle, a pseudo-religion arose in Nazi Germany. How else are we to interpret the following prayer, which was prepared for children in Cologne to whom the party was offering a free meal?

> Führer, my Führer, given to me by the Lord,
> Protect and preseve me as long as I live!
> You have saved Germany from its deepest distress.
> Today I thank you for my daily bread.
> Stay with me for a long time, don't leave me.
> Führer, my Führer, my faith and my light!
> Hail to you, my Führer!

And then after the meal:

> Thank you for this abundant meal,
> Protector of youth and friend of old age!
> I know that you have your cares, but don't worry,
> I am with you day and night.
> Lay your head in my lap.
> Be assured, my Führer, that you are great,
> Hail to you, my Führer![25]

It almost seems incredible that these words were placed in the mouths of children. Yet, isn't it just as incredible—but equally real—that within a matter of years all the people of this country adopted the custom of having people greet each other with the hollow words "Hail Hitler"? There were very few who dared to dissent; it became a standard greeting.*

The *method* used by the German authorities, however, was one of the great caution. It has been called an "indirect" method,[26] and also

---

*Some godly people had the courage to say: "Alles gute von Gott und alles Heil für Hitler."

a "slow process of pinching."[27] Dr. de Jong, who has used the latter phrase, points to the methods Hitler used in the occupied countries. A week after the invasion of Poland, an order was given to the SS in Germany to stop all actions against the Catholic and Protestant churches for the duration of the war. Hitler added later: "Once I have finished with the other question, I will settle accounts with the church. It will be an ear-splitting spectacle."

The same kind of order was issued in the Netherlands. "Do not provoke conflicts with the church, not even in matters of principle." This does not mean, of course, that there were no conflicts at all, or that there was no espionage in the church services. I will have more to say about that in a later chapter.

7

Religious Persecutions
in the Twentieth Century

Part I: Russia

Divergent views

By all appearances it seems to be extremely difficult to make unprejudiced, independent judgments about ecclesiastical freedom (or
the lack of freedom), tolerance or persecution in the Soviet Union and
other Communist countries. The German church historian K. D.
Schmidt calls the twentieth century "the bloodiest in the whole history
of the church" and states that the religious persecution inspired by
Communism is well-known all over the world.[1] On the other hand, the
provisional head of the Russian Orthodox Church, a man named
Sergius, declared at a press conference in February of 1930:
"Religious persecution never did take place and does not exist in the
U.S.S.R."[2] After the second world war, the patriarch Alexius called
Stalin a "true defender of the Holy Church,"[3] while Rev. M.
Zhidkof, a Russian Baptist leader, declared: "Mention is sometimes
made of religious persecution in our country. But this is not true.
Faith as such is not being persecuted in our country."[4]

The situation seems rather unclear, to say the least. Suppose we argue that the church leaders quoted above spoke with a knife at their throats. We would then still be faced with the task of explaining why so many theologians in the West take almost no interest in such persecution. And how is it possible for them to suggest that a Christian can truly uphold his Christian identity under the Soviet regime?* Those theologians were not alone in their convictions; numerous Western authors, artists, philosophers and utopians have dreamed of the coming of a new world through the Russian revolution of 1917-18. They believed they saw in it the outlines of a new Jerusalem. The Dutch poet Henriette Roland Holst, who translated the Internationale (the battle hymn of the socialists and Communists), was not speaking for herself alone when she expressed her (frustrated) expectations in the following words:

> The new world—yet it has been born,
> in blood and tears, yet it was born,—
> but it is quite different from what we thought,
> and no Paradise is to be found in her . . .
> And yet, and yet—our heart yearns for her.

The British journalist Malcolm Muggeridge, who was later converted to Christ, lived and worked as a reporter in Moscow at the beginning of the 1930s. In a fascinating essay he wrote:

> How marvelous the Russian revolution seemed when it happened! A little bearded man wearing a cap, Lenin, had taken over the vast empire of the Tsars on behalf of the workers and the peasants; his Jewish lieutenant, Trotsky, had created a Red Army of legendary valour, without officers, gold braid, bands or any of the other contemptible insignia of militarism. How we rejoiced and cheered and exulted at the time . . . In the distant, fabulous land of the steppes and vodka the proletariat had seized power and the millenium had begun.[5]

The Russian Communists, from their side, did everything possible to intensify the impression of an ideal socialist state. Solzhenitsyn writes in his book *The First Circle* about a visit to a prison in Moscow made by an American lady (Mrs. Roosevelt). In preparation for the visit the prisoners were given new clothes—and even Bibles. After the departure of the American lady, one of the prisoners concealed in his mouth some pages he had torn from the pocket gospel—the pages containing the Sermon on the Mount. He was caught and then

---

*I am not only referring to the "theologians of revolution" but also to such men as Karl Barth and Martin Niemoeller. I will come back to this matter later.

beaten—first on the right cheek, and afterward on the left as well.

At the end of Solzhenitsyn's masterful book, we find a description of how a group of prisoners was transported through the streets of Moscow. The prisoners were placed in closed vans which bore signs on the outside in four languages:

> KHLEB - PAIN - BROT - BREAD; MYASO - VIANDE - FLEISCH - MEAT. One of the vans stopped at an intersection. A shiny maroon automobile was waiting for the same red light to change. In it rode the correspondent of the progressive French paper *Libération* who was on his way to a hockey match at the Dynamo Stadium. The correspondent read the legend on the side of the van: MYASO - VIANDE - FLEISCH - MEAT. He remembered that he'd already seen more than one such van today, in various parts of Moscow. And he took out his notebook and wrote in red ink: "On the streets of Moscow one often sees vans filled with foodstuffs, very neat and hygienically impeccable. One can only conclude that the provisioning of the capital is excellent."[6]

In the relevant literature we are repeatedly struck by the credulity—or perhaps we could better say gullibility—of the churchmen from England and America. Dr. F. Schwarz mentions a number of instances of this. The following case is illustrative:

> A preacher visited Russia in 1938. He saw some splendid new buildings going up, and he reported that Russia was fulfilling the kingdom of God on earth. What was going on at that time was horrible to imagine. It was the period of the great Stalinist purges, when Stalin was watering the soil of Russia with the blood of the Communist elite. As a visitor, the clergyman did not see one execution or one trial. He saw only magnificent new buildings and on the basis of this he made his report.[7]

Without any doubt, the churches of eastern Europe have suffered atrocious persecution since the Communist assumption of power. But W. C. Fletcher rightly points to the "abysmal ignorance of Christians in the West concerning the situation of the Russian churches."[8]

A long, dark night (1917-29)

"This night will be very long and very dark." These words were spoken by a man who was at the point of death—the patriarch *Tikhon*, of Moscow. His office had been abolished by Peter the Great some two centuries earlier, but in Tikhon's time it was finally restored. For a period of some months there were high expectations.

The war had been lost and the tsar dethroned. The new provisional government of Kerensky allowed for the calling of a *sobor*, a national church meeting. Tikhon, who had served as a bishop in

America and in Vilna, was chosen by lot to be the patriarch, the ecclesiastical head of all the Russian Orthodox people. Apparently the
church, now free of state interference, could go its own way. And the
church was not unprepared.

It is not without reason that the church's weak points have been
exposed, e.g. the ignorance of the priests and the unconditional support the hierarchy gave to the political system. The overbearing influence of the monk Rasputin on the family of the Russian tsar has
been singled out as proof of this dishonorable condition. This man exercised a lugubrious influence on the crown prince when he was in
danger of losing his life. (He suffered from hemophilia, a blood
disease.) Still, as Michael Bourdeaux has rightly pointed out, Rasputin
was neither an orthodox clergyman nor a monk. Bourdeaux even
speaks of a Rasputin *legend* and emphasizes that this man cannot be
considered as representative of the Russian Orthodox Church in any
way.[9]

Since the beginning of the century, some of the men in this church
had been busy making plans for the renewal and reconstruction of the
church. In 1905 the members of the Theological Academy of St.
Petersburg* requested a reform of the church, which they hoped to see
achieved through the calling of a *sobor*. Soon there were literally entire books filled with suggestions concerning a more democratic form
of government for the church, decentralization, and a more important
role for the "layman." Therefore the *sobor* of 1917 had to deal with
an extensive program of church renewal.

Why was this program not carried out? Why was the Russian Orthodox Church not even given a chance to clean house and go to work
in a truly constructive way?

Symbolically, on the same day Tikhon was chosen patriarch, the
Kremlin, in which the *sobor* met, came under fire from the guns of the
Soviets. The October revolution that brought the Bolsheviks to power
meant a radical change. Its influence was not restricted to social,
political and economic matters; the relations between church and state
were also affected. (How could it be otherwise?)

On December 4 all landed property was nationalized, including
the church's property. On December 11 all schools were placed under
the supervision of the state, including the church's schools. In early

---

*There were no fewer than 58 seminaries and four theological academies. The
academies (in Moscow, Kiev, St. Petersburg and Kazan) were of a good quality (see N.
Struve, *Christians in Contemporary Russia*, 1967, p. 113).

1918 the absolute separation of church and state was proclaimed.

The separation of church and state might have turned out to be a blessing after all those ages in which the church was dominated by the state—but only if the church was truly allowed to be free. But how could the church be free under the administration of a leader like Lenin? He had already made this declaration: "All contemporary religions and churches, each and every religious organization, have always been considered by Marx instruments of the bourgeois-reaction, serving as a defence of the exploitation and paralyzing of the working class . . . there cannot be any good religion."[10] In 1929 the party newspaper stated:

> The religious ideology is one of the main obstacles in the way of the socialist reconstruction of the country. Religion and socialism are incompatible. To be an atheist only individually, and to grant others their own way of thinking, does not square with the proletarian-bolshevist methods of Marxism-Leninism. Such a passive attitude cannot be allowed in the ranks of the party, of the association of young communist workers, among the working men and women, in the Red Army or in general among the progressive elements of the proletarian Soviet-republic.[11]

Freedom of religion and freedom of conscience! The latter would soon be interpreted as "freeing of conscience from the fetters of religion,"[12] while the former would be amended in the constitution of 1929 so that there existed in Russia both "freedom of worship and of anti-religious propaganda."[13]

We should make sure we realize exactly what this meant. According to the letter of the law, the church was allowed to worship within the walls of its own building—and no more than that! The propaganda against religion, however, was completely unrestricted.

Soon it became only too clear what this implied. In January of 1918 Tikhon pronounced the anathema against "the open and clandestine enemies of the truth of Christ . . . who persecute that truth and are trying to ruin Christ's work." He added: "Echoes reach us every day of horrible and cruel massacres whose victims are innocent people, even those lying on a bed of sickness."[14]

We find eyewitness reports in the books of Dr. O. Schabert, who was the minister of the Lutheran church in Riga those days. It was not without reason that he wrote in the introduction to his book on the "victims of Bolshevism": "There are incontestable proofs of the persecutions of the Baltic Christians, whereas the Soviet power under no conditions permits complete information about the sufferings of the Christians to be reported to the West. The Baltic history of suffering therefore enables us to visualize the appalling drama is being played out behind the closed iron curtain on the other side of the eastern border of Europe."[15]

Then follows the description of the religious persecution in Latvia, which was occupied by the Communists in 1918. A black armored car was driven through the streets with the sign "Antichrist." Religious instruction and prayer in schools were forbidden. Communist spokesmen vented their blasphemies from the pulpits. Satan was hailed as the first successful revolutionary. The organists were forced to play the Internationale. For weeks the pulpits and churches were consecrated again by the ministers as a protest against the desecrations. When the churches were filled to capacity each Sunday in spite of all these threats, some ministers were arrested, and some were sentenced to death for "anti-revolutionary activities." Dean Marnitz and Rev. Treu were executed, just as in Estonia Prof. Hahn and the ministers Hesse, Paucker, Adolphi, Schwarz and Jende had been put to death. The Russian Orthodox bishop Platen and some priests of this church were killed as well.

Schabert tells the story of his own arrest and ill treatment and also describes what happened to some others, including Rev. Hesse:

> They brought him into court in the town. There they told him he had to sign a piece of paper in which he declared that everything he had preached was a lie. If he signed he would go free. Hesse took the paper, read it, tore it to pieces, and threw the scraps before the feet of the judges. After that he was horribly abused, although he did not utter a sound. They gouged out his eyes and cut off his ears. Not until they mutilated his tongue did he moan for the first time. After that they dragged him to the river, where they placed him with his back to the shore and shot him.[16]

In Russia it was no better. The famous author Alexander Solzhenitsyn, who received the Nobel Prize in 1970 in the field of literature, was born in 1918 in the Caucasian town of Kislovods. His early youth coincides with the period under consideration. He has written the following comments about those days:

> The sorrowful picture of the subjection and destruction of the Orthodox Church on our country's territory has accompanied me all my life from my very first childhood impressions: how armed guards stopped the liturgy and entered the altar; how people raged around the Easter service, snatching candles and Easter cakes; how classmates tore the little cross I was wearing under my clothes; how people threw the

church bells to the ground and dismantled the church to get the bricks.[17]

From the start it was a grim and evil time. Even before the adjournment of the synod or *sobor*,* the aged metropolitan Vladimir of Kiev had been killed. The country was laid waste by civil war and the terrorism that accompanied it. Monasteries and churches in different places were turned into dance halls and movie theaters. Monks and priests became vagabonds and beggars. The salary of the priests was not paid any longer; they were disenfranchised and allowed no opportunity to work.[18]

Solzhenitsyn

In the summer of 1921 a terrible famine broke out in Russia in conjunction with an epidemic of typhus. Tikhon asked for the help of the Pope, the Archbishop of Canterbury, the Greek Orthodox patriarchs and the head of the Episcopal Church in America. When money arrived, the relief committee of the church was disbanded by the state and the money was confiscated.

Tikhon offered to convert the treasures of the church into cash to help the starving population, except for the objects that were used regularly in the worship services. When the authorities confiscated *all* the treasures of the church without exception, the patriarch opposed the surrender of any object connected with the performance of the liturgy. He was immediately placed under house arrest. From then on Russia teemed with lawsuits against clergymen accused of a capitalist sin: instead of helping their starving parishioners, they stored up the gold and silver of the church!

---

*The decisions regarding church reorganization could not be implemented.

According to Struve's figures, some 269 priests, 1962 monks and 3447 nuns were killed in 1922.[19]

In June of 1923 Tikhon was released at the instigation of foreign powers, but not until he had signed a formal "confession of guilt." This confession was like many of the others wrung out by Communist regimes in Russia and other countries as well.* Included were the following words: "Having been educated in a monarchical society and to the very time of my arrest having been under the influence of anti-Soviet persons, I was indeed inimically disposed toward the Soviet government, and my enmity sometimes crossed over from a passive mood into active conduct . . . I repent of these misdemeanors . . . and ask the Supreme Court to change the suppressive measures for me . . . At the same time I assure the Supreme Court that I am henceforth not an enemy of the Soviet government."[20]

After Tikhon's "confession," the Russian Orthodox Church gave up her prophetic function with respect to the regime—at least as far as its highest leaders were concerned.[21] Tikhon kept silent, apart from the words he uttered on his deathbed in 1925 (see p. 105 above). His successors—first with the title of patriarch and then without it—agreed to all the demands of the Soviet government "for the sake of the church."[22] In time they began to promote both the ecclesiastical policy of the state as well as its foreign policy to such an extent that suspicions of collaboration were inevitably raised. Worse still, there were fears that these men represented Communist infiltration into the church.

Granted, there were plenty of human reasons for this breakdown. Ever since 1921 Russia had been covered with a network of concentration camps—places of hardship, maltreatment, exploitation and death. They have been impressively described for us by Solzhenitsyn in his *Gulag Archipelago*.

As early as 1922, a large number of bishops and priests of the Russian Orthodox Church were exiled to the Solowjetski isles in the White Sea. These isles, where a number of churches and monasteries were to be found, were places of terror.

> The communists silenced there the hymns of praise to God; the monastery was burned in 1923. — Finally the gate of the churchyard was broken open and that place was used for mass-executions. Behind

---

*One of the most notorious was the confession of the Hungarian cardinal Mindszenty (1949). Illustrative of the manner in which it was obtained is Arthur Koestler's book *Darkness at Noon*.

the walls, behind which formerly God had been praised in ecstasies and devotion, men now pined away in despair, waiting for the moment their names would be called.[23]

This portrayal of the situation might be called into question, however; the Soviets assumed a positive attitude toward certain forms of religion in those years. This was apparent from their policies with regard to the so-called *Living Church* and also the Baptists and Gospel Christians. The Living Church (also called the Reform Church) originated in 1922 when Tikhon was placed under house arrest. It was headed by the ambitious priest Vvedensky, who usurped the patriarch's place and called a *sobor*. In 1923 this *sobor* made the following declaration:

> The sobor declares that capitalism is a mortal sin and regards the struggle against it as sacred for a Christian . . . The Soviet regime, alone in the world, strives to realize, by governmental methods, the ideals of the Kingdom of God. Therefore every believing churchman should not only be an honest citizen, but also struggle, in every possible way, together with the Soviet regime, for the realization of the Kingdom of God on earth.[24]

That the Soviets supported such a "church" should surprise nobody. Neither should it surprise us that this "church" didn't last long. According to the statistics of 1925 it included some 12,593 parishes, 16,540 priests and 192 bishops. Somehow they all disappeared without leaving a trace, despite all the fanfare that accompanied their emergence.

The motives of the people involved in this "Living Church" can hardly be determined anymore. Obviously some of them were trying to get on the bandwagon of the authorities. Perhaps their talk about the realization of the Kingdom of God points to the influence of the social gospel and the religious socialism of the West.

As far as the Baptists and Evangelical Christians (see Volume VI, Chap. 12) are concerned, certain believers who had suffered persecution under the old tsarist regime initially entertained some good expectations of Communism, which they considered to be a "new democracy."[25] The Communists did not show much respect for these hard-working people, who did not include many of the noble and mighty. However, in line with their opportunism, they allowed these people certain privileges for some time, as opposed to the members of the "big church." So it came about that the Evangelical Christians were allowed to print a complete Russian Bible in Leningrad in 1926 and publish it in 25,000 copies. In 1928 they issued 10,000 copies of a concordance.

The future seemed full of promise when the Baptists cooperated fully with the state-organized collectivization of agriculture and founded Christian Kolkhozes (collective farms), one of which was called Gethsemane, and another Bethany. Bukharin, a committed Bolshevik who was to be disposed of by Stalin ten years later, expressed both respect and fear when he mentioned the youth movements of these two groups, which he called "Bapsomol" and "Khristomol," at the congress of the Komsomol in 1928.*

As a matter of course this was a temporary situation. In 1929 persecution started unexpectedly. Still, in the summer of 1928 the secretary of the Russian Union of Baptists expressed himself in very optimistic terms concerning freedom of religion in Russia when he attended a meeting of the Baptist World Alliance in Toronto. Only a few weeks after his return he was arrested and exiled to Central Asia. Many of his co-religionists fared no better. The language of the numbers is plain enough. In 1928 these groups numbered 3219 congregations, and in 1940 about 1000.[26]

Concentrated attack (1929-41)

The well-known, fearless Baptist minister Georgi Vins has written a short biography of his father, Peter Vins.[27] He recalls how his father was suddenly arrested in 1930. Born in Samara, Peter Vins had studied theology in America, worked as a Baptist missionary in Siberia, and visited Moscow in 1930 as a delegate to a congress of Baptist and Evangelical Christians. Immediately after his arrival in the city, he was summoned by the N.K.V.D. (the secret service operating in those years). He was advised to vote for two persons in the forthcoming meeting. He refused, and three days later he was arrested. The two persons mentioned were voted in as board members, and one of them subsequently turned out to be a traitor.

Peter Vins spent three months under investigation in jail, followed by three years in a labor camp. Also in that camp were ten Russian Orthodox priests serving sentences. Vins had good Christian contact with them. After his release he was arrested again in Tomsk. In 1937 the story repeated itself. He died in 1943 in a work camp in the far east. And this was only a reflection of what was going on in this

---

*Kolarz, *Religion in the Soviet Union*, p. 297. The Komsomol is the atheistic youth movement of the Communists.

age of the martyrs—one Baptist for every ten Orthodox priests in a house of the dead. Who could possibly count the number of victims?

The great change for the Baptists and Evangelical Christians, along with the intensifying of the persecution to cover *all* church people in Russia, was an outgrowth of the execution of Stalin's five-year plan (1928-33). This plan aimed at the enforced industrialization of Russia, the extermination of a free peasantry and the simultaneous, complete eradication of even the last traces of religion. Yaroslavsky,* the president of the League of Militant Atheists, described the situation in 1930: "It seems to me that the process of collectivization is linked with the liquidation, if not of all churches, then, in any case, of a significant part of the churches."[28] Certain points should be stressed here.

In the first place there was the effort to enlist the *young people*. At the eighth congress of the Komsomols in 1928 the members were exhorted to unmask the clergy as defenders of the kulaks. They were asked to become volunteer anti-religious workers so that they could urge the peasants to stop paying money for religious purposes.[29] This happened in the area of Communist-organized youth, but the idea was to get hold of *all* the young people. If that could be done, it would not be long before no one attended church!

Religious instruction in any form was out of the question. Atheistic slogans were supposed to be hammered into the heads of the children. The schools were to organize regular excursions to the numerous atheist museums. Christianity would be exposed with all its backwardness, absurdity, persecution-mania, obscenity and greed. In addition, the workers were forced to attend courses in which the fundamental rules of Marxism, of dialectical materialism, were imparted to them. Christianity was presented as a myth among the many other myths (with the whole apparatus of nineteenth-century unbelieving criticism). Natural science was played off against religion, and "priestcraft" was unmasked in all sorts of ways.

As a matter of course, things did not stop there. Priests were sentenced and either killed at once or transported along with millions of kulaks to Siberia, where many of them perished after first working as an unpaid labor force in the slave camps.**

---

*Emilien Yaroslavsky was a Jew whose real name was Gubelmann.

**It has been estimated that about five million peasants, most of them staunch supporters of the church, perished (see K. D. Schmidt, *Grundriss der Kirchengeschichte*, p. 567).

The manner in which a lawsuit would be brought against a clergyman can be learned from the Soviet press of the time. Sheldon Curtiss mentions several news items garnered from *Izvestia, Pravda* and *Bebozhnik* in 1929 and 1930. A certain standard procedure would be followed in which a clergyman was accused of capitalistic sins such as hoarding money, dodging taxes and carrying on anti-revolutionary propaganda. In numerous cases a death sentence followed.[30]

Many churches were razed, under a variety of pretexts. One such instance is described in the following account:

> The classical example, worthy of a high place in the annals of cynical hypocrisy, is that of the local Soviet which had heard rumours to the effect that the foundations of the parish church had subsided, making the edifice dangerous for the good parishioners. To verify this report it was necessary to inspect the foundations; to do this the church was torn down *instanter*. To the great relief of the Commissars, they found the foundations to be as solid as the Kremlin wall.[31]

The provisional patriarch Sergius, after being imprisoned twice, had expressed his unconditional loyalty to the Soviets in 1927. He persisted to the uttermost end in his claims of loyalty, and expressed them in an unworthy manner during a statement to the press in 1930. But it was all to no avail. One need only read the list of the 130 bishops of the Russian Orthodox Church, including names, titles and dates, who died as martyrs during this period[32] to be deeply impressed by the ferocity of the merciless persecution. Sometimes it died down for a period of time, only to break out again later with renewed strength. The persecution struck not only the bishops, priests, monks and nuns, but also many "anonymous" Christians.

In Solzhenitsyn's novel *One Day in the Life of Ivan Denisovich*, we find a description of a normal routine in a Russian labor camp. In passing, Ivan describes the conduct of the Baptist Alyoshka:

> What reason could he have to be happy? His cheeks were hollow, he lived strictly from his rations, he did not earn anything extra. Each Sunday he sat mumbling, together with the other Baptists. They shook off the afflictions of the camp life as a duck shakes water off its back.

The Roman Catholics were also subject to the yoke. Brave priests voluntarily assisted their fellow believers in the labor camps. We can read about their experiences in a book by the Jesuit Walter J. Ciszek.[33]

The waves of persecution soared to great heights. To give you some impression, I will pass along a few figures. In the peak year, 1937, some 1100 Russian Orthodox churches were closed, along with

240 Roman Catholic churches, 61 Protestant churches and 110 mosques. Between 1917 and 1941, the number of Russian Orthodox churches decreased from 46,457 to 4225, the number of priests from 50,960 to 5665, the number of deacons from 15,210 to 3100, the number of bishops from 130 to 28 and the number of monasteries from 1026 to 38.*

In that peak year of 1937, when both church leaders and dedicated Bolsheviks were being "purged" by Stalin, a striking phenomenon occurred. When a census was taken that year, the people were asked whether or not they believed in God. According to reliable sources, at least 45 percent of the population answered yes; they had kept their faith in God. The results of the census were not published, and a certain number of officials were immediately arrested.**

But Stalin learned his lesson well. When the German armies crossed the Russian borders on June 22, 1941, the League of Atheists was dissolved, the paper *Bebozhnik* (The Atheist) was suppressed, and contact was taken up with the remaining bishops. The country needed the help of the church, which had been persecuted to the point of death!

The people of God

In 1943 Stalin summoned Sergius, Alexius and Nikolai, the three metropolitans who were still alive, for a personal conversation. In September of that year *Izvestia* announced that the government was permitting the convening of a *sobor* in order to elect a patriarch. At that meeting, attended by 19 bishops (some of whom had apparently been picked up from prison or labor camp),[34] Sergius was chosen as patriarch. He was the first one to hold this title since Tikhon's death.

Nikita Struve, a member of the Russian Orthodox émigré community in Paris and a professor at the Sorbonne, offers the following comments about the situation: "In 1943, when the Communist Government agreed to a settlement with the Church, it did so because it had to reckon with 'the people of God,' with that very large propor-

---

*K. Scott Latourette, *The 20th Century in Europe* (1969 edition), pp. 497, 498. Latourette takes these figures from P. B. Anderson's *People, Church and State in Modern Russia* (1944) and N. S. Timasheff's *Religion in Soviet-Russia, 1917-42* (1942). He admits that accurate figures are not at our disposal.

**J. H. Nichols, *History of Christianity, 1650-1950*, pp. 362, 363. Bourdeaux, in *Opium of the People*, estimates the numbers of yes-voters at 50 million.

tion of the Soviet population for whom religious interests remained of primary importance, and who still, when they had been plunged in darkness, lived in the hope of seeing 'the great light' shine forth again."[35]

During the darkest hours there was still a people of God in Russia—and not only at that surprising moment of the census-taking in 1937. Struve points out how some of the Christians had to rebuild their churches from nothing, maintaining public worship and welcoming the missionary priests wholeheartedly.

Where did those priests come from? It is a very remarkable fact that although the official number of bishops never rose far above 130, more than 150 are mentioned at times. The latter figure is not an overestimation or exaggeration; some bishops actually appointed their own successors in the heat of the persecution. Those successors then took over immediately and with a great deal of courage when the office of bishop fell open because of persecution.

Priests who had to live from hand to mouth went on functioning. Children were baptized. In spite of new, oppressive persecution, the baptisms and the work of the priests continues to this day. Hedrick Smith, who spent several years in Russia, wrote about this matter in 1976:

Joseph Stalin

A Russian priest confiding to a Western pastor that he has little time to counsel young people because he is so busy doing 1,000 baptisms a year; a young woman who carefully draws out a visiting Catholic priest to explain his faith and then expresses her admiration for it; a young engineer who keeps ikons in the corner, the traditional place of worship, and who knows verses from the Scriptures. In 1973, *Pravda Ukrainy* reported that while one Party official was lecturing on atheism, his children were being taken for baptism by his wife and mother-in-law.

A writer told me that when Alla Tarasova, a leading actress of the Moscow Art Theatre, a Party official there for 19 years and a deputy in the Supreme Soviet, died in 1972, she shocked Party officials by leaving a will requiring a religious burial, and her husband, a secret police officer, fulfilled her wish. The late Ivan Petrovsky, for 22 years rector of Moscow State University, was another secret believer for years, this same writer informed me.[36]

In the same vein, Struve speaks of the many "Nicodemuses": a parish priest whose priesthood is unknown to those in adjoining flats; a Soviet colonel in Berlin who asked the Orthodox bishop to baptize him by night and with the utmost secrecy; and many more such cases.[37]

In this commitment to ikons and even the appreciation for the baptism of infants, we unquestionably have a continuation of the old and perennial Orthodox tradition. Still, we must say without reservation that God still has His people in the Russian Orthodox Church. As Struve puts it so beautifully: "The conditions imposed by the State upon the Church practically confine the religious life to its unalloyed expression, which is prayer. The people of God are essentially 'a people who pray.' "[38]

The Baptists and Evangelical Christians merged into one federation of churches in 1944. How are they faring? According to their own testimony: "The cross of Christ, Christ's sacrifice for sin, his precious blood, were and are the central theme of our doctrine and preaching." Also: "Most of our blessings were not granted to us in splendid and expensive houses of prayer, but in common rooms as those of Jerusalem. We pray without ceasing that our Russian Evangelical-Baptist churches will not deviate from the simplicity of original christianity."[39]

This does not mean, of course, that complete freedom of religion prevailed in Russia after 1941 or 1943. As matters stand, this is simply an impossibility under a totalitarian system.

Freedom with a question mark

The letter quoted above contains these remarkable sentences:

> Complete freedom of religion. We have mentioned all the marks that are characteristic as to the spiritual life and the activities of our fellowship, and we enjoy the complete freedom of religion to live that way each day. We regard our soviet-government very highly, which has given this freedom to us and protects it against all violation. In our country all churches and religions have the same complete freedom of religion. Because of this freedom we now have a flourishing spiritual life in our churches.

In five sentences the word *freedom* comes up five times in a row. That looks slightly suspicious; it leaves us with the impression it was dictated by someone eager to prove his point, or that orders were given by the government regarding the contents of this letter to America. And that was indeed the situation. Stalin was not "converted" at all; he was simply a realist. He had discovered that a great many Russians still appreciated the church and Christianity, and he did not want to run the risk of sabotage or counter-revolution, especially not in a critical situation. But he did ask a price.

The price was paid in the terminology of the letter from which I have quoted. It was implied even more clearly in the words of the patriarch Alexius, who called Stalin "a true defender of the Holy Church."[40] Alexius urged the church to pray for the authorities "presided over by the most wise Leader whom divine providence has chosen and established, to lead our country to prosperity and glory."[41]

In the course of time it became evident the Soviet government would try to make use of its new relationship with the Russian Orthodox Church in two ways. The Church would be asked to cooperate in the subjection of the other Slavic peoples to Moscow, and also to support with a clear voice the so-called peace offensive of the Soviets.

How was the first demand dealt with by the church? At a synod meeting in Moscow in January of 1945, the patriarchs of Alexandria and Antiochia assembled with representatives of the ecumenical patriarch (Constantinople), the patriarch of Jerusalem and the churches of Serbia and Rumania. This meeting, at which Alexius was elected the successor of Sergius, has been called the first attempt of the Russian Orthodox Church to gain hegemony over the entire Orthodox church.[42]

In April of that same year, a conference was held involving Stalin and Molotov and the church authorities, patriarch Alexius and the metropolitan Nikolai. Within three months of this conference, all the Orthodox churches of eastern Europe had been placed under the authority of Moscow.

Nikolai, who had diplomatic talents, then went on a propaganda tour to Jerusalem, Canterbury (where he was welcomed with open arms) and France. If the journey was not a complete success, it was because of blunders on the part of the K.V.D. and also because of the beginning of the "cold war."

As far as the second demand (the peace offensive) was concerned, the leadership role assumed by the Russian Orthodox Church was very unpleasant. While keeping its satellite states under iron control, Russia never abandoned the ideal of total world revolution. The Soviets considered it opportune to raise a plea for "peace" everywhere in the world with a loud voice and to display the peace dove, designed by Picasso, in all lands.

The Soviet government requested the assistance of the church in this matter—and received it. In 1952 the synod condemned the "imperialist aggression in Korea." In 1956 the patriarch condemned the Hungarian revolt in his New Year's message. In 1962 the patriarch censured President Kennedy because of the atomic tests. In all these matters the church showed it was the puppet of the state and was just as thoroughly discredited as it had been under the tsars.

Regrettably, the community of Baptists was also compromised in this matter—or a majority of the Baptists, at any rate. A minority made a resolute stand. Even in the Russian Orthodox Church clear protests arose here and there, especially after 1960 when the persecution (which had never stopped completely) increased again.

And, in fact, it never had stopped completely! The title and contents of *Three Generations of Suffering* (1975), a documentary book by Georgi Vins, testify to this. When the book was published (by Hodder and Stoughton, of London), Vins was sentenced to five years of imprisonment, and thereafter to five years of exile in Siberia. His father had died in a labor camp in 1943, and his mother had been sentenced to three years of imprisonment. Vins' children were excluded from attending high school and could not get work.

Until 1960 there had been a considerable degree of ecclesiastical freedom. The number of practicing Russian Orthodox believers has been estimated at somewhere between 30 and 50 million in 1959,[43] and the number of Baptists at 540,000 baptized members and another three million sympathizers. There were 20,000 Orthodox churches open in 1959, with some 30,000 officiating priests.[44]

This situation changed abruptly when Krushchev, the man who had initially announced the "de-Stalinization" and the "dew," put on the thumbscrews. Again the language of numbers is eloquent. In 1960 there were still 11,500 Orthodox churches open, with 14,000 priests in active service. By 1963 half of the parishes of this church had been discontinued, and it was estimated in 1975 that three-fourths of the church buildings open in 1959 had been closed.[45]

The prisons and concentration camps were again populated by substantial numbers of believers, as we can read, for example, in a letter of 1964 from the British businessman Greville Wynne, who was imprisoned in Vladimir:

> On the other side were some elderly women, very badly dressed; in the winter it was pathetic to see them wrapped up in newspapers and rags. Like most women in Vladimir, they had been convicted of "religious crimes" like trying to run a Sunday school. Later, when I was in a cell in which there was a crack in the window glass, through which I could see, I watched another group of women pass by on their way to the showers, chanting prayers and making the sign of the cross.[46]

How could this be going on when two of the Soviet churches were actually members of the World Council of Churches? (The Orthodox Church joined in 1961, and the Baptist-Evangelical Churches joined in 1962.) Didn't these churches emphatically disavow, in the Council, all criticism about lack of freedom in the Soviet Union? In order to answer such questions, we must look at two events of 1965.

The first was a visit made by a group of eight bishops, headed by Archbishop Yermogen of Kaluga, to the patriarch of Moscow. The bishops requested the head of the church to ask the state for a revision of the decisions of 1961.* The second was a letter to Brezhnev written by two courageous Baptist ministers. In the letter they asked for certain revisions in the constitution so that the way of "arbitrariness and force" would no longer be followed.[47] More protests were raised at that time, and some of them reached the West. I will mention only these two, both requesting a change in certain decisions or a change in the law.

As far as the law was concerned, I have already pointed out that the constitution guaranteed freedom of religion, while at the same time it guaranteed freedom of propaganda to the atheists. The screws

---

*Yermogen was thereafter removed from his diocese and placed in a distant monastery.

of such legislation were turned tighter. Let me give you a few instances.

In 1961 Archbishop Sushenko of Chernigiv was sentenced to eight years imprisonment because he was convicted of eluding taxation and engaging in religious propaganda among a group of miners. In reality he had refused to allow a large number of parish churches in his diocese to be closed.[48] A Baptist pastor received three years imprisonment because he had made converts in Alma Mata. His worst offense was that he had admitted his own son to full membership in the church.[49]

Several by-laws were added to the legislation mentioned above. The penal legislation of 1962 spelled out these two "crimes perpetrated on a religious basis": religious instruction given to children and non-performance of social duties. The Council of the Union of Baptists was instructed to announce to all congregations that the "worship" was not to be aimed at obtaining new members, the baptizing of young people between the ages of 18 and 30 was to be kept to a minimum and young children were not allowed to attend the public worship services.

These and other such by-laws were strictly enforced. (There were also rules for the registration of church members, of baptized members and of church buildings.) As a result, one could often read in the Soviet press about sentences given to religious transgressors, sometimes called religious parasites, complete with names and dates. Once more a large number of churches were razed.

In his well-known Lenten letter of 1972 addressed to the patriarch Pimen,* Solzhenitsyn wrote about the destruction of the Russian churches:

> Is there a more heart-rending spectacle than those skeletons populated now by birds and shop-keepers? The Northern part of our country, this age-old treasure-house of the Russian spirit . . . is now totally without churches.

And then the following words from the same letter:

> To this day, Ermogen of Kaluga is still exiled and confined to a monastery, the only fearless archbishop who did not permit the forces of a late-blooming and frenzied atheism to close his churches, to burn ikons and books, as had so frequently occurred in the years before 1964 in

---

*As untrustworthy as his predecessor Nikodim (see Bourdeaus, *Opium of the People*, pp. 221, 223).

other dioceses . . . We dare not even ask about the ringing of church bells—but why has Russia been deprived of her ancient adornment, her most beautiful voice? Would that it were not only churches: in our country we cannot even get hold of the Gospels. Even the Gospels are brought in to us from abroad, just as our missionaries once used to take them to Inidgirka.

A church ruled dictatorially by atheists—this is a spectacle unseen in two thousand years.[50]

In the Baptist churches, the servile obedience to the measures of the state finally occasioned the schism of the *Iniciativniki* or Reform Baptists. One of their main leaders was Georgi Vins, who has been mentioned before. These Christians, who made up an estimated 5 to 8 percent of the total Baptist community, protested against yielding to government pressure. Thereby they risked their lives.

Vins was one of the two Baptist ministers who wrote a letter to Brezhnev in 1965; it contained these powerful opening lines:

The persecution has become hereditary; our grandfathers were persecuted, our fathers have been persecuted; and now we ourselves are persecuted and oppressed, and our children are suffering from oppression and deprivation.

And then, at the end of this assessment of the crisis, we find these words:

Are we allowed to say that all nightmares are now behind our back? No, these criminal activities have not yet reached their end. They still continue. And this is the living proof of it: at this very moment, when you are reading our letter, many hundreds of believers are unlawfully deprived of their freedom; they are in jail, in concentration camps and in exile, while some of them have died a martyr's death; the children of believers have been taken away from them; thousands of members of Evangelical-Baptist congregations have no legal status, and meet in private houses which can accommodate only 25-30% of the membership; yes, even under these circumstances believers cannot meet in peace, because those meetings of believers are often dispersed by the police and the houses are confiscated.[51]

This is the face of the Russian church-under-the-cross in the second half of the twentieth century. And it is exactly this church that attracts the younger generation and the representatives of the intelligentsia. An eyewitness speaks of a service he attended in 1974 in Moscow led by a personal friend of Solzhenitsyn, the priest Dmitri Dudko, who has spent eight years in the Stalinist concentration camps. The church was full to capacity. Usually there were many young people and intellectuals in the Sunday night services. Dudko spoke straightforwardly about faith and conversion, condemned atheism, and protested against the interference of atheists in church matters. It should not surprise us that this witness to the truth was transferred to a small rural parish after a while. Only the international notoriety of his case protected him from much harsher punishment.[52]

Part II: East Germany

The crisis

In March of 1946, Winston Churchill declared that "an iron curtain had been lowered across the center of Europe." Anyone who visits Germany today can see the infamous Berlin wall with his own eyes. Moreover, from Lübeck at the Baltic all the way to Hof at the Czech border, there is a strip of land about five kilometers wide and staked off by barbed wire. This land is patrolled by guards with machine guns, and there are watchtowers all along it. This is the visible border between "the East" and "the West," between the Communist world and the free world.

It is also the border between the two disjointed parts of the German people, a people once so proud of their unity. The Germans had passed through a crisis. The gallows of Nuremberg testified to this, as did the many ruins. Finally, the wall that cut like a sword through the body of the country was proof of this crisis.

East Germany was occupied by Soviet troops in 1945. That meant a period of murder, manslaughter and rape for the civilians. More than half the Roman Catholic clergymen died, and a number of Protestant ministers as well.[53] In the ecclesiastical district of Berlin-Brandenburg, almost all the churches were destroyed.

In addition, there was a great moral disorder. Bishop Dibelius made this declaration in October of 1946, in a report to the Synod of Berlin-Brandenburg:

> Mothers are ordering their sexually diseased daughters out of the Berlin hospitals because they can't exist without the income these girls have been earning in their sinful trade. All over Berlin great numbers of people are plundering coal trains, claiming that at last they are getting what rightly belongs to them. Cases of exploitation of children are on the increase. Black-market dealings make up the main interest among half-grown boys, many of whom are not more than seven years old. Even among those who have not become involved in gross violations,

large numbers still draw the line at subjecting themselves to the law of God. One is constantly faced with the question of just how much the German people must go through before they begin again to take God seriously and to make a new beginning.[54]

Demoralization! At the same time, the new government kept putting more and more pressure on people to change sides and go over to the atheist camp. There is no need to tell the whole story over again, for the procedure already familiar in Russia was used in all the satellite states.

It was a story of Communist indoctrination, of campaigns against the capitalistic and militaristic West, of persistent efforts to get hold of the young people, of encouragement of "progressive" ministers and oppression of "reactionary" ones. Education was de-Christianized. As a provincial synod in Silesia put it in 1951, the schools became "confessional schools of the materialistic philosophy."[55] Pressure was brought to bear upon the young people to become members of the Communist "Free German Youth" organization.* The young people were also told to sign a paper in which they resigned their church membership.

This unrelenting attack met with success. Whereas no more than 15 percent of the young people participated in the Communist "Youth Dedication" (about which I will say more later) in 1955, this proportion rose to 25 percent in 1956, 32 percent in 1957, 47 percent in 1958 and 65 percent in 1959. In addition, a large stream of refugees succeeded in reaching the West by one means or another. According to official West German statistics, there were an average of 500 refugees per day in 1949, and by 1957 these figures had risen to an average of 700 per day.[56]

Perseverance

Although the church in East Germany suffered heavy losses,** it persevered. It was led by a number of fearless men, among whom Bishop Otto Dibelius deserves special mention. Once it became evident there was a shortage of ministers in various places, certain

---

*Refusal meant that one would not be allowed further education at a high school. Sometimes it also meant that the young person's father and/or mother would lose his/her job.

**Its official membership in 1950 was 15 million; in 1975 it was 8.5 million. By 1975 there were no church members at all in 116 villages close to Berlin (R. D. Linder in *Christianity Today*, Nov. 18, 1977, pp. 318, 319).

members of the church who had undergone a brief period of training began to give catechetical instruction. When the state would no longer pay the salaries, the freewill offerings provided for even more income than before.

Dibelius was not a man to mince words. In his autobiography he tells something about his preaching after the Russian takeover. On one occasion he declared that the introduction of house commissars, whose official duty was to check up on the occupants and spy on them, was devilish. The city councilors formally decided he had exceeded his authority. Dibelius's response can be found in his book: "I have never, perhaps, said a truer word."[57] Prime Minister Grotewohl said on one occasion that the generosity of the German Democratic Republic was never so clearly evidenced as in the fact that Bishop Dibelius was still permitted to preach in East Berlin's territory.

When religious instruction in the schools was forbidden, both Cardinal von Preysing and Bishop Dibelius wrote letters to the parents of the children. In the letter of Dibelius, dated October 25, 1945, we read: "The secular school which is now being introduced is not a religiously neutral school. In education there is no neutrality in respect to the great questions of human life. The children must be given answers to these questions, one way or another! The secular school is clearly and unmistakably a school opposed to the Christian religion. In this we have had ample experience."*

The conflict between church and state resulted in many cases of persecution. In the spring of 1953, for instance, more than 3000 young people were removed from the high schools for not participating in the *Jugendweihe* (Youth Dedication). The same year, 72 ministers and youth leaders were arrested.

Among the ministers arrested was Rev. Schumann of Chemnitz, against whom a "show trial" was arranged. Because he had advised the young people to use the Word of God as the standard for judging the films shown in the movie theaters (where they would doubtless find a great deal that was contrary to Christian teachings), he was accused of sabotaging public education. He also appealed to the young people to become "Christian anglers and fishermen," even among the People's Police and in the socialized factories, where they distributed church announcements. For these acts he was accused of violating Article 42 of the Constitution, which protected citizens of the

---

*Here Dibelius was referring to the Nazi era (Solberg, *God and Caesar in East Germany*, p. 39).

Republic against any compulsion to participate in activities of a religious nature. Rev. Schumann was given a six-year penitentiary term.[58]

For a time the persecution and oppression would slow down, and then it would increase again. It was a sign of the times that the old Francke foundations, which had preserved their Christian character even under the Nazis, were "taken over" by the Communists in 1956. Bibles and hymnals were printed there no more.[59]

A pseudo-church

The East German Communists realized perfectly well that they were going about their work in the heart of Luther's old territory, in an area with a deeply rooted Lutheran tradition. Even people who were estranged from the church still appreciated the baptism of their children, and also such ceremonies as confirmation, church marriages and funerals.

Such ceremonies really ought to be eliminated completely in an atheistic state. Still, who could object if attractive substitutes were offered? Earlier I mentioned the *Jugendweihe*, which was forced upon the youth. This rite closely paralleled other pseudo-church activities, and reminds us of "the beast that had two horns like a lamb" (Rev. 13:11).

The *Jugendweihe*, as introduced in 1954, was preceded by an instruction period of seven weeks in which questions relating to science and society were discussed. In the ceremony itself, an address would first be delivered to the assembled parents and candidates:

> Dear friends, these young people are now about to declare their solemn vows. With all their knowledge and the abilities they have acquired . . . with the help and protection of the entire community . . . they are to serve the unity of our fatherland and the building of Socialism.

Then followed a series of questions and answers:

> Dear young friends, are you prepared to devote all your strength together with peace-loving people everywhere in fighting for peace and defending it to the utmost?
>
> *"Yes, we promise."*
>
> Are you prepared to devote all your strength, together with all true patriots, in fighting for a united, peaceful, democratic and independent Germany?
>
> *"Yes, we promise."*

Are you prepared to devote all your strength to the building of a happy life, to progress in business, science and art?

"Yes, we promise."

Then the final word:

We have heard your vows. Receive in exchange the promise of the fellowship of all working people to protect, encourage, and help you, so that you may reach the high goals you have set for yourselves.[60]

To this imitation of confirmation or public profession of faith, a second pseudo-church ceremony was added—that of naming newborn children. This pseudo-baptism was celebrated for the first time at Christmas of 1957 in Altenburg, Thuringia. While an organ played and candles were lit, the baby would be carried into a special room at the city hall. After the parents pledged to bring up their child as a true socialist, they placed their signatures in a special book. Flowers would be offered them, and a savings book valued at 100 marks.

Similar things happened in connection with funerals and wedding celebrations. Solberg reports that in a town of 7000 people, there were two ministers and five secular funeral orators. Widows were often afraid they would lose their pension if they did not invite one of the secular orators to pay final respects to their departed husbands. And young mothers often asked some minister to baptize their little ones in secret.

Darkening of the eyes

In the next chapter we will see how much insight and firmness of mind Karl Barth and Martin Niemöller displayed as they protested against the Nazi infiltration of the German church in the 1930s. That's why we are surprised by the attitude they took in the East German church struggle. At the very least, some brotherly sympathy could have been expected. That such sympathy was not expressed, that there was not even a semblance of sympathy for the Christians in East Germany—all of this can only be called a darkening of the eyes.

About 1949 Barth was speaking and writing repeatedly concerning the situation of the church and the Christian under Communist government. He dared to say: "A man of the stature of Joseph Stalin cannot be mentioned in one breath with such charlatans as Hitler, Göring, Hess, Goebbels, Ribbentrop, Streicher." He spoke of constructive thinking in Russia and pointed to the solution of the social problems there.[61]

In 1958 Barth published his "Letter to a Minister in the German Democratic Republic." In scathing terms he spoke of the atheism of the West as more dangerous than the "atheist lion" of the East. He had been asked for advice concerning the pledge of loyalty required of the ministers of East Germany. Barth admitted he did not know the exact text of the pledge, but he assumed the pledge was not as far-reaching as the oath of allegiance once required by Hitler. In Barth's view, it was possible to pledge loyalty while reserving the right to disagree. "In your position I would see no difficulty in pledging loyalty to the German Democratic Republic in this sense, and therefore in signing the declaration required of you in all sincerity."[62]

Solberg recounts the contents of this letter and then exclaims: "After reading advice such as this to pastors who are being spied upon by unknown agents of the secret police, who are counseling young people being asked daily in their schools to pledge their total loyalty and strength to a system which denies both God and Christian morality, and parents being threatened with the loss of support for their families if they did not dedicate their newborn infants to Socialism instead of Christ, it is difficult to avoid asking the almost impertinent question: Does not Barth know what is going on in East Germany?"

Barth grossly underestimated the deadly peril of the demonic powers that had been unleashed over eastern Europe with the avowed intention of destroying the church and Christianity. Was this perhaps a consequence of his theology?

At one time he had rung the death knell of cultural Protestantism and, with it, any effort to label a human organization "Christian." In his opinion, all men without exception live in "the crisis"—under judgment. Barth must have seen some of that togetherness in the Communist-dominated society of East Germany. And who can speak of an "elect church of God" separated by a deep chasm from a "world that is in the power of the evil one"? (I John 5:19).

It is noteworthy that the so-called "breakthrough" was taking place at the same time in the Netherlands. The movement, strongly influenced by Barthian theology, rejected all Christian organizations and urged cooperation with the socialists and the acceptance of public schools.*

---

*In contrast to what had happened in the nineteenth century, when many "schools-with-the-Bible" had been founded.

Utter distress

In August of 1976 a shocking and dreadful act took place in the village of Zeitz in East Germany. A Lutheran minister named Bruesewitz burned himself alive in the public square in front of the church after drenching his body with combustible liquids. When he was buried, the Communist press suggested he had acted in an outburst of insanity.

Was that really true? A month later some 4300 East German ministers read a message from their pulpits on the text: "If one member suffers, all suffer together" (I Cor. 12:26). In this message they said Bruesewitz had wanted to be "a witness of Christ," and the question was raised "whether there was really enough freedom of religion and freedom of conscience, especially as far as the young people were concerned."

Bruesewitz's act of suicide was unjustifiable, but his death was a cry of distress. The pulpit message of his colleagues echoed that cry. Their intention was to awaken sleeping consciences on the other side of the Iron Curtain.

Part III: Other European Countries

"And what more shall I say? For time would fail me . . ." This exclamation in Hebrews 11:32 comes to mind as we continue our examination of the situation of the church in the countries behind the Iron Curtain in Europe. There is no need to make a long story of it, for the course of affairs always follows the same pattern to a certain extent. After the assumption of power we find the outward appearance of freedom of religion, but in reality we slowly see the thumbscrews being turned tighter. The illusion is democracy, and the reality is a bureaucratic dictatorship.

The term *illusion* is really the proper one to use. This becomes apparent from a Russian professor's lecture which Herman Gollwitzer, a German theologian who spent some time in Russian captivity after the second world war, once attended with his fellow prisoners in a barracks:

> If you say, "This is an old, badly painted wall of a barracks," you are pronouncing a metaphysical judgment, that is, you are absolutizing a moment that obtains. But if you say, "This is a perfectly white, beautiful new wall," then you may be wrong as far as the present moment is

concerned, because the wall is not yet white and beautiful, but dialectically speaking you are right, because tomorrow it will be so.

If you tell your people at home after you return to Germany that the Soviet people live in old, vermin-infested barracks, you will be lying, even though this is by and large the present situation. But if you tell them that the Soviet people live in beautiful new houses, you will be telling them the truth, even if only a few live that way today. To identify the day of tomorrow in the present day—that is what it means to see things dialectically.[63]

As a result of looking at things in this way, proponents of one of the many "theologies of liberation" in our days consider the present situation in China a new phase in the history of salvation.[64] Earlier I wrote about the course of events in the Baltic lands after the first world war (see p. 108 above). After the war these countries (Estonia, Latvia and Lithuania) enjoyed some 20 years of national freedom, and the churches shared in that time of liberty. Then they were occupied by the Soviets again, and then the Germans from 1941 to 1944, only to be definitively annexed by the Russians as the Germans were pushed out.

All these changes represented a period of hardship for the people. The small number of Jews in these lands suffered especially during the German occupation,* while the Lutherans and Roman Catholics suffered most under the Russians.

During the Russian occupation in 1940, Article 124 of the Constitution was immediately applied; it included the notorious freedom of worship and atheistic propaganda. This prohibited all religious instruction. Christian youth organizations were suppressed, and the theological faculties of Riga and Tartu (formerly Dorpat) were closed.[65] These measures were immediately applied again when the Russians took over once more in 1944. Many people were deported to the far east, and there were also many who marched away with the German troops to Germany. The number of citizens of Latvia dropped from 2.5 million to 1.6 million.

According to Shuster, some 500,000 Balts were exiled to Siberia in 1944, only 30 of the 250 Lutheran ministers in Estonia were left, and one-fifth of the Roman Catholic priests were left in predominantly Roman Catholic Lithuania. Shuster quotes a pathetic article from the Berlin monthly *Monat*, written by the Polish poet Milosz, who had

---

*The Jews were to be found mainly in Latvia, where, it is estimated, they made up about five percent of the population before the German occupation (K. Scott Latourette, *The Twentieth Century in Europe*, pp. 497, 498).

read a letter sent by a Baltic family to relatives in Poland. The family, consisting of a mother and two daughters, had been deported to Siberia in March of 1949. The last letter in several of the lines was inked in more heavily than the others. When read from top to bottom they formed the following words: "SLAVES FOREVER."[66]

The reports about the present situation are contradictory and leave little room for optimism.* As far as *Poland* is concerned, the country became a people's democracy in 1952 after the Russian pattern. This development was preceded by all sorts of maneuvering, including the infamous partition of the country in 1939 under an agreement reached between Hitler and Stalin.

The major difference between Poland and the other satellite states is that in Poland the overwhelming majority of the population was Roman Catholic. It was led by some very able cardinals: first, August Hlond (1881-1948) and after him Stefan Wyszynski (born in 1901). At first the Communist state exerted heavy pressure on the Roman Catholic Church (as many as 400 priests were in prison at one time), but in 1950 an agreement was reached between the bishops and the government. The bishops promised loyalty, and the government promised freedom of religious instruction in church and in higher education. The monastic orders and church organizations were also supposed to be free.

Despite the agreement, Roman Catholic activities were restricted that same year. Church estates were nationalized, schools were closed and religious instruction in public schools was prohibited. The celebration of the Sabbath was made impossible for many people. At the same time, the well-known methods used in Russia were also applied in Poland. The church was pressed to promote a peace campaign. Efforts were made to found a "progressive" church. In the course of time the new church had as many as 1700 priests. (The original Roman Catholic Church in Poland had 11,000 priests.)[67]

Cardinal Wyszynski was arrested in September of 1953 and confined to a monastery. After the Hungarian revolt of 1956, he was released, and the state took a more lenient attitude. Religious instruction could again be given to children if their parents requested it. In 1959 religious freedom was curtailed once more, as was the case in the Soviet Union, and so the ups and downs continued. In 1973 the

---

*According to newspaper reports in 1974, six priests in Lithuania were arrested and accused of spreading an underground Roman Catholic newspaper. That same year a clandestine printing shop in Riga was raided. Nine Baptists were arrested and 150,000 New Testaments confiscated (*The Gospel Witness*, January 23, 1975).

American theologian Carl F. H. Henry pointed to the remarkable fact that the Protestants in Warsaw were allowed to make use of the radio, read parts of Scripture and offer spiritual counseling. He added, however, that persecution and restriction of freedom were still the order of the day in Communist countries.[68]

In Czechoslovakia, Hungary and Yugoslavia, both the Roman Catholic Church and the various Protestant churches and groups were heavily persecuted by the Communist authorities, after first suffering the yoke of National Socialism. For a long time Karl Barth's friend Josef Hromadka, who was dean of the theological faculty at Prague, cooperated with the Communists. He withdrew from the scene in 1968 after the Russian tanks deprived the country of the last semblance of liberty. Several Protestants have been arrested or reduced to beggary since that time.

In Hungary a number of Reformed and Lutheran pastors were arrested. The Communists applied their well-known tactics of persuading the young people with ideology. In 1938 there were 1117 Reformed schools in the country, but by 1952 there were only five left. The Lutheran schools were reduced from 406 to two. In 1959 the first name-giving ceremony took place (shortly after the first one in East Germany).[69]

As far as the Roman Catholic Church is concerned, the names of Archbishop Beran of Prague, Cardinal Mindszenty of Hungary, and Archbishop Stepinac of Zagreb deserve honorable mention. All three provided their churches with powerful, fearless leadership, and all three became acquainted with Communist prisons from the inside.

In 1951, more than 3000 priests were arrested in Czechoslovakia, and 2000 of them were placed in "concentration monasteries."[70] In 1946 Archbishop Stepinac was sentenced to 16 years of forced labor.* The case against Mindszenty became world famous because of the "confession" extracted from him. Before his arrest he had scribbled on the back of an envelope:

> I have taken no part in any conspiracy of any kind. I shall not resign from my episcopal See. I shall not make a confession. But if despite of what I now say you should read that I have confessed or resigned, and even see it authenticated by my signature, bear in mind that it will have been only the result of human frailty. In advance, I declare all such actions null and void.[71]

---

*Because of his poor health, he was released in 1951. He was allowed to resume his priestly functions in his native village.

In a show trial in 1949, Mindszenty did indeed make a "confession." Apparently he had been subjected to the infamous brainwashing tactics also applied in Russia and China.*

During the Hungarian revolt of 1956, Mindszenty regained his liberty for a short time. After the Russian tanks crushed all budding hopes, he sought and found asylum in the embassy of the United States. In 1971, during the era of "détente," he was granted amnesty, but he refused to sign a document promising not to say or write anything jeopardizing the détente. In 1974, as part of an effort to improve relations between the Hungarian government and the Roman Catholic Church, the Pope removed Mindszenty as Primate of Hungary and Archbishop of Esztergom. He died in 1975, a deeply disappointed man.

As for the persecution in Rumania, Rev. Richard Wurmbrand has provided a great deal of valuable information.[72] The situation in Bulgaria has been described by Rev. Harlan Popov.

Wurmbrand has been accused of painting a "colored" picture of the situation behind the Iron Curtain,[73] and there may indeed be some truth to this accusation.** However, no one can deny that this man, who suffered incredibly because of his courageous witnessing, has disclosed some appalling facts about the ongoing persecution in eastern Europe. He has taken much of his material from the Soviet press, and he has shown—and continues to show—how the church in eastern Europe is living in something of a catacomb situation.

Part IV: China

Communist China, which is to be distinguished from nationalist China on Taiwan, has been surrounded by the Bamboo Curtain since about 1950. Reliable information about China is rarely available, especially where the situation of the church is concerned.

---

*He wrote in his autobiography: "I was abused, stripped to the skin, always kept awake, drugged, repeatedly trounced—without my own knowledge I had become another person" (J. Mindszenty, *Erinnerungen*, 1974³, pp. 217-29). On the method used, see R. L. Lifton, *Thought Reform and the Psychology of Totalism* (1961).

**R. Valkenburg's book *Rumoer rondom Wurmbrand* (1972) leaves the matter unsettled. An instance of apparently incorrect information is to be found in A. I. Kinnear's *Against the Tide* (1976), where we are told that Wurmbrand's description of the death of Watchman Nee does not square with the facts (p. 255).

Officially China grants freedom of religion and even guarantees it in the constitution. In reality, however, the voice of the organized church has been silenced. The old buildings are used for other purposes, and the occasional churches and mosques that one can still find in Peking simply serve the purpose of reassuring foreign visitors about the good intentions of the government.

In the summer of 1977, Prof. John Wang, a Roman Catholic teaching at the University of Montana, visited China, the country he had left in 1949. He could not find the churches and temples that had been so plentiful in his youth. The Roman Catholic church he used to attend was empty; it was decorated with pictures of Mao Tse-tung. A Buddhist monastery formerly used to house 500 monks was empty. His own brother, who had been educated as a Roman Catholic, was indifferent. Prof. Wang drew this conclusion: "If most of the members of my family practice Christianity no more, I can easily understand what has happened in the whole of China."[74]

There used to be some four million Roman Catholics in China, along with some 800,000 Protestants.[75] As we ponder this fact, we cannot avoid asking: What has become of all those Christians? What sort of tragedy has taken place in China behind the scenes?

I do not have room here to sketch in all the political developments. Suffice it to say that in 1949, when the Communists came to power under Mao, everything was brought into line and geared up for one purpose only: the building up of a new China and the consequent expulsion and erasure of all traces of imperialism and capitalism. The church was used temporarily to reach that goal, until it no longer served any useful purpose.

The Roman Catholic and Protestant churches both went through the same procedure. First the missionaries were warned that their presence was no longer appreciated. Typical of the warning was an article appearing in *The Christian Century* of March 29, 1950. It contained a "Message from Chinese Christians to Mission Boards Abroad." The "die-hards" were given a warning, and the following words of Mao were quoted:

> The whole world today looks to Communism for salvation and China looks upon Communism as a savior . . . Whoever chooses to oppose Communism must be prepared to be mauled and torn to pieces by the people. If you have not yet made up your mind about being mauled and smashed to smithereens, it would be wise of you not to oppose Communism. Let the anti-Communist heroes accept this piece of sincere advice from me, therefore.[76]

The vast majority of the missionaries left China. What happened to the few who stayed can be learned from the experiences of Dr. Frank Price, a Presbyterian missionary who was arrested in 1951 and accused of espionage.* According to Vatican reports, 23 bishops and archbishops, along with 300 priests, lay brothers and nuns, most of them foreigners, were in Chinese jails on December 31, 1951. According to other reports, 32 missionaries were in prison in May of 1952, while 193 American missionaries (153 Roman Catholics and 40 Protestants) were placed under various restrictions, charges and punishments.[77]

The Salvation Army was outlawed as a "reactionary organization led by imperialists." The Christian schools (13 colleges and universities, 236 high schools, and many more elementary schools) and hospitals (260 of them) were "taken over."

What happened to the native churches? Not all the churches had been organized by non-Chinese missionary societies. Some of them were of genuinely Chinese origin. Typical is what happened in the case of *Watchman Nee*, the leader of the so-called Little Flock Churches.

Watchman's grandfather had been baptized in 1857 and became a preacher. Watchman (his original name was Ni Shu-tsu) was born in 1903. He became an evangelist, and in several places he organized Bible circles. He also organized churches in several places. He did all of this as a Chinese layman completely independent of any foreign missionary group. In 1949 he urged the churches he had founded (there were 470 of them) to cooperate with the People's Republic as much as possible.

But even Watchman was arrested, on April 10, 1952. He was accused of being a "lawless, capitalist tiger" and sentenced to pay a heavy fine. He remained in prison until 1956. In those four years preparations were made to lay criminal charges against him.

Between January 18 and 30 of 1956, all the members of his church in Shanghai were assembled to take part in "accusation meetings." Those accusations were carefully spelled out in a document of no fewer than 2296 pages. Watchman was accused of imperialistic intrigues, espionage, financial corruption and immorality in his personal life. Those who dared to take his part were also arrested.

---

*Such accusations were drawn up according to a standard method. One should read the article of the YMCA Secretary Liu Liang-mo on "How to Hold a Successful Accusation Meeting," dated 1951 (see D. E. MacInnes, *Religious Policy and Practice in Communist China: A Documentary History*, 1972, pp. 238ff).

In June of 1956 he was sentenced to 15 years of imprisonment, with the term to include the years he had served since 1952. Still, he was not released in 1967. In 1972 he finally died in jail.[78] Watchman Nee was—and remained to the last day of his life—an exemplary Christian who had chosen as his motto for life: "I want nothing for myself; I want everything for the Lord."

Although several of the "accusers" had hoped to save their own freedom and also a certain measure of Christian freedom, and despite the fact that some Roman Catholics, caught in the same predicament, founded a "Catholic Patriotic Church," all the churches were put out of existence in the course of time. Today we hear some rumors about Christians who meet in private houses and Christians who pray without moving their lips, but a visible church is no more to be found in China.*

Something similar has happened to what we find in Europe, namely, the appearance of a *pseudo-church*. The materialized and intellectualized Marxism, which in China is called Maoism, created a vacuum, which had to be filled somehow. MacInnis, in his documentary history of method and practice with regard to religion in Communist China, speaks of a *new ritual*. He mentions, for example, the Morning and Evening Ceremonies for soldiers, Red Guards and workers on Tien An Men, the great public square in Peking.

In the morning, instructions are sought from a spiritually present Chairman Mao, and in the evening the achievements are reported to him. A poem describes the feelings of the multitude:

> Suddenly, like the eruption of a volcano,
> like the crashing of thunder in spring,

---

*This was written before 1978; it is too early to write anything definite about the most recent developments. According to recent data, "China is opening her doors to the world, to trade and technology, but definitely not to the Gospel." Further: "Also in 1979 the churches in this country remained closed" (Leslie T. Lyall, *New Spring in China*, 1979, pp. 19, 180).

Still, there are numerous house-churches. According to the China expert quoted above, it is highly probable that the number of Christians has increased since the revolution.

The following activities have been declared illegal by the government: (1) propagating religion to anyone under eighteen years of age or to government personnel; (2) giving speeches or publishing catechisms and religious materials without receiving prior approval from the Religious Affairs Bureau; (3) making any contact with religious organizations outside China or accepting financial help from them; (4) propagating religion or holding religious meetings outside of approved church buildings (*Christianity Today*, January 2, 1981). The parallels with Russian legislation are striking.

before Tien An Men
joyful shouts burst from our throats:
"Long live Chairman Mao! Long, long life to him!"
Chairman Mao has come!
Chairman Mao has come![79]

These rites take place all over the country. The analogy with morning and evening prayers is obvious. Also obvious is the analogy of the Meal of Bitter Remembering* with the Lord's supper, and that of the authority of the words of Mao with the authority of the Bible. Just listen to the following lines from the poem of a young Communist:

Mao Tse Tung

If for a single day we fail to study the works of Chairman Mao,
Selfish thoughts will raise their heads.
By studying Chairman Mao's works every day,
Public interest will take firm root, and self-interest will make away.
Studying Chairman Mao's works together, our family will quickly go forward,
On the broad way to ideological revolutionization.[80]

---

*In *China Pictorial* (1969, No. 2), a photograph of a group partaking of this kind of meal is to be found. The ceremony consists of eating a meal of wild herbs and vegetables and recalls the days before the liberation when this was often all the poor, starving people got to eat.

How was all this possible? This is the agonizing question posed by Outerbridge when he writes about the "lost churches of China." He gives the following answer: "The church lost to the enemy which sowed tares at night. Atheism, materialism, and Communism have choked the fields so carefully tilled by Christian missions, revealing the fallacy of the materialistic emphasis of the social gospel."[81]

Outerbridge continues to point to a number of significant facts. China was the greatest of the American missionary fields. (In 1928 there were 8,200 Protestant missionaries in China, mainly Americans.) Many of the later Communist leaders were educated in the missionary schools. The teachers in those schools included some who were not convinced Christians but simply clever intellectuals. Many of the students, especially after the anti-foreign agitation such as began in 1926-27 in Shanghai and Peking, left the schools in the same unbelieving state they were in when they entered. "Too often a priority has been placed, in the case of both teachers from abroad and Chinese staff, not upon the teacher's faith in the redemptive power of the gospel of Jesus, but in the teacher's competency in his particular field of knowledge." The author notes sadly that the first and great commandment was often forgotten in the missionary activities, and that Christianity was propagated as a success religion, a social religion. It was forgotten that man shall not live by bread alone.[82]

The work of the Chinese church was continued on a smaller scale in Taiwan. In 1959 the number of Protestants there was estimated at 230,000, and the number of Catholics at 170,000.[83]

Part V: Worldwide Persecution

The religious persecution in the twentieth century has been worldwide. We have not dealt with all areas, for there simply is not space to tell all the stories.

I could have gone on to write about the persecution in Assyria and Asia Minor, in the Sudan and in Uganda, in North Korea and in Celebes. In many cases we have no exact data to go by.

I must still mention the persecution in Mexico between 1926 and 1938. The Roman Catholic Church (with 22 million members out of a population of 26 million) was the special target of this persecution. The clergy was mainly of Spanish origin. The formalism was conspicuous, and the social consciousness below par.

When a new constitution was adopted in 1917 after seven years of great confusion, the document forbade religious instruction, celibacy was abolished, monastic orders were dissolved and processions were prohibited. And there were more anti-clerical measures. It was prescribed how many priests were allowed to work in a particular city. As a consequence, many priests and nuns were driven away and had to go into hiding or beg for a living. In 1926 all the churches were closed by government decree. Some Roman Catholics resisted by force of arms (under General Gonzalez), while others formed an underground church. No fewer than 5000 priests and other church members were killed.

After 1938, however, a complete reconciliation between church and state took place. In 1957, the number of Protestants in Mexico (Baptists, Presbyterians and Lutherans) was 911,000.

When we survey all these persecutions, we may choose to speak of the guilt of the church and point to its lack of economic justice and social mercy and its connections with all kinds of earthly powers. But we could also take a different approach and point to the church's failure to preach the real gospel. The church transformed the message of the Crucified One into a social program.

We should bear in mind the correction intended in both observations. But who could fail to be impressed by the words from Revelation to John which seem to begin taking effect in our age.

> The beast opened its mouth to utter blasphemies against God, blaspheming his name and his dwelling, that is those who dwell in heaven. Also it was allowed to make war on the saints and to conquer them. And authority was given it over every tribe and people and tongue and nation (Rev. 13:6-7).

8

Tribulation and Resistance: The Churches and National Socialism

---

An angel of light?

It is undeniable that various members of the church saw some definite glimmerings of light in National Socialism. They believed they were witnessing the dawn of a new day. For some time, at least, they looked to Hitler for "hail."

What did the Dutch journalist Mary Pos write in the Christian national weekly *De Spiegel* (The Mirror) in the 1930s? When she interviewed Mussolini, the Italian leader opened a drawer, took out a New Testament, and assured her he read it every day. What did a minister tell his congregation in Heilsbrunnen-Berlin in 1933? He told them he had it on the best authority that Adolf Hitler always carried a copy of the New Testament in his pocket, and that he read Bible verses and stanzas from a hymnal every morning.[1]

Otto Dibelius, who informs us of this fact, claims this myth was quite widely believed at the time. After all, the streets were safe again! In the view of many, this fact alone was sufficient to tip the scales in favor of National Socialism. Life had seemed no longer livable, but now Hitler's program opened new perspectives.

The situation after the first world war had indeed been chaotic. Among the most valuable documents from postwar Berlin were the drawings of George Grosz, who portrayed "aimlessly strolling demobilized men," as well as "beggars, showily dressed up women, street musicians, undernourished children—very many pale, shivering children—luxury cars and well-groomed true-bred dogs." P. J. Bouman, who uses these expressions, speaks on the same pages of the "Berlin of the nudist colonies, pornographic magazines, brothels for homosexuals, séances, marriage bureaus of a very special kind, ads for fortune-tellers and quacks—the triumph of asphalt culture."[2]

Germany, once so proud of its "Kultur," had lost its moorings. The economic depression had been total in its impact. (Witness the bewildering devaluation of the mark.) The social misery was most distressing. (Witness the unheard-of unemployment figures.) The feelings of resentment, of being humiliated and offended, were running high. A growing number of workers and intellectuals believed they saw light dawning in the East, and so the membership rolls of the Communist Party of Germany grew alarmingly. In the course of time street fighting became the order of the day.

Into this situation walked Hitler with his message: one people, one *Reich*, one Führer. He seemed to be the man who could create order in the chaos, suppressing the threat of anarchy with a strong hand and restoring honor to Germany, while ending the dominance of the immoral filth *(Schmutz)*. He would respect the church—the Roman Catholic Church in which he was baptized—as well as the Protestant churches.

Was it surprising that Hitler was hailed as an angel of light during this period? Article 24 of the National Socialist party program of 1925 embraced "positive Christianity." After Hitler assumed power in 1933, the government issued a statement on March 23 containing the following decrees: "The national government will acknowledge and guarantee to the Christian confessions their due influence in school and education. It desires a sincere cooperation of church and state."[3]

There were both Catholics and Protestants who gladly joined the Nazi party. I will have more to say about those Protestants a little later. As far as the Roman Catholics are concerned, it is typical of the situation that both Mussolini and Hitler managed to conclude concordats with the Vatican.

The Lateran Pact of 1929 solved the so-called Roman question. The Pope was granted a private piece of ground on which he was sovereign and the "Catholic and Apostolic Roman religion" was recognized as "the only religion of the state." In the Roman Catholic world press, Pope Pius XII was acclaimed as "a new Constantine who has brought peace to the world."[4]

The concordat between the Third Reich and the Holy See likewise seemed a promising arrangement from the standpoint of the Roman Catholic Church when it was concluded in 1933. The concordat guaranteed complete freedom of religion for the Roman Catholic people of Germany, including freedom of religious instruction and freedom for organizations promoting religious, cultural or charitable purposes. The bishops would be appointed by the church with the approval of the state and would be required to swear an oath of allegiance. On Sundays and on public holidays, there would have to be prayers in the churches for the welfare of the German Reich.[5] No wonder Cardinal Faulhaber wrote to Hitler after the concordat was concluded: "With regard to Germany's prestige in East and West and in the eyes of the whole world, this handshake with the papacy, the greatest moral power in the history of the world, is a boundlessly blessed achievement."[6]

Five days after the signing of the concordat, the law on sterilization was issued in Germany.* This interference in the area of personal freedom was diametrically opposed to the agreement that had just been reached. Five days later, Dr. Erich Klausener, the leader of the Catholic Action organization in Germany, was murdered. Great was the disenchantment. Many honest people (including some original members of the party) could not imagine how the Nazis could appear to be so completely unreliable.

The "German Christians"

The "Faith Movement of the German Christians" can be compared to the "Living Church" in Russia, described in Chapter 7. Just as the "Living Church" expressed its homogeneity with the Communist authorities, the "German Christians" wanted to combine Christianity and National Socialism. And just as the "Living Church" was initially favored by the Soviet government, the German Christians at a given moment received Hitler's personal support. In spite of the official support, the "Living Church" remained a foreign element in a materialistic state, and so it finally expired, slowly but surely. The "German Christians," likewise, went down without honor after several setbacks. In the minds of Hitler and Rosenberg, there was no place for even this kind of Christianity.

---

*It was called the "Gesetz zur Verhütung erbkranken Nachwuchses" (Law to prevent the birth of children with hereditary taints) and was applied especially to the Jewish party in a Jewish mixed marriage.

During 1932 and 1933 in particular, the so-called faith movement gained considerable ground. For some time, its adherents formed a majority in the synods of several of the ecclesiastical provinces of Germany. The movement had its roots in the German national way of thinking, which was already present in the nineteenth century. This way of thinking tended to idolize the people and the fatherland, and it had given its blessing to the weapons of war in 1914.*

A number of ministers joined the ranks of the National Socialists when this movement emerged. Various members of the church wore the brown shirt. Ecclesiastical and religious organizations were founded. The most prominent of them was the "Faith Movement of the German Christians" established in 1932 by *Rev. Joachim Hossenfelder.*

The first words of the movement's basis formula, adopted in 1933, were: "God has created me a German. Being a German is a gift of God. God wants me to fight for my being-a-German." These words struck home. They seemed to establish a bridge between Christianity and the rehabilitation of the German nation anticipated under Hitler. Many Germans who were scattered throughout the different churches agreed with Hossenfelder's plea; he called for one Protestant State Church under the leadership of a single state bishop *(Reichsbischof)* who would apply the Führer principle within the church.

Many people joined the movement. Some of them believed in all honesty that the gospel of Jesus Christ would thus be preserved in its purity. Among them was Gerhard Kittel, the well-known editor of the *Theological Dictionary of the New Testament.* In correspondence with Karl Barth, Kittel said he had prayed for years for the deliverance of his people from distress and shame, and for a Christian the choice between the Soviet star and National Socialism could not be a difficult one to make.[7]

There were others who saw an unmistakable connection between the ideas of the German Christian theologians and the liberal theology that had captivated so many minds in Germany since the days of Schleiermacher. Among them was Walter Nigg, who wrote in 1937 that there was "an unmistakable connection between religious liberalism and the German Christians," in part because "the latter were prepared to remove the Old Testament from the canon and also discussed Paul as a Jewish figure."[8] Other Germans, who had been

---

*It should be noted that Germany was not the only country with tendencies in this direction.

baptized in infancy but were already unchurched for years, were only too happy to cooperate with the powers seeking to make the church a department of the totalitarian state.

A grand-scale effort to realize this ideal was made in a meeting held in the Berlin Sportpalast on November 13, 1933, about half a year after Hitler's rise to power. Some 200,000 German Christians were present. Sixty banners were consecrated, and the speaker of the day was Dr. R. Krause, who was called the *Gauleiter* (district leader) of the movement. Krause declared:

> The multitude of those who want to return to the church should first be persuaded. Therefore one needs to feel at home in his own country, and the first step in this homecoming is that we must be purged of all that is non-German in liturgy and confession, purged of the Old Testament with its Jewish morality . . .

Then follow the words that were quoted in Chapter 6 (see p. 98 above.)

This was clear language. In the ears of some, it was all too clear what was going on. "Reichsbischof" Müller immediately withdrew as protector of the Faith Movement of German Christians. This kind of cooperation was not what he had in mind.

Now the eyes of many hangers-on were finally opened. According to some, an earthquake had struck the church. Because of the unvarnished language of Krause, the days of the "Faith Movement" were numbered—in the Evangelical Church, at least.

The church struggle

Karl Barth was the man who realized from the start what a deadly danger National Socialism was to the church. In 1937 he addressed the churches in the West in a very candid way, especially the churches of England and America. He expressed regret that the German churches had not been quicker to perceive the demonic nature of National Socialism, for the Nazis preached a new faith based on a new revelation. He even spoke of "the German Islam or the German Bolshevism." Barth noted with gratitude how Scripture was being studied anew and more intensively, and he pointed out the need for repentance and conversion, even in the Western part of the world. Perhaps the discovery would then be made that people in the West should also return to the sources of the evangelical faith and repudiate the errors of which all the churches of the world have been guilty. Barth went on to say: "We have but to think of the remarkable passivity with which the political world has accepted the suppression of the Church in Russia, and with which it now appears to be willing to accept that of the Church in Germany, without the Churches having done so far anything worth mentioning in opposition to this indifference."[9]

These words do not reflect Barth's later attitude toward churches under a Communist regime, about which I spoke in Chapter 7. In 1937 he was certainly qualified to speak the way he did, for he had not bowed the knee before the idol to which the entire country paid homage day after day by crying, "Hail Hitler." Moreover, he had exhorted others to serve God alone.

As early as June of 1933, shortly after Hitler's rise to power and when the "German Christians" began to call for one national church and one national bishop, Barth wrote a flaming protest in the form of a brochure entitled *Theologische Existenz Heute* (Theological Existence Today).* In this brochure he rejected unconditionally the ideology of National Socialism. He wrote:

> The communion of those who belong to the church is marked not by blood and therefore not by race but by the Holy Spirit and by baptism. If the German Evangelical Church were to exclude Jewish Christians, or treat them as second-rate Christians, it would cease to be a Christian church.

Also:

> *If* the office of national bishop *(Reichsbischof)* is to be possible at all in the Evangelical Church, it must be regarded as comparable to any other ecclesiastical office; that is to say, it must not be exercised in accordance with political ideals and methods (general elections, membership in the Party, etc.), but only by means of the regular office-bearers of the church who, when they are appointed to office, are qualified exclusively by virtue of ecclesiastical capacities.

In a more positive note he declared:

> In the church we all agree that it is good for man to cling to the Word of God with all his heart, with all his soul, with all his mind, and with all his power, and that in time and eternity only this can be good for him. In the church we agree that God is only present in our space and time in His Word, and that His Word has no other name for us or any other content than Jesus Christ, and that Jesus Christ is to be found for

---

*After the German invasion, the same idea was expressed in the Netherlands by Klaas Schilder in an article in *De Reformatie* on the theme "Leave your shelter, show your colors."

us nowhere in the whole world except each day anew in the Scriptures of the Old and New Testaments.

These words of Barth were not written in a vacuum. They found a response especially when the government threatened to force the notorious "Aryan paragraph" upon the church. Matters even went so far that the Prussian general synod, meeting on September 5, 1933, adopted the following ruling: "Whoever is not of Aryan descent or whoever is married to a person of non-Aryan descent may not be appointed clergyman or office-bearer of the general government of the church. Clergymen or office-bearers of Aryan descent who marry a person of non-Aryan descent must be dismissed."

When this happened, the Ministers Emergency Association *(Pfarrernotbund)* was established under the leadership of *Rev. Martin Niemöller.* Each member signed the following declaration:

> I pledge to perform my office as minister of the Word only in obedience to the Holy Scripture and to the confession of the Reformation as the pure interpretation of Holy Scripture. I pledge to protest fearlessly against each violation of the confession. I acknowledge my co-responsibility, as far as it lies in my power, with regard to those who are persecuted because of this confession. In accordance with this pledge, I declare that through the application of the Aryan paragraph within the church, the violation of the confession has become a fact.

This was a courageous testimony, but Martin Niemöller was a courageous man. In the first world war he had served as the captain of a submarine.* After the war he wandered about the moorlands of Westphalia and sought peace with God. Finally he decided to become a minister, for only in preaching the Word of God could he find a way out of all of Europe's misery. Only gradually did he learn to appreciate Barth, but once he was converted to his ideas, he followed his leadership heart and soul, including his plea for unconditional obedience to the Word of God.

In 1933 Niemöller was the beloved pastor of Berlin-Dahlem, and there he founded the Ministers Emergency Association when the sky became black with clouds of oppression. In spite of the dangers connected with membership in this organization, 2000 ministers immediately applied. The number swelled to 7000 after Dr. Krause's notorious speech at the Sportpalast.

Essentially all these men were in a dilemma. It seemed to them as

---

*He was well-known for his book *Vom U-Boot zur Kanzel* (From Submarine to Pulpit), published in 1934.

if love for the fatherland and love for the church of the Lord were in competition. On no account were the members of the Association revolutionaries.

At a meeting at Niemöller's house on October 15, 1933, they sent Hitler a telegram on the occasion of Germany's retirement from the League of Nations. They thanked him for his "manly deed and clear word" and assured him at the same time, "in the name of 2500 pastors who did not count themselves among the German Christians," of their loyalty and prayers.[10]

But then lightning began to flash in the sky. Dr. Krause's speech on November 13 roused many sleepers. On November 19 the pastors of the Ministers Emergency Association read a message from their pulpits in which they protested. In more than 2500 Evangelical churches, the following words were heard: "Paganism has invaded our church . . . We, the preachers of the gospel, don't want to become worthy of the prophet's accusation that we have become dumb dogs."

Martin Niemöller

Then came the year of many synods. The most distinguished of them was the Synod of Barmen (May 29-31, 1934). The significance of those synods was that not only ministers but the *churches* of Germany —including both Reformed and Lutheran churches — unanimously raised their voices against the penetration of the demons of darkness.

The Synod of Barmen has been called the first "Confession Synod." In contrast to the official national church under a national bishop and under the supervision of a Ministry of Church Affairs, a "Confession Church" now took shape.*

Both for theology and the church, the *Declaration of Barmen* adopted at this synod and composed largely by Karl Barth was very important. Here the church was speaking out and condemning the spirit of the time, which meant more than the spirit of the National Socialist time. Hans Asmussen, in his explanation of the Declaration set forth at the synod, has this to say: "We protest against a phenomenon that for more than 200 years already has been in the process of preparing the degeneration of the church."[11]

He was referring to the practice of "natural theology" since the second half of the eighteenth century, and also the theology of experience which arose in Schleiermacher's wake. The first of the six Barmen theses was vigorously opposed to such a way of thinking:

> John 14:6, John 10:1, 9. Jesus Christ, as He is attested for us in Holy Scripture, is the one Word of God which we have to hear and which we have to trust and obey in life and death.
>
> We reject the false doctrine, as though the Church could and would have to acknowledge as source of its proclamation, apart from and besides this one Word, still other events, powers, figures and truths, as God's revelation.

The other theses were also composed as positive declarations of faith followed by a rejection of errors. I mention only the following from theses 3 and 4, the relevance of which is obvious.

> We reject the false doctrine, as though the Church were permitted to abandon the form of its message and order to its own pleasure or to changes in prevalent ideological and political convictions.
>
> We reject the false doctrine, as though the Church, apart from its ministry, could and were permitted to give itself, or allow to be given to it, special leaders vested with ruling powers.[12]

All these words sound rather theological to untrained ears, but a good listener heard in the Declaration a definite rejection of the demands of a totalitarian state.

I must refrain from giving a detailed description of the course of events up to 1937. It is sufficient to note a few facts. Regional

---

*At an earlier date an exclusively Reformed synod met in Barmen (January 3-4, 1934), in which 167 churches were represented. Barth exercised a great influence on that synod. A statement of faith was adopted in which the totalitarian state was rejected. On February 18 and 19, an Evangelical synod then met in Barmen and expressed its agreement with the declaration of Barmen I. Then, on March 7, an Evangelical synod met in Berlin-Brandenburg (see F. W. Kantzenbach, *Christentum in der Gesellschaft*, Vol. II, pp. 300, 400).

"Brother Councils" were founded, and also a national "Brother Council" (under the leadership of Barth, Breit and Asmussen), for the purpose of giving advice and counsel in special cases. A provisional church government was set up for comparable purposes, chaired by the Lutheran bishop Marahrens. Barth was dismissed from his professorship in Bonn when he refused to take the oath of allegiance to Hitler. Nevertheless, he continued his struggle against the Hitler regime from Basel. At the instigation of the church, *Reichsbischof Müller*, Hitler's favorite, had to resign in 1935. But on May 1, 1937, Hitler brazenly declared:

> There are old dotards of whom nothing can be made. But we are taking the children from them! We are educating the children to be new German men. When the youngsters are ten years old, we take them and form them into a new fellowship [the so-called Hitler Youth]. At eighteen years we do not yet leave them at peace. At that age they enter the S.A. or the Labour Front, and then we stick them into the Labour Service, and then for two years they come to the Army.[13]

These words were cast in the same mold as the method applied by the Communists in Russia and to be applied in all the countries they occupied. In vain the Confessing Church protested. It was increasingly placed under restraints, and it could not always maintain its own unity. On more than one occasion, the Lutherans, in line with their tradition, appeared more inclined than the Reformed members to comply with the demands of the state.

Numerous ministers were arrested. I will mention only three of them here. The first is Dr. Weiszler, a baptized Jew who was chosen as president of the Provisional Church Government. He was arrested in 1936 and transferred to a concentration camp, where he died in February of 1937.[14]

The second one is Martin Niemöller, who was arrested on July 1, 1937. To get an impression of the situation, we should listen for a moment to the following words, which are drawn from the sermon he delivered on the Sunday before his arrest (June 27). The sermon is based on Acts 5:34-42.

> It is the message of the Cross which places before us the question: Either-Or; belief or unbelief; salvation or destruction; life or condemnation. Thus all neutrality, even that which is well meant, turns one into an enemy.
>
> The pressure is growing; anyone who has gone through the fiery ordeal of the tempter in these last days—I think, for instance, how on Wednesday the Secret Police penetrated into the closed church of

Friedrich Werder, and arrested at the altar eight members of the Council of Brethren there, and took them away; I think how yesterday at Saarbrücken six women and a trusted man of the Evangelical Committee were arrested . . . I repeat, he who has suffered all this, cannot be far from the words of the prophet; he also would like to say: Now, O Lord, take away my life.[15]

Niemöller was held without trial until February of 1938. In March he was sentenced to seven months in prison, which he had already finished serving, but he refused to sign a paper promising to never preach again. By direct order of Hitler he was therefore consigned to a concentration camp in Sachsenhausen (1938-41). Later he wound up in Dachau (1941-45). Somehow he survived, but later he said of those years that it would have been easier to die fearlessly before the firing squad than to be forced to spend day after day in the camp.

In 1937, another 806 people, almost all of them ministers, were imprisoned. *Dietrich Bonhoeffer*, a man of notable theological qualities and great integrity, should be mentioned as the third of the ministers. It would be out of place in this context to discuss his theology in which he called for both an unconditional following of Christ and an interpretation of the Christian message in non-Christian terms for a world alienated from Christ.

As late as 1939, Bonhoeffer was teaching in America (at the request of Reinhold Niebuhr). Still, he wanted to share the destiny of his people, and so he returned to Germany be-

Dietrich Bonhoeffer

fore the outbreak of the second world war. He grew more and more convinced that it was his Christian calling to contribute actively to the resistance against Hitler. As he himself put it: "When a madman rages through the streets with his car, I can do something more than comforting the persons who have been knocked down or burying the dead, when I, being a minister, happen to be present. I must jump in front of the car and stop it." Bonhoeffer took part in the resistance against Hitler. He was arrested on April 4, 1943, and hanged on May 9, 1945, in the concentration camp at Flossenburg. In a letter from the camp he wrote: "My life has been abundantly filled with the goodness of God in the past, and above all guilt stands the forgiving love of him who was crucified."[16]

In the course of time, the Roman Catholics also came to share in the persecution and the resistance. Deluded in the expectation raised by the concordat, curbed in their associational activities, silenced in their press, and bereft of their young people, they listened with agreement to the papal encyclical "Mit brennender Sorge" (With Burning Care), issued on March 2, 1937. In this encyclical Pope Pius XI exposed the sinfulness of the doctrine of race and the myth of blood and the soil.

Among the members of the Roman Catholic hierarchy, Von Galen, the Bishop of Münster, and Cardinal von Faulhaber, the Archbishop of Munich,* played a leading role. In 1945 there were 245 Roman Catholic clergymen among the inmates of Dachau.**

The fate in store for all the churches after the full triumph of Nazism becomes fully apparent from some secret instructions given to the German district leaders in June of 1941 by Hitler's collaborator Martin Bormann:

> National Socialist and Christian concepts are irreconcilable. The Christian churches build on man's ignorance, and are endeavoring to keep the greatest possible number of people in a state of ignorance. For it is only in this fashion that the churches can maintain their power. National Socialism, on the other hand, rests on scientific foundations . . . Just as the harmful influences of astrologers, fortune-tellers, and other swindlers are being eliminated and suppressed by the state, so all possibility of ecclesiastical influence must be totally removed.[17]

---

*Von Faulhaber had initially assured Hitler of his sincere cooperation (see P. E. Lapide, *De laatste drie pausen en de joden*, 1967, pp. 115, 116).

**Especially after the rise of the "Confession Church," there were generally a good number of Evangelical ministers in prisons and concentration camps at any one time.

The folly of war

I have already described the effort the German people made to stand on their own feet again after the debacle of 1918. Nevertheless, we can only speak with bewilderment of the "will to power" that overcame Hitler when he found himself in command of the finest army in Europe, the army he put into operation on all fronts in order to attain his demonic goals.

The man who was most outspoken in raising his voice against all of this in 1938 was Karl Barth. Austria had been incorporated into the Reich, and German troops stood at the borders of Czechoslovakia. No one raised a finger to save Czechoslovakia from its fate. The country was simply thrown to the wolves, much the way Hungary was in 1956.

It was against the background of the Czechoslovakian situation of 1938 that Barth wrote a letter to his friend Prof. Hromadka of Prague, in which the following words are to be found: "I dare to hope that the sons of the old Hussites will show impotent Europe that even today there are men. Each Czech soldier who fights and suffers in those circumstances will do so for us—and, I say it now without any reservation—he will do so also for the church of Jesus Christ, which in the atmosphere of Hitler and Mussolini can only lapse into ridicule or extirpation."[18]

These were not only cutting words which placed the background of the struggle for or against Hitler into sharp perspective, they were also debatable words, words equating the Czech soldiers with the soldiers of Jesus Christ. Even so, Barth was and remained fully convinced of the rightness of the point of view he had adopted at that time. Twelve years later he wrote: "I am no pacifist, and I would do the same thing now in the same situation."[19]

In the German situation of that time, however, his letter, which was published internationally, backfired. The whole German National Socialist press branded him a warmonger, although this did not upset him. But when he was estranged from his brothers, who could not understand why he would say such things—*that* was upsetting.

This applied especially to the Lutheran theologian *Hans Asmussen*, who had cordially cooperated with Barth until then. Afterward, however, he turned away from Barth more and more.

At the request of the Provisional Church Government, Asmussen had prepared a humble Order of Prayer. In case of war all the congregations of the Confessing Church would join together in praying not for victory but for the grace to resist all hatred and vindictiveness. The prayer to be used was a prayer for *all* people threatened by the great suffering.

Compared with Barth's letter, Asmussen's prayer was not a political document at all. All Evangelical Christians could have joined together in praying such a prayer, and it might have served the purpose of enhancing their cooperation. But when fragments of Barth's letter were published at the same time as this Order of Prayer, the National Socialist authorities immediately suspected there was some connection between the two. The Lutheran bishops Wurm, Meiser and Marahrens were summoned by Kerrl, the minister responsible for religious affairs, who intimidated them to such an extent that they condemned the Order of Prayer on "patriotic grounds."

Dibelius, who tells this whole story in his autobiography, describes how he visited the bishops immediately afterward and found them completely despondent. In later years Wurm wrote about this incident: "None of us had the inner strength at that moment to do and set forth only that which would have been right. There are certain moments in which the power of darkness is greater than that of light, and for that reason we must humble ourselves before God and men."[20]

When various acts of war followed each other quickly, there was not much elbow room left for the churches. As a matter of course, not only civil life but also church life was badly disrupted. Forty-five percent of the Evangelical clergymen served in the army, and the hand of the government weighed heavily on their churches. By 1941 no religious books or periodicals or Bibles could be printed anymore because of the shortage of paper. Christian youth work, which had already been curtailed, was all but stopped. In the final period of the war, many churches were devastated.

Two things should be added, however. In the first place, *revival* took place in several churches as a result of oppression and distress. Earlier there had been a decline in churchgoing, but now the houses of prayer in many areas were proving to be too small. A great act of courage on the part of many Christians was the signing of the so-called "red card"; signers were witnessing to the fact that they were living members of the Confessing Church. By signing the card, they were confessing Holy Scripture to be "the only foundation of the church and its proclamation" and promising to contribute on a regular basis, to stick to the Word and sacraments, and to have the intention of leading a Christian life. In some congregations practically all the members signed this card. In the Rhineland there were 300,000 who signed, and in Westphalia there were 500,000.[21]

It was no accident that when the war broke out, all members of the Provisional Church Government were placed under arrest. Between August of 1939 and January of 1945, no fewer than 24,559 members of the Army were condemned to death.[22] Doubtless there were various reasons behind the executions, but we know conscientious objectors were shot as a matter of course.[23]

Consider this moving letter, written by a farm boy to his parents on February 3, 1944:

> Dear parents,
>
>   I must give you bad news. — I have been condemned to death, I and Gustave G. We did not sign up for the SS, and so they condemned us to death. You wrote me, indeed, that I should not join the SS; my comrade, Gustave G., did not sign up either. Both of us would rather die than stain our consciences with such deeds of horror. I know what the SS has to do. Oh, my dear parents, difficult as it is for me and for you, forgive me everything; if I have offended you, please forgive me and pray for me. If I were to be killed in the war while my conscience was bad, that too would be sad for you. Many more parents will lose their children. Many SS men will get killed too. I thank you for everything you have done for my good since my childhood; forgive me, pray for me . . .[24]

Consider also the words of Prof. Hermann Stöhr, secretary of the German Union of Conciliation, in a letter to his sister-in-law, written June 3, 1940:

> This is my situation: ever since March 2, 1939, I have been explaining to the military authorities, that I could serve my country only with work, not with arms (Matt. 5:21-26, 38-40) nor with an oath (Matt. 5:33-37, Jas. 5:12). And God's commandments have force for me unconditionally (Acts 5:29). For this I was sentenced to death on March 16, 1940, and the judgment was confirmed on April 13, 1940.
>
>   To be daily prepared to die is of course enjoined upon every Christian. Therefore this present state is for me a discipline. In the midst of it I rejoice in my leisure, which I use above all for Bible study.[25]

Bonhoeffer was prominent among those who proceeded to engage in active resistance. The leader of the plot against Hitler's life, which failed in an almost miraculous way on July 20, 1944, was *Carl Friedrich Goerdeler*, a former mayor of Leipzig. Goerdeler had resigned this post in 1937 when the statue of the Jewish composer Felix

Mendelssohn-Bartholdy in front of Leipzig's great concert hall was removed by vandals.

Goerdeler was one of the approximately 5000 men of the resistance, some of whom had strong Christian convictions, who were killed in 1944 and 1945. Consider these words from his last letter:

> Is there a God who takes a part in the personal destiny of man? It becomes difficult for me to believe so, for this God has now for years permitted torrents of horror and despair to be engendered against mankind by a few hundred thousand bestialized, spiritually diseased, and deluded individuals . . . Is it not possible that with our arbitrary nationalism we have affronted God and practised idolatry? Yes, in that case the things that are happening would have meaning: God desires to root out in all nations the propensity to harness him to their national ambitions. If this be true, we can only beg God to let it suffice, and in the place of tears and death, to give ascendancy to the apostles of reconciliation who have recognized this spirit in God and his purpose in his judgments. For this I pray to him.[26]

It is certainly incorrect to hold all Germans without exception responsible for the crimes of the Hitler regime. It is important to emphasize that the Confessing Church (not the whole church, and not all the members of the church) was the only fellowship—as contrasted with organizations of intellectuals and workers—to protest against Nazi crimes and keep on protesting. Moreover, honest men such as Otto Dibelius and Helmut Thielicke have contended—not unjustly—that the men of the church in many cases simply did not know the terrible facts.[27]

Confession of guilt

In a ruined Germany ploughed up by bombs, representatives of the German churches met in several gatherings in 1945. The Evangelical Church in Germany was founded to take the place of the German Evangelical Church. Bishop Wurm became the chairman, and Niemöller the vice-chairman.

At a meeting of the council of the new church held in Stuttgart on October 18 and 19, 1945, with representatives of the Ecumenical Movement present (including Visser 't Hooft and Kraemer), the following confession of guilt was made:

> With great pain we say: Through us, infinite suffering has been brought upon many peoples and countries. What we have often declared before our congregations, that we now declare in the name of the whole church: For long years we struggled in the name of Jesus Christ against

the spirit which found its frightful expression in the National Socialist regime of force; nevertheless, we accuse ourselves of not having confessed more courageously, prayed more faithfully, believed more joyfully and loved more ardently. Now a new beginning must be made in our churches.[28]

This declaration became the foundation of a new cooperation between the churches in Germany and those in other parts of the world. In the next chapter I will talk about the problem of the Jews, which requires special treatment.

The church in occupied countries

On April 9, 1940, German troops invaded Denmark and Norway. On May 10 they continued their *Blitzkrieg* against the Netherlands, pushing on at once to Belgium and France as well. On June 10 they entered Paris without having fired a shot. Hitler was lord and master of most of Europe.

The weak defenses in this part of the world, where the idealistic pacifism of a Sermon-on-the-Mount-Christianity modeled after Tolstoy was preached, had attracted Hitler and his armies like a magnet. In Denmark there was no resistance at all. In Norway there was resistance until June 12, and in the Netherlands the resistance lasted five days. When Rotterdam was mercilessly bombed, resistance ceased.

Once the occupation began, freedom in the broadest sense was gone. There was no more civil-political freedom or freedom of the press. Freedom of education and instruction was gradually taken away. The freedom enjoyed by the churches was restricted as much as possible. The octopus-like tentacles of the totalitarian state suffocated all human expressions of opinion. In all the occupied countries, resistance was offered. Here I will touch on some of the main points.

In *Denmark* there was only a small number of collaborators among the ministers (not more than 12). The bishops pleaded for freedom in preaching and opposed anti-Semitism. The best-known of the resistance leaders was *Kaj Munk* (1898-1944).

Munk (his real name was Kaj Harald Leiningen Petersen) was a talented man—a preacher, author and patriot. At the end of December, 1943, he preached in the main church at Copenhagen and called for resistance against the persecution of the Jews. When he lashed out against the lax attitude of the members of the church of Vedersø, who, it was said, had voluntarily cooperated in the construction of German coastal defenses, he was arrested on January 4, 1944 and shot.

The leader of the resistance of the churches in *Norway* was the bishop of Oslo, *Eivind Berggrav* (1884-1959). A group of seven Lutheran bishops and ten clergymen from various churches, headed by Berggrav, formed a Christian Council for the Church of Norway on October 25, 1940.

When various measures were taken against the Norwegian population under the traitor *Quisling*—measures representing violations of conscience—this Council protested in a letter of January 1941 and publicly declared the measures in question to be in conflict with the law of God. When the Norwegian Nazis took possession of a cathedral in Trondhjem in February 1942, Berggrav and six other Norwegian bishops sent in their resignations as state officials. At the same time, however, they declared that "the spiritual calling entrusted to me at the altar of the Lord remains mine in accordance with God and with justice." At Easter of the same year, a letter was read from the pulpits of the churches. The letter included a strong protest against the effort to indoctrinate the children with National Socialistic principles. On April 9 of that year, Berggrav was arrested and severely manhandled. He spent the rest of the war in jail.[29]

Even before the invasion of 1940, the Reformed Churches of the Netherlands (Gereformeerde Kerken) had discerned the anti-Christian character of National Socialism clearly, and they decreed membership in their churches to be incompatible with adherence to such an ideology. In a report submitted in 1936 to the Synod of Amsterdam dealing with the question of disciplining members of the National Socialist Movement, it was stated that "old, pre-Christian, pagan ideas and ideals, supported and abetted by philosophical conceptions of modern times," had come to new life in this movement. There was evidence of this in the struggle for a power state founded on brute force. Further evidence could be found in the obsession with the economy, because common citizens were now officers and soldiers in the production army. Other pagan ideals included the exclusive nationalism, the glorification of war and the presence of totalitarianism. The directives of the report were accepted at the synod, and it was decided that "members of our Reformed Churches should not participate in organizations which expose the unscriptural errors mentioned in this report."[30]

Generally speaking, this discipline was maintained in the Reformed Churches before the invasion. But how would things go when the men-of-Mussert* could count on the support of the men of Hitler, possibly by acts of terrorism?

The official answer was given by the Synod of Utrecht (1941), which upheld the decision of Amsterdam as it stood. The synodical reporter, Prof. Klaas Schilder of Kampen, was certainly entitled to speak as he did. Schilder was the man who had encouraged the Reformed people and, through them, the entire Dutch population. Shortly after the occupation, he wrote two bold articles in his weekly *De Reformatie* (The Reformation).** Schilder declared:

Klaas Schilder

Our people will look forward to the future to come; they will set their eyes on the day in which the Wilhelmus [the Dutch national anthem] will resound again before the balcony of the palace in The Hague.

[Our people] will continue to pray for the Jews and not exclude them from the baptismal font if they are converted. They will declare that blood, race and soil are subordinate to the Word of the Spirit.

If they wear their uniforms [the Nazis used to wear black shirts], should we then let ours be motheaten?

O Christians, out of your shelters! Put on your uniforms! Remember the text used so often on the high days of the church: For Zion's sake I will not keep silent.

Fortunately there is and will remain a difference between power and authority. When all is said and done, the Antichrist has power only, and the church has authority only. Thereafter the day of the great harvest will come. Come, O Lord of the harvest, yes, come quickly! Come from the other side of the Channel and over the Brenner Pass.

---

*Mussert was the Dutch Quisling, the leader of the National Socialist Movement in the Netherlands.

**Copies of *De Reformatie* were passed from hand to hand in those days.

Come via Malta and Japan. Yes, come from the ends of the earth and take with You Your pruning knife and have mercy on Your people. Your people have authority, indeed, only by You, by Your sovereign grace.[31]

Naturally Schilder was arrested before long. He was one of the first ones. After three and a half months he was released. Others would fare much worse.

Resistance to the Nazi ideology on the basis of principle was not offered only in the "Gereformeerd" churches. There was also a group in the "Hervormd" churches* that resisted, especially under the influence of the theology and activities of Karl Barth. This group formed the "Lunteren circle," in which such men as J. Koopmans and K. H. Miskotte were prominent.

In the fall of 1940, Koopmans wrote his (illegal) brochure *Almost Too Late*, in which he called upon people to take the side of the Jews. He accused the many who had signed the so-called Jew-declaration** of having taken a first step in the wrong direction. He called for a firm stand against the forthcoming measures aimed at dismissing the Jews from all employment.

Then followed Miskotte's secretly printed brochure, entitled *Better Resistance*, in which he claimed a totalitarian Holland was impossible. In the process he called on the illustrious names of "Marnix and Coornhert, Bogerman and Hugo de Groot, Daendels and Hogendorp, Groen and Thorbecke, Schaepman and Kuyper, Troelstra and Nolens, Calvinists and Humanists and Catholics." Miskotte wrote:

> The totalitarian state is in conflict with the first commandment: you shall have no other gods before Me. It appears as an anti-church, in which all that the church worships is despised, all that the church liberates is persecuted, all the virtues that the church praises are trodden underfoot, while the vices are praised.[32]

Miskotte appealed to the great Dutchmen of the past with their various religious and philosophical insights. Interchurch cooperation had already existed since June 25, 1940, when the delegates of the Dutch Reformed *(Hervormd)* Church, the Reformed *(Gereformeerd)* Churches, the Arminian Brotherhood, the General Mennonite Society, the Reformed Churches (Renewed Federation), the Evangelical

---

*The Reformed free churches were the ones called "Gereformeerd" in Dutch. The "Hervormd" (Reformed) Church was the original state church.

**By signing the declaration, people declared themselves to be of Aryan descent and isolated themselves from their Jewish fellow citizens.

Lutheran Church and the Restored Evangelical Lutheran Church began meeting in order to decide on a common policy with regard to the measures of the German forces of occupation. Two men in particular came to the fore: the Reformed delegate, Dr. J. Donner, and the Dutch Reformed delegate, Dr. K. H. E. Gravemeyer. By the end of 1941, the meetings were also being attended by a representative of the Archbishop of Utrecht—Msgr. F. van der Loo.

The Convent of Churches established through these meetings accomplished an enormous amount of work. Its most prominent members risked their lives and were arrested repeatedly. The Convent often "sustained with a word him who is weary" (Is. 50:4). According to some, it was too cautious at times.

It was a great moment when a pastoral letter was read from most of the pulpits in the Netherlands on March 23, 1941.* In this letter the people heard these forthright remarks:

> How much we have been shocked and moved in recent times by so many things which are in conflict with what has been taught in our midst from of old and which we would like to hand over to generations to come, that the name of Jesus Christ is decisive for all of human life. In our time the idea is increasingly emphasized that not our relationship to the Name of God but the connection with a certain people or race draws the line of division between men. When you live close to Holy Scripture you should never fail to give an answer to this doctrine which is accepted by so many. It is the privilege of the congregation that it realizes that Christ was born in the history of the Jewish people, and only for that reason already it can never limit the love to our neighbor and the mercy that is required of us to the confines of a certain race.

In many addresses the Convent directed itself to the representatives of the occupying power or to the functioning secretaries of state of the Dutch government. The Convent presented requests and statements concerning the growing legal insecurity and stability, the interference of the state in the affairs of the church, the efforts to engage the churches and the people in the German "winter assistance" plan, the infamous treatment of the Jews, the recruitment of young

---

*The Convent had decided that the letter was to be read on that date. Donner and Gravemeyer had been arrested in the meantime. Donner did not yield to pressure, but Gravemeyer agreed that the reading of the message should be postponed. As a result there was some confusion in the Dutch Reformed Church (Delleman, ed., *Opdat wij niet vergeten,* pp. 81, 512ff; L. de Jong, *Het koninkrijk der Nederlanden in de 2e Wereldoorlog,* Vol. V, 1974, pp. 681, 682).

people for the Labor Service and the attacks on Christian education. The totalitarian state was opposed to its face.

Still, not everyone realized the precarious position of the spokesmen of the churches, and not everyone thought they were acting as firmly as they ought to. Think of what happened in 1942 with regard to the Labor Service.* The Reformed Synod declared in October of 1942 that it had to "object most seriously against this service, to the extent that consistories [the local councils of the churches] ought most earnestly to advise young people and their parents against any active cooperation and to yield only to coercive measures."

This last expression was criticized by the well-known illegal paper *Free Netherlands.* In no uncertain terms, this paper censured the even laxer attitude of the Dutch Reformed synod and the Roman Catholic hierarchy. "Our only hope is that more faith will be found with our people and our youth than with our church leaders."[33]

This generalizing expression was not quite fair. However Classis Utrecht of the Reformed Churches was much more courageous and dared to speak straight language when it sent a letter to all the other classes (May 1943) containing this decision:

> When Classis considers the following facts:
> 1) that the majority of Christian parents, among whom nota bene ministers, elders and deacons, send their children to the Labor Service, which professes to be a National Socialist institution of education;
> 2) that many Christian policemen are disloyal to their heavenly King by readily executing godless measures against the people of the Jews and by the unlawful detention of thousands of innocent hostages;
> 3) that many civil servants cooperate in the unlawful and inhuman deportations of workers;
> 4) that there are so few traces of serious reflection on the question whether it is permitted to serve in the building up of a world that can never be ours;
> it questions whether we still find the serious reflection of faith which may be expected from confessors of Christ.[34]

In spite of all this, the resistance of the churches was effective. After examining all the data at his disposal, Delleman concluded: "As far as the Reformed people are concerned, only a small percentage

---

*It was decided by decree of the occupying power (May 26, 1941) that all young Dutchmen (male and female) would have to serve their people in the Dutch Labor Service. Without any doubt, the Labor Service was a Nazi educational institution.

yielded in the face of the threat of German repression. And those who went to work camps resisted even while they were there, many of them deserting."[35] In January of 1945 it became apparent that 90 percent of the workers in the Dutch Labor Service had gone underground.

It would take too much space to go into detail about the personal resistance of the many office-bearers and members of the church. De Jong tells us the touching story of the arrest, imprisonment, suffering in a concentration camp and ultimate death of Rev. D. A. van den Bosch, a Dutch Reformed minister in The Hague. He also describes how 136 of the approximately 2000 Dutch Reformed ministers were imprisoned for a longer or shorter period of time; 12 of them died in the concentration camps. We read further that 106 of the approximately 500 Reformed *(Gereformeerd)* ministers were arrested, 20 of them died, and 400 of the approximately 4500 to 5000 Roman Catholic clergymen lost their freedom, and 49 of them died.[36]

I will mention only three typical incidents. First, there was the Stijkel group, which was one of the first resistance organizations. Its leader, Dr. J. A. Stijkel, wanted to continue the fight underground immediately after the Dutch army capitulated. The whole setup was betrayed. After extensive interrogation, Stijkel and 32 of his associates were shot in Berlin on June 4, 1943. According to the chaplain of the prison in Berlin, they met death together, singing the hymn "A Mighty Fortress Is Our God."[37]

Secondly, I would mention Rev. J. Overduin of Arnhem, who was involved in the resistance offered by the Christian schools. In January of 1942, some members of the board of a Christian school in Arnhem were imprisoned because of the dismissal of a Nazi teacher who, according to the German authorities, was to be appointed as principal. On Sunday, February 8, Rev. Overduin preached in one of the Reformed churches of Arnhem. At the very last moment he saw two agents of the German police (the Gestapo) entering the building. The text of his sermon was: "Blessed are those who are persecuted for righteousness' sake . . ." (Matt. 5:10-11). Overduin did not mince the truth: "Children belong to their parents, not to the state, and because these children have been baptized, only Christ has a right to them; no one else. No one has the right to rob us of our children . . . We experience our oneness with all believers, with all the martyrs of all ages."[38] When the sermon was over, the congregation rose and sang the words of Luther's hymn:

> Take family and friends
> take goods and life away,

you'll never take the throne,
for heaven is our own,
and heirs are we to kingdoms.

That same Sunday Overduin was arrested. He was detained first in the camp at Amersfoort, and then in the notorious camp at Dachau. He survived, remained steadfast and witnessed courageously. In October of 1943 he returned to the Netherlands. It had been a divine miracle.

> When the special Christian school in Arnhem was closed on August 1, 1942, because the parents refused to send their children to the Nazi principal Feenstra, Rev. Overduin was a human wreck in Dachau already. His weight had dropped to forty kilograms. His legs and hands were covered with wounds caused by hunger oedema. Almost every day he spit up blood. His memory was weakened by undernourishment. His back was covered with wounds because of the heavy coal bags he had to carry. Every day a petty officer kicked with his heavy clogs against the swollen legs of the imprisoned preacher.[39]

An S.S. man shoots a Jew squatting on the edge of a mass grave.

Finally I would mention the brave and devout Roman Catholic priest Titus Brandsma, who was a Carmelite father and a Nijmegen professor. In consultation with the Archbishop of Utrecht, Brandsma had advised all Roman Catholic newspapers to refuse advertisements favoring the National Socialist Movement and all other Nazi organizations. For this he was arrested on January 19, 1942.

Brandsma was a mystic. After spending a week in prison in Scheveningen, he wrote:

I am quite at home here in this little cell

of mine. I have not felt bored here—on the contrary. I am alone here, indeed, but never has our dear Lord been closer to me. I would be able to shout for joy because He enabled me to find Him solely. He is my only support, and I feel safe and happy. I would like to stay here always if it is His will. Rarely have I been so happy and content.

Brandsma was moved from Scheveningen to Amersfoort. There, with his weak and sick body, he comforted others with the words: "God grants you the *privilege* to be worthy of this sacrifice." From there he went to Dachau. (I will have more to say about that region of death later.) He was maltreated by sadistic block-elders and room-elders,* and on July 26, 1942, he was disposed of by the camp doctor by means of an injection.[40]

Dachau was a "Vernichtungslager" (annihilation camp). It was much worse than Amersfoort, which was already bad enough. Rev. K. G. Idema, who was confined at Dachau from June 26, 1942, to April 14, 1943, wrote the following comments about it:

> The day started at 4 a.m. and ended at 9 p.m., during which time we had almost no opportunity to rest. The sparse food had to be eaten while we stood. Add to this the fact that life was tense all day long. Many of the room-elders and block-elders (though fellow prisoners) and the capos (chiefs when we worked) were petty tyrants. Among them were the camp criminals, who have the death of many "comrades" on their conscience. In this period humor disappeared and we did not laugh any more. The last remnants of our spiritual and physical power were consumed, and God in heaven was our only refuge. Our faith tried to hold on to Him, even when the spirit was too tired or too preoccupied for intensive prayer.
>
> . . . the invalids . . . bodies wasting away . . . skeletons living cautiously . . .
>
> Dachau with its Revier (sick-ward) and its invalid-blocks, with its hideous medical tests on the prisoners, Dachau with its crematory that worked each Thursday—it was one of the many regions of terror which revealed the meaning of National Socialism.[41]

National Socialism and Communism agreed with each other in their reliance on a network of such camps.

One more characteristic of the church in the occupied countries should be mentioned; more and more, the churches became *praying* churches. We hear that in Denmark and Norway, the churches were

---

*The technical name of the officers in charge of the sections and rooms of the camp.

more crowded than ever. Alas, this situation did not continue after the liberation.

In the Netherlands, interdenominational prayer services were held in various places, especially during 1944 and 1945. People sighed for deliverance and sought refuge with God. How they sang on the Sunday after the liberation:

> Here in Thy house I give to Thee
> the life that Thou dost bless;
> and pay the solemn vows I made
> when I was in distress (Ps. 66).

Distress had taught people to pray. But in the Netherlands, too, it appeared to be difficult to continue to thank God.

9

The Mystery of Israel

Requiem for a nun

It does not happen often that a Jewess is baptized in the Roman Catholic Church. It is even more exceptional to see a female Jewish philosopher converted to this church. Still, this was the step taken by *Edith Stein* when she chose with all the sincerity of her heart for Christ as He is professed in this church and for unmarried life as practiced in the convents of the Carmelite Sisters. The name she took for herself was *Theresia Benedicta a Cruce.*

She did not retire completely from the world, however. She was a woman with keen insight into foreign affairs. In April of 1933 she wrote a letter to the pope in which she urged him to rouse the people of his church. She told him it was high time to issue an encyclical through which the eyes of Roman Catholic believers would be opened to the great dangers threatening the Jews. She asked the pope to speak with authority "about Catholic indifference in regard to the increasing vexation of the Jews."[1]

We have seen that she had good reason to make such a request (see p. 142 above). However, she received no reply. The pope, who knew perfectly well what was going on, considered it wiser to chart a different course. He was about to conclude a concordat with Nazi

Germany, hoping to allay the growing storm that way. The concordat was indeed finalized on July 20 of that year. Shouldn't that be sufficient for Sister Theresia? It wasn't, and she felt very unhappy. Four years later she wrote in her diary: "I have often wondered what the holy father has thought of my message, for everything I had anticipated concerning the German Catholics has come true."

She was well informed, and she would become even better informed. The anti-Jewish fury of the Germans literally knew no limits, and after 1939 it swept the occupied countries as well. In 1940 it entered the Netherlands.

Especially in the Netherlands, Protestant and Roman Catholic churches protested repeatedly and urgently against the increasing infractions of the law. To their credit, those churches never stopped voicing their indignation over the persecution of their Dutch fellow citizens. Earlier I quoted part of the pulpit message of March 23, 1941, in which the churches rejected the Nazi ideology concerning the Jewish "race" (see p. 147 above). On April 19, 1942, another such declaration was read. In the Roman Catholic churches it was couched in the form of a pastoral letter from the bishops. The message contained the following comments:

> You are acquainted with the absence of justice, the mercilessness toward the Jewish part of our population and the advance of the National Socialistic life-and-world-view, which is diametrically opposed to the Gospel. It becomes ever more difficult for the Church to exert its blessed activities, and many have been forced to sacrifice their freedom.[2]

For many, the sacrifice of freedom became the sacrifice of life. On July 26, 1942, Titus Brandsma was killed in Dachau. In August of that same year, the Gestapo arrested Sister Theresia in a Dutch convent. Her nun's attire and her religion afforded her no protection. Her indelible crime was her Jewish blood. She was transported to Auschwitz and gassed there—one of the millions.

What was Auschwitz?

I wrote about Dachau earlier and used the term *Vernichtungslager* on that occasion (see p. 165 above). Yet there were people who survived the "hell of Dachau." Auschwitz, a camp situated in the southern part of Poland (its original Polish name was Oswiecim) was an annihilation camp in the most literal sense of the word.

Rudolf Hösz, the commander of the camp, declared after the war that he had been summoned to Berlin in 1941 by the national leader of the SS, who told him the Führer had decided on a definitive solution *(Eindlösung)* to the Jewish problem. Since the camps then in existence were not suitable for such a purpose, Auschwitz was chosen. It was favorably located in terms of accessibility and it could easily be camouflaged. The outside world would not easily be able to detect what was going on.

The national leader told Hösz about the difficult things that lay ahead for him, tasks requiring his total commitment. More information would be provided by "Sturmbannführer"* Eichmann. For the rest, Hösz was not allowed to speak to anybody about this matter, not even to men who were higher in rank than he was. The national leader of the SS explained what was at issue: "The Jews are the eternal enemy of the German people and must be exterminated. If we do not succeed now in destroying the biological foundations of the Jewish people, the Jews will one day destroy the German people." Then follow some terrible matter-of-fact words from Hösz:

> The destruction procedure in Auschwitz was the following. As calmly as possible, the Jews who were destined for destruction were conveyed to the crematories—the men separated from the women. In the room in which they had to undress, they were told in their own language (by prisoners of the SS assigned for this purpose) that they had come here to take a bath and be deloused. They were supposed to lay their clothes in good order at a spot they could remember well so that they could find their own property back as soon as possible after the delousing. The prisoners assigned to do the explaining had a personal interest in a quick, quiet and unperturbed dispatch of this business.
>
> After undressing, the Jews entered the gas room. Because it was provided with shower baths and water pipes, it made the impression of a washing place. The women and children entered first, and after that the men, always a somewhat smaller number of them. Almost invariably this took place quietly; any people who might have been afraid and might have had some misgivings about what was going to happen to them were set at ease by the SS prisoners. Those prisoners stayed in the room until the last minute, along with an SS man. Then the door was rapidly screwed shut, and the gas was immediately . . . let in . . . by a ventilating shaft. Through a peephole in the door one could see that those who were closest to the place where the gas entered fell down at once. It can safely be said that about one third died instantly. The others fell down and began to cry and gasp for breath. Soon the crying

---

*A high rank in Hitler's elite troops, the SS.

became a rattling, and within minutes all lay down. After twenty minutes, at most, nobody moved any longer.

By a special SS command, the golden teeth were removed from the corpses, and the hair of the women was cut. Then the corpses were brought up by an elevator in front of an oven, which had meanwhile been heated. Depending on the size of the bodies, a maximum of three corpses could be placed in one of the chambers of the oven. How long the cremation took depended on the number of bodies. On the average it took about twenty minutes.[3]

It is usually assumed that a total of some six million Jews were killed in Auschwitz and the other camps and by all sorts of acts of violence. Although this number has been disputed, the figures are still staggering, and the act was one of unparalleled barbarity.

Many questions could be raised here, but they can hardly be properly discussed within the framework of this book. Certain basic questions, at least, cannot be evaded. Where did this anti-Semitism come from? What was it?

Anti-Semitism

The name *anti-Semitism* has come into general use only in the last century. It was used for the first time in 1879 by Wilhelm Marr, a German who hated the Jews.[4]

It should be noted that there is something essentially arbitrary about this term. Strictly speaking, the Arabs should be regarded as Semites along with the Jews, but in our century Arabs have been among the most pronounced of anti-Semites. Nevertheless, the name is based on such an irrefutable historical reality—namely, the aversion to the Jews that has flared up so often and in so many places—that the term has come to be generally accepted. People know what it means.

Bible readers will remember the persistent efforts made by the Egyptian Pharaoh in Moses' time to liquidate the young and growing people of Israel. Readers will also remember the attack made by Haman on "a certain people scattered abroad and dispersed among the peoples" (Esther 3:8), as well as the attempt made by the emperor Claudius to remove all the Jews from Rome.[5]

Church history describes how the Jews were repeatedly viewed with disfavor by the church. On the other hand, the synagogue was not favorably inclined toward the church either, as we see clearly from the book of Acts. At the end of the first century, the Jewish prayer book was supplemented with a curse on all Jews who accepted Jesus as their Messiah.[6] Nevertheless, there was no excuse for hatred of the

Jews, for their isolation, or for the recurring persecution, often promoted by the men of the church.

Constantine the Great did not make room for the Jews in his famous Edict of Toleration of Milan (313). Two years later they were officially branded a "godless sect." Since then there have been pogroms in every century.*

OOK U MOET DEZE FILM ZIEN

The poster title reads: The Eternal Jew. It advertises a so-called documentary designed to stir up anti-Jewish sentiment in countries occupied by the Third Reich.

Elsewhere I have written about the outrageous acts the first crusaders committed against the Jews (see Volume II, Chapters 6 and 12). Let me add here that Pope Innocent III called them slaves who were damned from eternity. He consigned them to the ghetto and commanded them to be distinguished from the Christians by their way of dressing.

Both the Reformation and Humanism meant a certain amount of liberation for the Jews. Reuchlin took their side, and the young Luther offered them his hand. But in one of his last works,[7] Luther passes a severe judgment on them for refusing to listen to the gospel and trying to establish their own righteousness. This judgment impaired the Lutheran tradition, although it should be added that the Jews found no better friends in Lutheran areas than among the Pietists (Spener) and the followers of Zinzendorf.

As far as Calvinism is concerned, William of Orange was the great advocate of a tolerance extended to the Jews. In Cromwell they

*This term originated in a later age.

found a protector, and in the Netherlands a place of refuge.

In the time of the Enlightenment of the eighteenth century and the post-revolutionary period in the nineteenth century, the hour of liberation seemed to have struck for the Jews. Moses Mendelssohn was the man whose image was in Lessing's mind when he wrote his *Nathan der Weise* (see Volume V, Chap. 5). Mendelssohn epitomized the tolerant Jew whose highest aim was virtue. This man, who has been called the father of Reform Judaism, modified the prerequisites of Judaism since the enlightened Christians of the time were in favor of an undogmatic and, above all, practical form of Christianity. Why not shake hands with each other?

After the French Revolution, the time of great emancipation and assimilation commenced for the Jews. In all countries (with the exception of eastern Europe) and in all areas of life, the Jews cooperated as good patriots. It has been said that they joined the Frenchmen in singing the Marseillaise, and the Germans in singing "Deutschland über alles."

Yet the Jews did not really belong to the nations in which they happened to live. In the mouths of many, the word *Jew* remained a term of abuse. In eastern Europe the pogroms continued.* France had its Dreyfus case, and there were anti-Jewish sentiments in circulation in the Vichy government. Germany had its racial doctrines as promoted even by the court chaplain, Stöcker. Later they were mapped out in detail by Rosenberg and carried through by Hitler to their gruesome consequences.

Even in the camp of the socialists and Communists, the Jews did not manage to keep out of harm's way, although there were always Jews to be found among the most radical left-wing figures. One of the very first essays by Karl Marx, who stemmed from an emancipated Jewish background and was baptized when he was six years old, was entitled "A World Without Jews." In this essay we find these sentiments:

> What is the object of the Jew's worship in this world? Usury. What is his worldly God? Money. Very well then; emancipation from usury and money, that is, from practical, real Judaism, would constitute the real emancipation of our time . . . The social emancipation of Jewry is the emancipation of society from Jewry.[8]

---

*Comparisons have been drawn between the Romans, who cast the Christians to the lions when they were in trouble, and the Russians who unleashed a pogrom whenever things looked dark.

Marx wanted to liberate the world from the Jews. He dreamed of a world without Jews—not because of any racial theory but because the ideal of a stateless and classless society was always present in his mind. He believed that the function of the Jews in the society of his own time was mainly their thorough mastery of financial affairs.

We find the same line of thought in Lenin, who once wrote: "A Jewish-national culture is the slogan of the rabbis and bourgeois, the slogan of our enemies."[9] In the Stalinist period, anti-Semitism broke out again in Russia as if it was a contagious disease. It was an incredible state of affairs, but the eyes of the world were opened when the Slansky trial took place in Prague in 1952 and the doctors' trial in Moscow in 1953.

In the case of the former trial, the secretary-general of the Communist party in Czechoslovakia was a man named Rudolf Slansky. Slansky had received the highest honors on July 31, 1951, on the occasion of his fiftieth birthday. He was the most faithful aide to President Gottwald, but he was also a Jew. When the economy of the country ran into trouble, a scapegoat had to be found. Four months later, Slansky was arrested.

When Slansky and 13 others were put on trial, all of them were expressly called Jews, and there were accusations of Trotskyism and Zionism, of espionage and sabotage. On December 3, 1952, most of the defendants were hanged; three were sentenced to life imprisonment. The Party, industry and all government offices were subsequently purged of all Jews. A wave of Jewish suicide swept the country. Eleven years later, during the brief "thaw," the High Court of Justice in Czechoslovakia declared the entire affair to have been a falsification prompted by the spirit of the Stalinist era.[10]

Even more sensational was the doctors' trial staged in Moscow shortly before Stalin's death. Nine doctors, six of them Jews, were accused of having killed two members of the Politburo, the leading policy-forming committee in the Soviet Union. Only the death of Stalin on March 5 of that year prevented the death sentence. Then there was a short period in which Christians and Jews could breathe more easily again. However, since that time there have been many instances of discrimination against the Jews in Russia, and Russian politicians support the Arabs by all possible means in their struggle against Israel.[11]

I have not told the whole story, but by now it should be clear that anti-Semitism is centuries old and is still a force to be reckoned with in our time. Hans Habe, a Hungarian-German Jew, expressed himself in a highly ironical way after a visit to Israel: "One should not say that the world can be divided into Arabs, Turks, Greeks, Christians, and Mohammedans—as soon as the word *Jew* is heard, they all agree."[12]

How is anti-Semitism to be explained?

Much has been written about anti-Semitism, and many attempts have been made to explain this phenomenon.

We have already been confronted with the *economic* motive stressed by Marx. This approach allows for either of two conclusions. Some people have viewed the Jew as the essential capitalist whose prototype was the shrewd Jacob and whose highest expression is to be found in the international Rothschild bankers. Others view the Jew as the essential Communist who proclaims the gospel of dialectical materialism. The names that come to mind are Marx and Lasalle, Rosa Luxemburg and David Wijnkoop (a Dutch Communist leader), Trotsky and Litwinov.

Once this motive is assumed, a particular question must be answered: Is it the natural disposition of the Jew to make use of the economic situation or to dominate the situation, as Joseph did in Egypt, for example? Or has the Jew become what he is because of necessity, when all other means of subsistence were denied him on religious grounds? In other words, is the Jew a born Shylock, or is he the ill-fated victim and doomed scapegoat?

I have also referred to the explanation in terms of *racial theories*. Again, either of two approaches are possible. It is possible to consider the Jews a superrace, and in almost every Jewish book written on this subject, the impressive number of Jews who have won the Nobel prize is mentioned—not without pride or without reason. But some authors have also looked upon the Jews as an inferior race, the parasites of human society. Among the proponents of this idea one could mention such names as Voltaire and Richard Wagner,* Count de Gobineau and H. S. Chamberlain, Goebbels and Rosenberg.

Anti-Semitism has also been explained in *evolutionist* terms, that is, in connection with Darwin's theory of science.[13] And it has been *psychologically* explained as a reaction against feelings of inferiority.[14]

Karl Barth was on the right track when he connected anti-

---

*To Louis II of Bavaria, Wagner wrote: "I consider the Jewish race the natural enemy of all undefiled mankind and of all that is noble in it; . . . . we Germans particularly will perish by it" (Arendt, *The Origins of Totalitarianism*, p. 105). Hitler's predilection for Wagner's operas is a well-known fact.

Semitism with Israel's *election*, but his dialectical doctrine of election makes it impossible for us to follow him here and agree with him completely. In Barth's opinion, the Jew is a mirror of the election of each of us; he reflects the pattern of divine world government. The Jew, in his self-righteousness, is the most human of us all. The Jew shows us what we are—and exactly for that reason we detest him. Barth further speaks of the Jew as the ineradicable witness of God's constant grace. That grace applies to each one of us as well, but we do not want it. We are irritated by it. This is the reason for the phenomenon of anti-Semitism.[15]

At this point we are on the track of the only explanation that, in my opinion, can be deemed valid. This explanation ties in with God's free election of His people, as we read in Amos 3:2: "You only have I known of all the families of the earth." God made the people who are descended from Abraham His own in His sovereign grace. But then immediately follow these words: "Therefore I will punish you for all your iniquities."

The Jews had a unique position as a people elected to bring forth the Savior of the world. The reprobation of this people who rejected the Savior was also unique. Their abandonment is accompanied by a persistent *hardening*, as Paul explained it in the great Israel chapter of the New Testament: "God gave them a spirit of stupor, eyes that should not see and ears that should not hear, down to this very day" (Rom. 11:8). He adds that they cannot escape this situation despite all efforts at friendship and assimilation: "Let their table become a snare and a trap, a pitfall and a retribution for them."

In some quarters it is customary to speak in this connection of anti-Semitic tendencies in the New Testament. It is sometimes argued as well that it would be unfair to make all Israel responsible for the sentence imposed on Jesus.[16]

Clearly, the New Testament is not anti-Semitic. It could better be said to be pro-Semitic. Salvation in Jesus Christ is "to the Jew first and also to the Greek."* But it is salvation in Jesus Christ *only*. All of Jewish history after the last warning in the 40-year period that preceded the destruction of the temple shows there is nothing but disaster outside of Him when He is rejected.

Even so, the last word has not yet been spoken. Romans 11 tells

---

*Romans 1:16. It should be added that Jesus certainly has announced a coming judgment on the people of Israel for the sin of rejecting Him (Matt. 11:20-4; 21:33-43; 23:37-8; Luke 19:41-4; 23:27-31).

us something more. We should underline the remarkable words in verses 25 and 26: "A hardening has come upon part of Israel, until the full number of the Gentiles come in, and so all Israel will be saved; as it is written: the Deliverer will come from Zion, he will banish ungodliness from Jacob."

There has been much discussion and argument about these words. Many pre-millenarians regard this as an announcement of the Millennium. Although I for my part find no such announcement here, there is indeed a limit indicated in the little word *until*; this limit coincides with "the coming in of the full number of the Gentiles," and it is marked by the salvation (instead of the rejection) of Israel and the reign of the Deliverer in Zion. In this connection we should discuss Zionism.

Zionism

When we survey the relevant nineteenth and twentieth century history, we must conclude that the Jews have been driven back to Israel against their own objections, as it were. It all happened in an extraordinary way!

The Jews in western Europe were emancipated. As far as eastern Europe is concerned, the Jews emigrated by the hundreds of thousands to the freedom and openness of America.* They adjusted their religious customs to the new situation. The majority of them became Reform Jews. In their national life they were in favor of complete assimilation. Disraeli was an Englishman, Felix Mendelssohn was a German, Offenbach and Saint-Saëns were Frenchmen, and Israels and Querido were Dutchmen, to mention only a few.

Still, it didn't work! When the Hungarian-Jewish reporter Theodor Herzl attended the Dreyfus trial in 1891, he could see and hear that it was not working. In enlightened, liberal France, the monster of anti-Semitism raised its head. Herzl saw only one way out; in 1896 his book *Der Judenstaat* (The Jewish State) appeared. Herzl sketched the ideal of Zionism, which he also expressed at the first Zionist congress in Basel in these words: "The creation of a homeland for the Jewish people in Palestine, protected by public legislation."

---

*During the reign of Alexander III (1881-1894), under whom a horrible pogrom took place, about 100,000 Jews emigrated to the United States each year (E. H. Flannery, *Twenty-three Ages of Anti-Semitism*, pp. 189, 190).

Understandably, this movement did not gain much momentum at first. Generally speaking, the Jews were well off, as they are today in America. As for Palestine, it had been Turkish territory for ages. But both situations changed. I need not demonstrate again how the Jews in many parts of Europe were crushed to the point of perdition. Moreover, Turkey entered the first world war on the side of the loser, and as a result the League of Nations handed Palestine over to England to administer. In the process the Jewish people were given the right to establish a national home in Palestine.*

Between 1918 and 1936, approximately 150,000 Jewish immigrants arrived in the Holy Land, mostly from eastern Europe. The result was that "the desert began to blossom as the rose." Towns, villages, factories, trees and orange orchards covered the fields between Haifa and Askelon, an area that had been neglected and backward for centuries.

Actually, it was only a handful of Jews, and they did not receive much sympathy in their new environment. The Arabs often cast envious glances at them because of their growing prosperity, while at the same time shunning the Jews because of their religion. As for the English, they tried to restrict Jewish immigration as much as possible to keep peace with the Arabs. But things could not stay that way, of course, especially when the Jews proved themselves to be faithful allies of the English in the second world war in the struggle against Rommel in North Africa.

At the beginning of 1947, England placed the question of Palestine on the agenda of the United Nations. On November 29 of that year, the General Assembly of the United Nations decided to partition the country into two independent states—one part for the 1.1 million Arabs, and the other part for the 650,000 Jews.

The result was immediate warfare. It is fascinating to consider how the young Jewish state, attacked by five armies, managed to defend itself with such great courage. It appeared as if the age of David and his heroes had returned—not just in 1947 and 1948 but repeatedly in future years when the Jews were attacked by superior forces. Each time they held out and enlarged their territory. To all appearances, they were being preserved in a miraculous way. Unfortunately, a

---

*In the so-called Balfour Declaration, the British government had pledged to view with favor the establishment of such a national home for the Jews, but it had also made promises to the Arabs concerning national sovereignty (see M. I. Dumont, *Jews, God and History*, pp. 397ff).

description of the wars fought by the new Jewish state falls outside the scope of this book.

I will mention only two touching moments. The first of them is May 14, 1948. All 650,000 of the Palestinian Jews were listening somewhere, wherever they could, to the radio. At exactly 4 p.m., the well-known voice of their beloved leader, David Ben-Gurion, came through. He spoke these words: "By virtue of the national and historic rights of the Jewish people and the resolution of the United Nations, we hereby proclaim the establishment of the Jewish State in Palestine, to be called Israel."

The people who heard those words jumped up, and from the mouths of thousands was heard "Hatikva," the song of hope. Immediately afterward the sirens shrieked in Tel Aviv. The announcement of liberty was followed by the signal of the first air raid.

Secondly, I should mention the prayers that are recited on the anniversary of Israel's Independence Day:

> May it be Thy will, O Jehovah our God and the God of our fathers, that as we have been granted the dawn of redemption, so may we be granted to hear the trumpet of the Messiah.
>
> He who performed miracles for our fathers and for us and who redeemed Israel from servitude to freedom, may He speedily redeem us with a complete redemption and gather our dispersed ones from the four corners of the earth, and we shall sing before Him a new song. Hallelujah.[17]

All of this does not mean, however, that all Israelis are equally orthodox in their faith. That is simply not the case. Many of them continue to be liberal or leftist Jews as they were before. Only with much difficulty and diplomacy does the government manage to maintain the unity of the people as far as keeping the Sabbath and respecting dietary laws is concerned. But it is encouraging to see the Old Testament being read and studied diligently as the book of national history.

Neither should we assume that the doors to missionary work among the Jews in Israel have been thrown wide open. Wherever the door is left open even a crack, the government does everything it can to seal it off again.

In spite of all this, however, everyone who has eyes to see cannot fail to notice that something is happening in Israel. We should ponder the words of Paul: "Even the others, if they do not persist in their unbelief, will be grafted in, for God has the power to graft them in again." "As regards the gospel they are enemies of God, for your sake; but as regards election they are beloved for the sake of their forefathers." "For God has consigned all men to disobedience, that he may have mercy upon all" (Rom. 11:23, 28, 32).

Does this mean we may believe in a new primacy of Israel? No, but we do believe that God still has something in reserve—for them and for us together.

10

Continuation
and Confusion:
The Roman Catholic Church

The popes

In the twentieth century, the Roman Catholic Church remained the *church of Rome*. Therefore we must speak in the first place of the popes, and also of the adoration of Mary, which all of them promoted. We should also bear in mind, however, that this church wished to be a *catholic* church with all the means at its disposal. Hence its continuing missionary activities and its contacts with the Greek Catholic patriarchs, with the Anglican Church and with the ecumenical movement. This also helps to explain the infiltration of the "New Theology," which some regard as a hopeful sign and others as a depressing sign. Whatever it may be, the New Theology brings with it some major difficulties.

Who were the popes during this period, and what kind of influence did they exert? Earlier I wrote about the drastic measures Pope Pius X (1903-1914) took against the rise of Modernism in the church (see p. 31 above). I also mentioned the anti-Modernist oath he required. This man, who has been called a priest on Peter's throne, wanted to protect his church against the upsurge of new ideas conflicting with its character and confession. It has been said that when

181

Modernism was forbidden upstairs, it went on living downstairs for the ensuing 40 years.

Pius X was succeeded by Benedict XV (1914-1922), who tried to maintain a strict neutrality in the first world war, a war in which members of the Roman Catholic Church fought on both sides. He did his best to alleviate the suffering of soldiers and citizens during and after the war. The pacifist Romain Rolland was even led to speak of the Roman Catholic Church as "a second Red Cross." Benedict agreed with his predecessor as far as the condemnation of Modernism was concerned, and he spoke some plain words about the Mosaic origin of the Penteteuch.

The task of Benedict's successor, Pius XI (1922-1939), was very difficult. He had to steer the ship of his church over the waves of the post-war depression and the subsequent dictatorial states. In almost every one of those states, the leader was a Roman Catholic by baptism (Mussolini, Hitler, Franco, Peron). Pius XI has been called the "concordat pope" because he made pacts with so many states.* Through the pacts, he secured the most favorable conditions possible for the Roman Catholic Church, sometimes in exchange for certain concessions on his part. That his reliance on these political agreements was a mistake in some cases is apparent from his encyclical "Mit brennender Sorge" (see p. 152 above). It is particularly regrettable how he cooperated with the Fascist authorities in Italy.

The Roman Catholic church historian Bihlmeyer laconically declares that Mussolini's campaign against Ethiopia (1935-36) was viewed by the pope in part as a "mission project."[1] It was even more deplorable when Pius XI spoke of the conquest of Ethiopia as "a contribution to the peace of the world."[2]

On the other hand, we can appreciate the pope's encyclical "Quadragesimo Anno"[3] (1931), in which he elaborated on what his great predecessor Leo XIII has said about Christian social action. In this encyclical he condemned both laissez-faire liberalism and socialism that decrees the state must own everything. He endorsed collective wage contracts and the idea of having the workers share in the profits earned by an enterprise, but he opposed strikes and lockouts.

His successor, Pius XII (1939-1958), did everything he could to avoid taking sides in the great world conflict of his time. He has been

---

*With Latvia, 1922; Bavaria, 1924; Poland, 1925; Lithuania, 1927; Rumania, 1927 and 1929; Prussia, 1929; Italy, 1929; Baden, 1932; Austria, 1933; Germany, 1933; and Yugoslavia, 1933.

accused of manifesting a callous attitude in the matter of the terrible plight of the Jews,[4] but the Jewish author Lapide has come to his defense and has shown that "Pius XII saved more Jews than all the church leaders and all the politicians of the West put together."[5]

Pius XII issued several encyclicals, two of which I would mention here. In 1943 there was his "Divino Afflante Spiritu," in which bishops were urged to promote the knowledge and love of Scripture. This document has been termed cautiously progressive. According to the personal recollections of the well-known Swiss theologian Oscar Cullmann, a number of Roman Catholic exegetes believed some sort of liberation was taking place.[6]

Liberation from what? From the yoke of the anti-Modernist oath and the uncertain atmosphere of the years since the oath was decreed. "The exegetes who were working in a cautiously progressive direction were given an official pat on the back through the encyclical of Pius XII."[7] The question at issue here is: What is progressive? With regard to this point, G. C. Berkouwer speaks of the problem of the historicity of the first chapters of the Bible and of the dangers of a naive understanding of what we find written there.[8]

I would also mention the encyclical "Humani Generis" (Of the Human Race, 1950), in which many errors were rejected.* Roman Catholic believers were exhorted to believe that the mystical body of our Lord should be identified with their church.

The pronouncements of Pope John XXIII, the successor to Pius XII, were a great contrast to the spirit of this encyclical. With great cordiality the new pope stretched out his arms to his "separated brothers" and, as much as possible, to all mankind.

The original name of this simple man was Angelo Roncalli. Not without reason, he has been called "Good Pope John." On August 15, 1961, he wrote in his diary:

> Vicar of Christ? Ah, I am not worthy of this name, I, the humble child of Battista and Marianna Roncalli, two good Christians to be sure, but so modest and humble! Yet that is what I must be: the Vicar of Christ. "Priest and victim"; the priesthood fills me with joy, but the sacrifice implied in the priesthood makes me tremble.
>
> Blessed Jesus, God and man! I renew the consecration of myself to you, for life, for death, for eternity.

---

*Among them: existentialism, distrust of Thomism, and the denial that Adam existed as a historical person and that original sin has reached us through direct descent from him.

In the devout Roman Catholic tradition, he writes on the same date: "My dominant thought is expressed in the familiar but precious phrase: 'To Jesus through Mary.' "[9]

This pope, who was popular in the proper sense of the word with both Roman Catholics and Protestants, opened the Second Vatican Council on October 11, 1962, with an address in which "he pointed to the perspective of reconciliation that would characterize this pastoral council."[10] He died during these sessions on June 3, 1963, and was succeeded by Pope Paul VI. To him now fell the difficult task of steering the ship of the church through the tempests and past the rocks of the post-Vatican period.

Pope John XXIII, wearing the Triple Crown, blesses the City and the world, from the balcony of St. Peter's, Rome, after his coronation on 4 November, 1958.

Adoration of Mary

More than once we have had occasion to look at the popular and typically Roman Catholic adoration of Mary, who is preferably called "Our Lady" or "the Holy Virgin." All the popes in our century have promoted this devotion.

A number of prayers of John XXIII addressed to Mary have been published.[11] In the week before the opening meeting of the Second Vatican Council, the pope undertook a pilgrimage to the shrine of Mary in Loreto where, according to an old legend, the house in which Mary lived in Nazareth now stands. (It was carried to Loreto by angels.) There he prayed: "O Mary, O Mary, Mother of Jesus and our Mother too, we have come here this morning to pray to you as the first star above the Council that is about to be held, as the light that shines propitiously upon our way as we proceed trustfully towards the great ecumenical gathering which the whole world awaits."[12]

John's predecessor, Pius XII, had performed a spectacular act on October 31, 1942; in a radio message to the people of Portugal, he dedicated the entire world to the immaculate heart of Mary.[13] Why had this message been broadcast to *Portugal?* Twenty-five years before, on October 13, 1917, a miraculous appearance of the Holy Virgin had taken place there, according to many believers. This appearance, which took place in the village of Fatima, was accompanied by a sensational meteorological phenomenon.

Three peasant children who were seven, eight and ten years old respectively had witnessed a certain appearance five times in a row, always on the thirteenth of the month. What they seemed to see was a pure, shining white lady, who told them she would express her demands the last time she appeared, on October 13. The news spread by mouth, and when October 13 rolled around, there were no fewer than 50,000 people on hand, including many with high hopes and also some who were totally skeptical. Only the children saw the lofty figure, but all the others are said to have viewed a miraculous phenomenon. That phenomenon has been described by the non-Catholic editor of the daily *Seculo* in the following words: "Before the astonished eyes of the people, who behaved like people of Biblical times, looking up into the blue sky with great respect, their heads uncovered, the sun trembled. It experienced shocks that have never been observed before, shocks beyond all cosmic laws. The sun 'danced,' as the peasants used to say in their typical fashion."[14]

The scenes at Lourdes in 1858 almost automatically come to mind. Whatever explanation we might offer of this phenomenon,[15] the results were about the same. Pilgrimages increased, healings were recorded and a magnificent basilica was built. In 1946 a statue of the Lady of Fatima was crowned by a cardinal in the name of the pope. And just as the Immaculate Conception of Mary was announced as an infallible dogma in 1854, Pius XII added the dogma of her Assumption* to it in 1950.

Even Roman Catholic theologians acknowledged that this doctrine, properly speaking, cannot be proven from Scripture. But this is not a major objection, given their point of view concerning the primacy of the Church with regard to Scripture. They claim it is fitting that she who was born without original sin should be physically taken up into heaven. Mary was adorned with many new names: the new Eve, the mother of Christ and of believers, the mother of God and of men, the queen of the universe.

Outside the Roman Catholic Church this doctrine met with no positive response. The archbishops of Canterbury and York, who were usually inclined to make ecumenical gestures, published a joint declaration in which they expressed their concern that Rome, pleading for an ecumenical front, had taken an action having the opposite effect. In their judgment, the new dogma was lacking in appeal to Scripture and to history and was built on *a prioris*, that is, unproven assumptions.[16]

The New Theology

Everything we have noted up to this point was in line with traditional Roman Catholicism. At the same time, however, a silent revolution was taking place. For the time being it escaped the attention of the common man, but in the course of time it made itself conspicuous.

As far as the Netherlands is concerned, this province of the Church had for years enjoyed the reputation of being "more Catholic than the pope." Yet Rogier, the church historian at the Roman Catholic university at Nijmegen, referred in later years to a "passion for destruction which, since the twenties, was directed against the fortress of the institute of the Roman Catholic Church."[17]

To an increasing degree, the Dutch Catholics looked at Rome in critical terms. Sometimes they insisted on more input from their own

---

*The term *Assumption* is used here as distinguished from *Ascension*.

circles, where, as often as not, the thinking was not in keeping with the authority of the Holy See. As a result, the pope sometimes felt compelled to interfere, which in turn caused discontent among many of the "progressive" members of his church.*

Although Catholics in other countries tended to consider the Dutchmen forerunners in either a restoration or a revolution in the Church,** they were not at all an isolated group in their thinking and acting. They were part of a wider Roman Catholic revolt which came to expression in the New Theology, originally called the "théologie nouvelle" because it originated in France.

Hans Küng

The name *New Theology* seems more innocent than *New Modernism*, but there is doubtless a direct line of communication to be drawn between men such as Loisy and Tyrrell, whom we have met before (see p. 29f above), and the Jesuits in the seminary at Lyon-Fourvièvre, who became known in the 1940s. Well-known among them were F. Bouillard, J. Daniélou, H. de Lubac and Y. Congar. In the course of time they picked up close contact with such Swiss theologians as H. Urs von Balthasar and H. Küng, the German theologian K. Rahner, and such Dutch theologians as P. Schoonenberg and E. Schillebeekx. Some English and American theologians were also involved in these discussions.

---

*Think of the appointments of the bishops Simonis (Rotterdam, 1970) and Gijsen (Roermond, 1972), which were handed down directly from the Vatican.

**Witness the striking comment made by Prof. F. D. Wilhelmsen of Dallas in the symposium *The American Catholic Exodus* (1968): "Many contemporary theologians speak in all sorts of languages, but all with a Dutch accent" (p. 178).

All these men, like their predecessors at the beginning of the twentieth century, wanted to put the Church in living contact with the culture of their time. But whereas Loisy and Tyrrel had been influenced by the Protestant liberalism of the beginning of the century, the men of the "new theology" appeared to share the ideas—or in their own way to participate in the ideas—of the dialectical, liberal, Protestant theologians of *their* days, and also the existentialist philosophy of their time.

There was also another motivation present, however. Europe had gone through the crisis of two world wars. During the occupation of France, the Roman Catholic clergy there made a disturbing discovery. Priests who tried to take up contact with the French prisoners of war or the *maquis* of the underground resistance observed a total estrangement from church and religion—a pronounced, practical atheism.[18] France, the "eldest daughter of the Church," appeared to be de-Christianized as far as two-thirds of its population was concerned.

Earlier I pointed out how this phenomenon also manifested itself in other church communities. To its credit, the New Theology tried to reach out to the common man again by speaking his language, by listening to what he had to say, and by making an effort to share with him. This, after all, was the background of the priest-worker movement in France, a movement promoted by the New Theology. It was also the reason why some priests sided with Marxism *against* the old forms of organizations under the direction of the church, opting instead for a total, utopian renewal of society.

At its base, however, there was much more at stake. Each of the "new" theologians went about his theology in a unique way—as a matter of principle. Together they adopted the existentialist principle that the building of systems belongs to the past; man's way of thinking should be authentic, that is, a matter of genuine personal experience. Still, these theologians did have certain things in common.

They were characterized by a return to the Bible, which was hailed with joy by many Protestants. However, this return was combined with a disappointing, strongly time-bound way of criticizing the Bible. They were also characterized by a return to the Church Fathers of the first five centuries. They studied the Fathers with great professional skill, but at the same time they kept their distance from the ancient dogmas of the Church. Finally, they were characterized by an aversion to the rigid Roman Catholic hierarchy, favoring an emphasis on the "layman" instead. They combined this emphasis with the erection of a new intellectual hierarchy made up of scholarly exegetes and philosophers.

Bible study! With gratitude we should note that daily Bible reading was now being recommended as never before. New translations of the Bible appeared, some of them published by Roman Catholics and Protestants jointly. The Papal Bible Institute, originally established in Rome to refute Modernism, was headed in 1930 by an able man named A. Bea, who later became a cardinal.

At the same time, there was refined Biblical criticism, parallel to the form-criticism current among prominent Protestant exegetes (see p. 30 above). In his encyclical "Divino Afflante Spiritu," Pius XII permitted the new criticism in a very moderate form. But where was one to draw the line? Some Roman Catholic exegetes went far beyond any previous bounds. The creation story was called a myth, as were several of the miracles. The story of the empty tomb was branded a legend. The resurrection was said to be related to the experience of the disciples—not something that had happened to Jesus Himself.[19]

New interest in the Church Fathers! Some of their writings, especially those of the Greek Church Fathers, were translated anew. There was a desire to go back behind Trent, behind earlier and later scholasticism, to the original sources, as the Roman convert Newman had done in the nineteenth century (see Volume VI, Chap. 8). We should note that Y. Congar emphasized the importance of the writings of Origen, for Origen manifested a marked preference for typological, allegorical, non-literal exegesis.[20]

At the same time there was criticism of the ancient Christian dogmas, the same kind of criticism practiced in earlier Protestant circles by Harnack, who spoke of a blending of Christianity and Hellenism. The Roman Catholic theologians of the new variety now went further down this path. True, H. Küng claimed he accepted the confession of Chalcedon, but he added that he could not find any passage in the Bible where Jesus made Himself known as the eternal Son of God. He also argued that the first Christians had not held this belief. In this context one can well understand the cry of sorrow raised by the French opposition bishop Lefebre: "Nobody knows anymore what words mean!"[21]

A new intellectual elite! I call upon Rogier as a witness who is beyond suspicion. In the essay referred to earlier, he defended with all his ability the Roman Catholic revolution in his country, but he also dared to write about a "new rationalism." He compared the "passionate renewers" of his time to the priests of the eighteenth century who, influenced by the spirit of their times, played an instrument with only one string. The music they produced resounded with the excellence of human reason and the pleasures of virtue and tolerance. Likewise, in our time we always hear the praise of universal benevolence. Consequently we find a "chilliness within the church, as if the hearths have been quenched one after the other."[22]

A similar complaint is uttered by James Hitchcock, an American professor who went along with the church reformers at first but turned his back on them when he saw they accepted the infallibility of the radical theologians instead of the infallibility of the pope. He writes: "What is often called the 'revolt of the laity' in the Church is in reality closer to a revolt of the experts, who use a democratic rhetoric to mask an elitist conception of religious reform."[23]

The New Theology criticized papal infallibility in a subtle way, but it wound up directing criticism at all forms of infallibility—whether of the Bible, the church, the councils, or the pope.[24] The New Theology radically denounced the old Roman Catholic exclusivism; the reformers found sparks of the knowledge of God everywhere, even in the non-Christian religions, as a saving revelation of God.[25] The New Theology tried to build bridges everywhere, but in its extremist form it came out in favor of dynamiting bridges, for leftist adherents of the New Theology joined with the Marxists in preaching the gospel of liberation.

In America the Berrigan brothers, both Jesuits, stood out for the efforts they made to try to heal the diseases of society by civil disobedience. In France Father Cardonnel declared during the weeks of Lent, 1968: "I have no hesitation in saying it: the only Lent in which I believe would be that of a general strike that would paralyze a society based on profit."[26]

A special place was occupied by the well-known evolutionist theologian and archeologist Pierre Teilhard de Chardin, who spoke of a cosmic Christ and of a universe on its way to becoming the organic body of Christ in accordance with the laws of evolution. Transubstantiation on the altar is a sign of the coming transubstantiation of the universe. His doctrine, which was condemned by the Roman Catholic Church during his lifetime, has rightly been called more Gnostic than Christian.[27]

The Second Vatican Council

It was all very impressive. Listen to this eyewitness report of what happened on October 11, 1962, in Rome:

> The streets of the city teem with traffic, as they do every morning. Everyone knows that for the past two and a half thousand years, the *ubiculus mundi*, the navel of the world, is to be found here on the *Forum Romanum*, along with the *millenarius aureus*, the golden milestone, the end of all the world's roads. A special day of the church in one of the provinces causes more sensation than an ecumenical council in Rome.
>
> It is clear, at any rate, that on the other side of that red traffic light a bus with hoary bishops is expected, bishops who cannot get to the Vatican by foot anymore. In front of St. Peter's Christian people from all over the world assemble quietly, as if in passing—people who talk or keep silent, people who pray or laugh, curious people and bashful ones, meaningless and lively faces. They fill the proud—or rather, princely—square above the bones of the martyrs.
>
> The people are singing! They are not singing an opening march or a hymn of loyalty but a quiet song of praise. They are singing the words of the Nicenum: credo in unum Deum partem omnipotentem.*
>
> Then the solemn entry of the Council begins. A choir of priests sings psalms at the portal of the dome. Some companies of soldiers in uniforms dating back to the beginning of the nineteenth century march on, while a military band presents the papal march of Gounod. Also, medieval knights in sparkling armor present themselves. Spanish grandees, seemingly straight from the court of Philip II, open the procession.
>
> All of this does not cause surprise. The people gathered here remember the *saecula* [i.e. the ages], and all this belongs here.
>
> Neither is it surprising, now, that we see a long procession of men shrouded in cloaks of Latin shepherds, in the tunics of Roman citizens, in the togas of senators, and in the solemn robes of state of the Byzantine emperors: in that manner, the *patres conscripti*, the bishops, prelates, abbots, the shepherds of the Christian people of the whole world, and finally the papal retinue, stride slowly to the gate of the church. Against his wishes, the pope is carried on a chair. He would rather have walked humbly on his feet, but with greater humility he must renounce his own wishes because they are out of order and such a show of humility on this particular day would be too loud.[28]

This whole scene looks like the première of a fantastic movie, but even if we pay no attention to all the unusual features, something of

---

*I believe in one God, the Father Almighty.

that little word *fantastic* stays with us. Isn't it fantastic that at this council, which the Roman Catholics count as the twenty-first in the series of all general councils, East and West meet each other? Isn't it fantastic that bearded observers from the Orthodox Churches of the East, which have been separate from the West since 1054, are officially present? Isn't it fantastic that there are Protestant observers to be found in addition to the Roman Catholic cardinals, observers who have been invited in the name of the pope? And shouldn't this pope, John XXIII, be called a fantastic man because of his great dream of unity? In his opening address he declares that he cannot agree with the voices of the prophets of doom, because "in the present order of things Divine providence is leading us to a new order of human relations which, by men's own efforts and even beyond their very expectations, are directed toward the fulfillment of God's superior and inscrutable designs."[29]

John XXIII was the man of the "aggiornamento," of the updating of his church, of the signs of a new future. He hoped new winds would blow through the old church, and a new, world-embracing unity would be achieved.

The Vatican: The Ecumenical Council: An event of world-wide significance. In the foreground, the twelve cardinal presidents of the Vatican Council.

Has that hope indeed been fulfilled? Let's try to get an overview of the principal events of the Council.

The first session lasted from October 11, 1962, to December 8 of that same year and can be called a period of provisional discussion without palpable results. Pope John died on June 3, 1963, and his successor, Paul VI, opened the second session on September 29 of that year. The second session was concluded on December 4, 1963, with a solemn promulgation of the Constitution on the Sacred Liturgy and the Decree on the Instruments of Social Communication.*

The third session lasted from September 14, 1964, to November 21 of that year and concluded with the promulgation of the Constitution on the Church, the Decree on Ecumenism and the Decree on the Eastern Catholic Churches. In the final public session, Paul VI emphasized the primacy of the pope, buttressed by the principle of the collegiality of the bishops and the significance of the Virgin Mary: "Therefore we declare to the honor of the Holy Virgin and for our comfort that Holy Mary is Mother of the Church."[30]

The last session lasted from September 14, 1965, to December 8 of that same year. Several declarations were promulgated. The ones attracting the most attention concerned the bishops' pastoral office in the Church and the declaration concerning religious freedom. Also important were the Constitutions on Divine Revelation and on the Church in the Modern World.

In this short survey I have touched only on the main points, given the fact that the documents produced by the Council have been calculated to contain more than 103,000 words.[31] In the context of my aims in this volume, I will say a few more things about two important Dogmatic Constitutions, dealing with the Church and Divine Revelation respectively.

Both Constitutions, like all the other decisions of the Council, begin with the words: "Paul, bishop, servant of the servants of God, together with the Fathers of the Sacred Council, for everlasting memory."

During this great council, which clearly stated the collegiality of all bishops in its Constitution on the Church, the pope appeared to be aware of his dignity as the successor of Peter and the Vicar of Christ. He also expressed such an awareness on June 10, 1970, on the occa-

---

*The decisions of the Council are distinguished as Constitutions, Decrees and Declarations. Although the difference is hardly definable, the Constitutions appear to be of foremost importance.

sion of his visit to the headquarters of the World Council of Churches in Geneva. He introduced himself there with the words: "Our name is Peter."

But what are the contents of this constitution? It should be noted with gladness that Christ is called the only Mediator of the Church (Chapter 1), and the Church's existence as the people of God is emphasized, sharing the priestly and prophetic office of Christ (Chapter 2). This is clearly a shift of emphasis in Roman Catholic thinking. The church member had stood more or less in the background before, but is now placed in the foreground.

This does not mean, however, that the sacramental power of the Church—and, with it, the power of the priest—is disowned. With great clarity, the seven sacraments of the Church, with their grace-producing character, are maintained:

> The faithful are incorporated into the Church through baptism; — reborn as sons of God, they must confess before men the faith which they have received from God through the Church. Bound more intimately to the Church by the sacrament of confirmation, they are endowed by the Holy Spirit with special strength.
>
> The ministerial priest, by the sacred power he enjoys, molds and rules the priestly people. Acting in the person of Christ, he brings about the Eucharistic Sacrifice, and offers it to God in the name of all the people.
>
> Taking part in the Eucharistic Sacrifice, which is the fount and apex of the whole Christian life, they offer the divine Victim to God, and offer themselves along with it.
>
> Those who approach the sacrament of penance obtain pardon from the mercy of God for offenses committed against Him. They at the same time are reconciled with the Church, which they have wounded by their sins.
>
> By the sacred anointing of the sick and the prayer of her priests, the whole Church commends those who are ill to the suffering and glorified Lord, asking that He may lighten their suffering and save them.
>
> Finally, Christian spouses, in virtue of the sacrament of matrimony, signify and partake of the mystery of that unity and fruitful love which exists between Christ and His Church.[32]

This Constitution continues to speak about the Church being linked with those baptized Christians "who do not profess the faith in its entirety or do not preserve unity of communion with the successor of Peter," and also with those who have not yet received the gospel, mentioning the Jews, the Mohammedans, and "those who in shadows and images seek the unknown God." Those who sincerely seek God can attain to everlasting salvation.

The third chapter of this Constitution deals with the *hierarchical structure* of the Church. In the bishops, for whom the priests are assistants, the Lord Jesus Himself is present in the midst of those who believe.[33] The collegiality of those bishops is emphasized, but the Constitution immediately adds:

> The college or body of bishops has no authority unless it is simultaneously conceived of in terms of its head, the Roman Pontiff, Peter's successor, and without any lessening of his power of primacy over all, pastors as well as general faithful. For in virtue of his office, that is, as Vicar of Christ and pastor of the whole Church, the Roman Pontiff has full, supreme, and universal power over the Church. And he can always exercise this power freely.[34]

The final chapter of this Constitution (Chapter 8) speaks of "the Blessed Virgin Mary, Mother of God." She is called the mother of all members of Christ. Her immaculate conception and her assumption are promulgated once more. Among the names she is given we are struck by the address *Mediatrix* (i.e. she who is a mediator). At the end of the chapter the following words stand out: "Let the entire body of faithful pour forth persevering prayer to the Mother of God and the Mother of men."[35] We note furthermore how the veneration of images *expressis verbis* (explicitly) is maintained: "Those decrees issued in earlier times regarding the veneration of images of Christ, the Blessed Virgin, and the saints, be religiously observed."

As far as the Constitution on Divine Revelation is concerned, it is noteworthy that on the one hand we should recognize with gratitude that Scripture is called the "soul of sacred theology," and the believers are urged "to move ahead daily toward a deeper understanding of the sacred Scripture." On the other hand, Scripture has been dethroned as the sole rule of faith and life.[36]

These two statements are not as completely contradictory as they appear to be at first glance. We already dealt with the double face of the New Theology, which advocated a return to the sources, including the Bible, but at the same time advocated criticism of the Bible.

What, now, do we find in this Constitution? In one instance it does not uphold the old "two-sources doctrine" any longer. Scripture and tradition are no longer considered sources of revelation alongside each other. No, there is only *one* Revelation, which comes to us by "transmission." In this transmission, Scripture, tradition and *magisterium* (the teaching authority of the church) go hand in hand.

Nevertheless, it is stated in plain words:

> To the successors of the apostles sacred tradition hands on in its full
> purity God's Word . . . Consequently, it is not from sacred Scripture
> alone that the Church draws her certainty about everything which has
> been revealed.[37]

And further:

> Those who search out the intention of the sacred writers must, among
> other things, have regard for "literary forms." For truth is proposed
> and expressed in a variety of ways, depending on whether a text is
> history of one kind or another, or whether its form is that of prophecy,
> poetry, or some other type of speech. The interpreter must investi-
> gate what meaning the sacred writer intended to express and actually
> expressed in particular circumstances as he used contemporary literary
> forms in accordance with the situation in his own time and culture.[38]

In these words, the Council was accepting form-criticism of the Bible
with all its consequences, as the pope had already done in 1943. In the
final analysis, however, the criticism of the Bible was still controlled
by the *magisterium*, the teaching office of the successors of the
apostles. The well-known Lutheran scholar J. W. Mongomery exclaims after describing this course of affairs: "When Roman

Patriarch Athenagoras I, spiritual leader of Orthodoxy (left), and Pope Paul VI meet in
Jerusalem, breaking a silence between the two churches that had lasted for centuries.

Catholicism continues to insist that the Holy Scriptures were dictated by the Holy Ghost and are inerrant, while at the same time allowing internal contradictions through source conflation, external contradictions with known fact, employment of Midrash fictions, etc., the Church speaks nonsense.''[39]

Pope John meant well, and we have no reason to doubt the good intention of his successor either. Neither would I deny that the Second Vatican Council has built bridges to the Eastern churches and the churches of a modern-Protestant character.

However, if we inquire into the relation of this Council to the great, powerful principles of Protestantism (i.e. *sola fide, sola gratia, sola Scriptura, soli Deo gloria*), we are forced to voice our deep disappointment. The Roman Catholic principle of human cooperation, represented in the Virgin Mary, is fully maintained. The saints are still invoked. The sacraments remain channels of God's grace. The sinner is not justified by faith alone, and Scripture is not exclusively the Word of God's revelation for us.

Advances were made toward the "separated brothers," but the term "separated *churches*" was avoided. A very remarkable change was made in the Decree on Ecumenism. The original text read: "*Moved* by the Holy Spirit they (the separated brothers) find in these very Scriptures God speaking to them in Christ." The final, corrected text reads: "Invoking the Holy Spirit they seek in these very Scriptures God as if (quasi) speaking to them in Christ."[40]

After the Council

The period after the Second Vatican Council has been characterized by the Dutch bishop Gijsen as follows: "Now it becomes clear that the foundation under the house of faith has been largely destroyed, that often little more than a facade of the church is sustained by all sorts of tricks, and that a pseudo-Christianity is being preached vociferously by many."[41] The gloomy mood expressed in these words is shared by quite a number of Catholics—and not without reason.

What did the Council mean? How should we interpret its decisions? We are directly confronted with this important question when we read the book *The Crucial Questions*,[42] written by a number of the "new" theologians. Y. Congar writes:

> What do the Scriptural texts *intend* to convey, which of their affirmations must be maintained, what is the historical reality of the words and

deeds recorded there? This is the whole discussion set in motion by
Rudolf Bultmann. But this question of interpretation (hermeneutics)
is *just as valid in regard to the pronouncements of the Church's magisterium.*

And E. Schillebeekx:

> Thus, in its express and understandable context the dynamic of faith's
> understanding is both "demythologizing" (dissolving the previous
> formulas of faith) and "remythologizing" (constructing ever new
> formulas of faith). The unassailable element of the context of faith lies
> in the inexpressible objective perspective which presents itself ever anew
> in and on the basis of the constantly changing historical profile of
> human existence.[43]

The permanent reinterpretation never stops. The influence of existential philosophy is unmistakable here. Still, there is no avoiding
the question: Doesn't all of this lead to endless relativism?[44]

Questions arise concerning the authority of Holy Scripture. The
Council officially allowed form-criticism within the limits of the
church's teaching authority, its *magisterium*, which has the final say.
But does the *magisterium* really wind up with the final say? Shouldn't
the intention of its words and terms always be questions again? Don't
we face the same burning question today, yesterday and tomorrow,
namely, what is truth? And isn't the answer to that question a very
personal one?

Closely connected with this are the questions concerning the
authority of the pope. The Council talked about the collegiality of the
bishops, and the pope, after all, is one of the bishops. Can the *intent*
of papal authority ever be discussed?* Rogier, at any rate, concludes:
"The history of the Dutch province of the Church since the closing of
the Second Vatican Council amounts to the story of a series of conflicts with Rome."[45] In 1968 the Dutch bishops declared straightforwardly in a communiqué regarding the encyclical "Humanae Vitae"
that one should take the words of the pope very seriously, but one's
own conscience should settle the matter.[46]

In the Netherlands, 75 percent of all the priests declared
themselves to be opposed to celibacy in 1968. In America there are
also some remarkable figures to report. Statistics of the mid-1960s
reveal that only 29 percent of the priests there agree with the pope's

---

*See especially Hans Küng, *Structuren van de Kerk* (1962). Küng writes:
". . . when the pope acts and teaches against the gospel of Jesus Christ . . . the Church is
allowed to defend itself against him" (p. 285).

position on birth control. Only 54 percent believe in the divinity of Christ, and 52 percent foresee the possibility that conscience might have to be followed instead of obedience to the church. As far as the "laymen" are concerned, 53 percent said they never read the Bible at all, while only two percent claimed to read it daily. Yet 83 percent pray at least once a week.[47]

To those who enjoy the theologies of secularism and liberation, this might seem an ideal situation. But others who have tried to find a shelter in the old Catholic church find it a cause of heartache.

A striking example is the Dutch professor C. J. de Vogel, who left the Dutch Reformed Church for the Roman Catholic Church. She conveyed her heartfelt disappointment in her book *De grondslag van onze zekerheid* (The Foundation of Our Certainty). In this book she expresses her appreciation for the Second Vatican Council, but she claims its decisions have been wrongly applied in many churches, and as a result many believers wound up confused. She points to the fatal results of form-criticism, which moved Schillebeekx to say that the resurrection stories do not tell us what happened to Jesus but what happened to His disciples, and moved Küng to say that the resurrection is not a historical event but a legend. In the face of such thinking she asks a pointed question: "Do you think that an exegete is infallible?"

De Vogel finally reaches a heart-breaking conclusion: "In fact everything has changed with those who have abandoned the dogma. God is God no longer, the almighty Creator of heaven and earth. Jesus Christ is no longer the eternal Son, our Lord, but a perfect man. As for the Spirit, who, sent by Christ, keeps the Church in the truth of faith—He is absent in the contemporary presentation when it is expressed in the form of a dogma."[48]

We are confronted with the same kind of disappointment when we read John Eppstein's book *Has the Catholic Church Gone Mad?* (1971). Eppstein was born in 1895, the son of an Anglican clergyman, but in 1919 he became a Roman Catholic. He retired from the office of secretary-general of NATO in 1961. Truly at one with the church of his choice and appreciative of the Second Vatican Council (just as Dr. de Vogel was), he expresses a deep concern regarding the many revolutionary tendencies in doctrine and life, which he documents at great length in his book.

Apparently the Roman Catholic Church has fallen into a crisis. The impressive series of documents issued by the Second Vatican Council sometimes seems a mausoleum. Only the future can tell whether this is indeed so. But this much we can say for sure: the Roman Catholic Church is not the only one in this situation. Many large Protestant churches are manifesting similar signs of decay.

Appendix

Some notes should be added about the situation of the Roman Catholic Church since the completion of the original Dutch edition of this book in 1978, the year that has been described as the year of three popes. Pope Paul VI died that year. His successor, John Paul I, died only a half year later and was succeeded by the Polish cardinal Karol Wotjyla, who took the name John Paul II.

The present pope has tried to curb the liberal trends in his church. Hans Küng has been removed from his teaching office. Edward Schillebeekx was summoned to Rome and admonished. The effort to have women ordained as priests has been resisted. The use of contraceptives is still forbidden.

The pope has stirred the enthusiasm of millions of Roman Catholics on his tours of South America, Mexico, Germany, and Africa. He has taken a firmer stand against Communism than his predecessors, especially in relation to Poland, his homeland. Still, he follows in the footsteps of his predecessors in his adoration of Mary, whom he has called the "Mother of the Church," the one to whom God entrusted "the whole of His mystery of salvation."*

---

*In his book *Sign of Contradiction* (1979), pp. 112, 205.

11

Continuation and Confusion: The Ecumenical Movement

Amsterdam 1948

Again an eyewitness report, but this time describing something that amounts to a great Protestant council:

> The bells in thousands of American church steeples rang joyously the morning of Sunday, August 22, 1948. They had reason to ring, for they were announcing the first meeting of a momentous assembly, the first Assembly of the World Council of Churches. No other meeting of the Churches of the world for centuries was so important, for the Assembly had convened in Amsterdam, first city of the Netherlands, for the purpose of establishing a continuing world fellowship of the churches, dedicated to co-operation and unity. Though still morning in the United States, it was afternoon in Amsterdam when the official delegates of 147 branches of the Christian Church—representatives of every communion save Rome—gathered in the historic Nieuwe Kerk (the "New Church," built in the 1400s). As was fitting, they gathered for praise and prayer—praise to God for having led them to that hour, prayer that his will might be done through them and so his kingdom come on earth in greater measure.
>
> The Nieuwe Kerk was thronged with visitors from all parts of the globe. Eagerly they awaited the entrance of the delegates. The great

organ announced the stately procession and for nearly twenty minutes archbishops, archimandrites, bishops, priests, pastors, deacons, elders, Doctors of Divinity, and plain laymen and laywomen made their way around the church to their appointed places.

The worship began with the singing of the familiar tune of "Old 100th" of the French hymn by de Beze (1519-1605) — *"Vous qui sur la terre habitez."* Those who could used the original tongue. Others sang in English, "All people that on earth do dwell" or in German, "Nun jauchzet Herrn aller Welt." The fact that different languages were used did not spoil the harmony of the hymns, for music is a universal language.

A minister of the Dutch Reformed Church called the Assembly to worship and penitence. The Archbishop of Canterbury led in prayer. The Holy Scriptures were read in French and Swedish by the president of the French Protestant Federation and the primate of the Church of Sweden, respectively.

There could have been but one choice for the first speaker of the Assembly. In his person, John R. Mott incarnated the ecumenical movement, and he was an active participant in every one of the great conferences from Edinburgh, 1910, on. In his address he recalled the past and paid tribute to former comrades who had labored beside him in the task of furthering the unity of the church. But he did not rest upon the past. From his vantage point of eighty-three years, he could look forward with hope and courage, though he had to warn the Assembly that the most *exacting days* for the Church lay ahead.[1]

It was an impressive service. Although the Greek Catholic churches were not yet represented and the Roman Catholic Church remained aloof and various Protestant churches raised objections, it appeared that a beginning had at last been made in reuniting Christianity, which already had been ruptured and fragmented for so many ages.

What was the character of this meeting? Was it a *council?* No, this could not be said. The differences in conviction were only too apparent when the Lord's supper was celebrated at four separate tables (i.e. Reformed, Anglican, Lutheran, and Eastern Orthodox). Moreover, it was stated at the meeting that no super-church was being established and no decisions binding on all the participating churches were made.

Was the meeting no more than a conference, then? No, the slogan regularly heard at the Amsterdam meeting indicated otherwise: "We intend to stay together." That the meeting was more than a conference was also apparent from the fact a new organization was created at the Amsterdam meeting—an organization with a general-secretary, headquarters in Geneva and committees meeting regularly.

That same year, 1948, the Dutch expert Dr. H. van der Linde explained the official position in the following words:

> The World Council of Churches is less than a world church and more than a theological conference. It is a meeting place and conference place of the churches that are officially represented, where they can talk together about the way to achieve more unity, the way the churches themselves should take. We pray and hope that it is the place where we may grow together toward a world church of Christ.[2]

If this was the clearest language spoken on the subject, a number of questions remained unanswered. Some people preferred to speak of the World Council as a platform for *discussion*. It was usually added that the Council provided opportunities for cooperative *action*. There were those who were opposed to calling the Council a *faith communion*, because of the differences between the delegates, some of whom were orthodox and others liberal. And it was emphasized that the basis formula which had been accepted was *not a confession*.

Yet this basis formula was undeniably confessional in character. As formulated in New Delhi in 1961, it read: "The World Council of Churches is a fellowship of churches which confess the Lord Jesus Christ as God and Savior according to the Scriptures, and therefore seek to fulfill together their common calling to the glory of the one God, Father, Son, and Holy Spirit."*

The Council does not concern itself, however, with the manner in which the churches interpret the basis.** This would be virtually impossible because there is no doctrinal unity with regard to the divinity of Christ.

In the title of this chapter I have spoken once again of "confusion." I trust you can now see that sense of confusion becoming visible in many ways. But I also spoke of "continuation." Amsterdam meant the end of a long road, and the beginning of a new one as well.

Origins and pioneers

There have been many attempts to establish the *pedigree* of the World Council of Churches by drawing up a list of consecutive events relating to international contacts between churches and reunions of

---

*An extension of the basis of Amsterdam, which confessed no more than Jesus Christ as God and Savior.

**"The basis is not a creedal test to judge churches or persons" (*Documents of the World Council of Churches*, 1948, p. 16).

churches since the beginning of the nineteenth century. I will mention two ecumenical pioneers and then discuss three organizations that have paved the way for the establishment of the World Council.

Ecumenical pioneers! The word *oikoumene*, which occurs repeatedly in the New Testament (e.g. Luke 2:1; Matt. 24:14), refers to the whole world or the whole *inhabited* world—or more specifically, to the world-touched-by-the-gospel and the Church gathered by Christ in the whole world. In the parlance of the ancient church, the first great meetings in the first centuries were called ecumenical councils.

The first ecumenical pioneer who should be mentioned here is *John R. Mott* (1865-1955). Mott was an American, but at the same time a cosmopolitan. In his travels throughout the world, he manifested a strong interest in Christian work among students and also in missionary work. He saw the drawbacks of all the ecclesiastical and confessional divisions, and he urged them to cooperate.

Mott was an evangelical Christian and a student of history and political science. Because he held a law degree, the road to a high government position seemed to be open before him. But he was converted and deeply influenced by the well-known Methodist preacher *Moody*. At a student conference in 1886 at Mt. Hermon in Massachusetts over which Moody presided, Mott was captivated by the slogan: "The Evangelization of the World in our Generation." Mott was one of about 100 students who volunteered for missionary work, and at once he was elected chairman of the "Student Volunteer Movement for Foreign Missions."

All through his life Mott zealously advocated the cause of missions and Christian student organizations. He inspired young men and became their beloved leader. He was largely responsible for the formation of the World Student Christian Federation, which was in turn influential in the rise of the ecumenical movement.

Henry Van Dusen talks about this matter when he describes the Oxford Conference of 1937, about which I will say more later. The leadership of this conference was in the hands of about 20 men, including Archbishop Temple, Bishop Azariah, Hendrik Kraemer, J. H. Oldham, W. A. Visser 't Hooft and Reinhold Niebuhr. Van Dusen wondered how such a diverse collection of men could appear to be old friends. He found the answer when he was reminded about their student years; it was "a reunion of old school-mates. The great majority had been educated in the fellowship of the World Christian Student Federation."[3]

Mott became chairman of the missionary conferences of Edinburgh (1910), Jerusalem (1928) and Tambaran (1938). He was appointed honorary president of the World Council in Amsterdam (1948). Mott was the embodiment of one of the original motives of the ecumenical movement. He combined the energy, the optimism of faith and the persuasive power of American Moody-Methodism (see Volume VI, Chap. 10) with a downplaying of the divisive elements and an emphasis on the unifying elements—in other words, a minimum of theology.

The other ecumenical pioneer who should be mentioned here is the Swedish archbishop *Nathan Söderblom* (1866-1931), who has been called "the ecumenical patriarch" by his countryman Aulén. In his childhood, Söderblom regarded the infallibility of the Bible as the only foundation of faith.[4] As a student, however, he was influenced by the Biblical criticism of the Wellhausen school and Ritschl's horizontal expectations concerning the Kingdom of God. He became an expert in comparative religions and found in the history of all religions a manifold, evolutionary revelation of God, the highest form of which was Christianity.[5]

A liberal theologian, Söderblom followed the modern way of thinking, and could no longer cling to the conviction of faith that Christ is both true God and true man.[6] In his younger years he had been a Swedish pastor in Paris. Later, he made a trip to America, taught in Leipzig from 1912 to 1914, and made numerous international contacts with students, theologians and "civilized persons."*

Like Mott, Söderblom attracted persons with divergent convictions by means of his outgoing personality. He made them enthusiastic about the ideal of unity by which he himself was animated, using the motto: "Doctrine divides, service unites," or, as he wrote in his book on "true brotherhood":

> We see new life-giving powers entering larger or smaller segments of Christianity without dividing it into new churches. I might refer to Pietism, to the insights of Schleiermacher, and to the modern theological research that has not been arrested by theological borderlines but has entered the hearts of those who are spiritually awake and those who are intellectual authorities in almost every church.

---

*O. Dibelius says this in passing regarding the conference of Stockholm (1925), which was inspired by Söderblom: "Of course the Scandinavians were all represented as if they were genuine Lutherans: Sven Hedin, Selma Lagerlöf, Hjalmar Hammerskjöld . . ." (*In the Service of the Lord*, p. 252).

What is it that unites us? The imitation of Christ. Indeed, it should be a sufficient bond of unity that all of us together and everyone for himself in all honesty wants to follow in the footsteps of the Master.[7]

It was especially as a result of Söderblom's activities that the World Conference on Life and Work took place in Stockholm in 1925. At this conference the problems of Christian action were emphasized, without much attention to the dogmatic-theological background.

Söderblom represents the embodiment of another original motive of the ecumenical movement, but a different one from Mott. Söderblom called for the confessional differences to be more or less minimized; "messages" should be promulgated in which all Christians could join in speaking about Christian behavior with regard to social, political and economic problems.

Some organizations also paved the way for the World Council. I want to draw your attention briefly to three of them: the International Missionary Council, the Conferences on Life and Work, and the Conferences on Faith and Order.

Nathan Söderblom

It should come as no surprise that missionaries have been especially ecumenically minded. The nineteenth century was the age of missions, and it was on the mission field that the negative effects of divisiveness were felt most keenly. Another factor here was the increasing influence of liberal missionaries, especially from America, who all essentially brought the same message regarding culture and society.

In 1910 the great missionary conference of

Edinburgh was convened. It was marked by enthusiasm and optimism, but also by a certain one-sidedness. Three-fourths of the participants were Anglo-American. The Anglican Indian bishop Azariah
had urged a more deeply experienced communion of missionaries and
natives without the "condescending love" of the West.[8]

Because of the disaster of the first world war, the plans for extension and renewal could not be carried out. In 1921 the International
Missionary Council was founded at Lake Mohonk in New York. It
convened its first great conference in Jerusalem in 1928.

At this meeting there was more representation than before from
the churches founded by missions, the so-called younger churches.
The representation from these churches increased again at the next
conference, held at Madras in 1938.

This did not only mean a more equitable representation, it also
meant a more liberal representation. Henry Van Dusen, the chairman
of the study department of the World Council of Churches, explained
in 1948:

> Those who professed what might have been called the theology of
> liberalism constituted the majority of the leaders of the universal
> church. The consequence of this fact is clear: the young churches have
> developed, in a large measure under the guardianship of the mission-
> aries from England and America. The spirits have been framed by an
> interpretation of the Christian faith nearer to "Liberalism" than to
> "Orthodoxy" or "Neo-Orthodoxy." The theology of the Christian
> missionary movement is in the majority that of liberal Christianity.[9]

These meaningful words require some further comment, even if this
takes me away from my line of thought for a moment.

New missionary ideas

Was Van Dusen right when he asserted that the theology of world
missions had become liberal? In general there was more variety than
he seemed prepared to admit. He overlooked the worldwide Roman
Catholic missionary activities, and also the many Protestant missionaries who preached the pure gospel of Christ. Still, he was not
totally wrong.

In the first quarter of the twentieth century, a radical change had
taken place in leading American missionary circles. The change was
marked by an increasing antipathy to the call to conversion in the
Biblical sense, and increasing sympathy for cooperation with people
of different religions, especially in social and cultural areas.

To the bewilderment of some and the joy of others, this change became visible to everyone in 1932 when the book *Rethinking Missions* appeared. The subtitle of the book was: "A Laymen's Inquiry after One Hundred Years." The book contained a report written by 35 so-called laymen under the leadership of Prof. W. E. Hocking of Harvard, who had studied the question: What direction should missions take in this modern era? The entire enterprise was financed by a generous donation from the well-known millionaire J. D. Rockefeller, Jr.

The question was answered in plain language; the purpose was no longer "to save men from eternal punishment." At the core of every pagan religion there was something good to be found: "the inalienable religious intuition of the human soul." Then follow these words of the report: "The God of this intuition is the true God; to this extent universal religion has not to be established, it exists."

I wrote that some people were bewildered by this report. (I will have more to say about them in the next chapter.) Others, however, were very happy with it. Among them was the well-known American novelist Pearl S. Buck. She was the daughter of a missionary in China and had herself served as a missionary for some time. She called the book "a masterly statement of religion" and expressed her expectation that it would lead to "the greatest missionary impetus that we have known for centuries." In a subsequent article she confessed her liberal faith in the following words:

Hendrik Kraemer

Even though it is proved in some future time that there never lived an actual Christ and what we think of as Christ should some day be found as the essence of men's dreams of simplest and beautiful goodness, would I be willing to have that personification of dreams pass out of men's minds? . . . . Others live it also, many who have never heard the name of Christ; but to know the meaning of Christ's life, to know how he lived and died, is an inestimable support and help.[10]

This was nothing but modern idealism—idealism because it attached more value to manmade ideas than to the facts of salvation given and revealed by God.

In spite of the approval which had been voiced for the laymen's report, the International Missionary Council was not pleased with it. This became clear at the following missionary council, at Tambaran in 1938. The focus of the discussion there was the book *The Christian Message in a Non-Christian World*, written by the Dutch missionary expert Dr. H. Kraemer.

In this book, objections were raised against the laymen's report, and the necessity of conversion was reaffirmed. In the Message of Tambaran, mention was made of the love of God revealed in Jesus Christ, and also of His life and work, His suffering, death and resurrection. Later in his life, however, Kraemer felt impelled to declare: "The responsible agencies to which I appealed in 1938 for practical measures to combat syncretism have not responded even to this day. What I do hope and pray for is the awakening of responsible agencies to the fundamental necessities."[11]

The Conferences for Life and Work

The Conference for Life and Work that met in Stockholm in 1925 might well have been called "Söderblom's conference." It was completely in line with his thinking, because questions about Christian *doctrine* were disregarded as much as possible, while questions about the Christian *life* were placed in the foreground—as if the word *Christian* did not at once give rise to questions about its exact meaning.

All sorts of questions—economic, industrial, social, moral and educational—were raised. Yet, an assuredly unprejudiced observer says there was a "naiveté which was absolutely incompetent in view of the numerous and comprehensive problems." Also: "the fundamental error was made that there might be a thoroughly different dogmatic view of faith and world, without having cumbersome consequences in the areas of the practical cooperation and social witness of the churches."[12]

The next conference, with the same character, met in Oxford in 1937. Because of the situation in those days, the problems of race and nation, war and peace, and church and state were added to the topics mentioned earlier. The Oxford conference was more realistic than the Stockholm conference because it acknowledged the existence of fundamental differences. It spoke of "the tragedy of our disunity" and also of an essential unity in Christ.[13] It is also significant that the Oxford conference addressed the German Confessing Church in an encouraging way, and that it declined to cooperate with the movement for Faith and Order in its efforts to establish a World Council of Churches.

The Conferences for Faith and Order

The movement for Faith and Order runs parallel to the Life and Work movement in an interesting way. The questions on the agenda at its conferences were the ones circumvented as much as possible at the Life and Work conferences. It should be added, however, that it was often very difficult to draw the line between matters of faith and matters of church order in the strict sense. The Anglicans, for example, considered the office of bishop to be a matter of faith. They were inclined to tolerate all sorts of errors, but in no way would they tolerate the exclusion or non-recognition of this office.*

At the conference of Lausanne in 1927, which was convened especially through the persistent efforts of the Canadian-born Anglican bishop C. H. Brent, no fewer than 400 delegates from different churches were present. When they talked about unity, offices, sacraments and the proclamation of the church, they discovered the great differences between the delegates. The delegates from the Eastern Orthodox Churches, for example, were convinced that seven sacraments were necessary, while the Quakers wanted no sacraments at all. Questions about the essence of grace seemed to pose almost as many problems as questions about church order, offices and sacraments.[14]

At the ensuing conference held in Edinburgh in 1937, similar differences arose. In spite of these differences, however, the unity of faith in the Lord Jesus Christ was pronounced. According to Van der Linde, the main result of this conference was that the participants realized the *direct* method of discussion led nowhere. From then on they would use *indirect* method, which consisted of listening to each other with great patience, assisting each other spiritually and so pro-

---

*Since 1867, all Anglican bishops meet almost every tenth year at the residence of the Archbishop of Canterbury (the Lambeth Palace). These meetings are called the Lambeth Conferences. Since 1888, these conferences have accepted the following four points as the essential basis for a reunited Christian church: (1) Holy Scripture, (2) The Apostolic Creed and that of Nicea, (3) the two sacraments of baptism and the Lord's supper, and (4) the historical episcopate (the so-called Lambeth Quadrilateral).

ceeding together. This method was to be applied in the World Council of Churches, the Council to which both series of conferences looked forward. In 1948 the World Council was finally convened in Amsterdam.

From Amsterdam to Nairobi

There have been meetings of the World Council (since Amsterdam they have generally been called "Assemblies") in Evanston (1954), New Delhi (1961), Uppsala (1968) and Nairobi (1975). There are six presidents, but most of the influence in exercised by the secretary-general and the executive committee, which is made up of 12 people. The so-called headquarters are to be found in Geneva, while the Ecumenical Institute is in Chateau de Bossey, close to Geneva. This is also the site for many conferences and much study.

In 1948 there were 147 churches at the meeting, representing 44 countries. By 1975 the number had increased to 280 churches from 90 countries. The World Council had indeed become a global movement, although the Roman Catholic Church did not participate and a number of Protestant churches were still opposed.

It is impossible to offer even a capsule review of all the reports, acts, messages and decisions of the Council, for they fill many volumes. I will only touch on some pertinent points. Then I will go on to draw some main outlines, indicating the basic development of the movement.

The theme of the Amsterdam Assembly was: "Man's Disorder and God's Design." Discussion was focused on the struggle for new forms of society in the postwar climate. This was expressed in the final conclusion of one of the reports, where we read that "the Christian churches reject the ideologies of both communism and laissez-faire capitalism, and should seek to draw men away from the false assumption that these are the only alternatives." In another report we find the following words in capital letters: WAR IS CONTRARY TO THE WILL OF GOD.

At the first session Karl Barth issued a remarkable warning:

> I do not wish to weaken the earnestness, the good will and the hopes that have brought us here, but only to base them on their proper foundation, when I now say: We ought to give up, even on this first day of our deliberations, every thought that the care of the Church, the care of the world, is *our* care. Burdened with this thought, we should straighten out nothing, we should only increase disorder in the Church and world still more. For this is the final root and ground of all human

disorder: the dreadful, godless, ridiculous opinion that man is the Atlas who is destined to bear the dome of heaven on his shoulders.[15]

Barth justly condemned any human effort to establish the Kingdom of God on earth. As much as he could, he objected to discussions about Christian principles for political and social life.

Precisely at this time, some of Barth's adherents in the Netherlands turned their backs on the Christian political parties and joined the Labor Party. (They called this action the "breakthrough.") As church members they wanted to show their solidarity with the world. They did not acknowledge the validity of a Christian pattern of behavior but acted according to their own insight in the concrete situation.* We will see later how such ideas gained ground in the World Council.

When the next Assembly met in Evanston, a suburb of Chicago, in 1954, the theme was: "Christ, the Hope of the World." Before and during the discussion of this topic, a fundamental difference of opinion became apparent regarding the meaning of this "hope." European theologians tended to emphasize the expectation of Christ's return, while American theologians were inclined to expect a Kingdom of God on this earth in the way of development.[16]

A new theology had come upon the scene, maintaining the old terminology but radically changing its meaning. Prof. J. Hastings Nichols brought this point out in his vivid description of the meeting:

> To many newspapermen it was a surprise to discover that the theologians, continental and otherwise, no more thought of heaven and hell as *places* than they did, in fact less so. Heaven is communion with God. Hell is alienation from Him. But what then of time? When is the age to come? One can understand that in a sense the End is Now, that the Coming King meets men today and every day, that the dimension of the last things is to be seen in all present and passing things.[17]

We read in the "Message of Evanston": "We are thankful that, separated as we are by the deepest political divisions of our time, here at Evanston we are united in Christ."

In 1961 the World Council met in New Delhi. Earlier I mentioned that the basis was reformulated at this meeting, to include a reference to the Trinity and the Scriptures. Nevertheless, the new "affirmations are not inconsistent with grossly objectionable views of both divine Trinity and scriptural authority."[18]

---

*Barth spoke of being obedient to "das Gebot der Stunde" (the commandment of the hour).

The predominantly Protestant character of the Council was drastically changed by the admission of the Greek Orthodox churches of Russia, Rumania, Bulgaria and Poland. Earlier I mentioned the objection registered by the Hungarian Reformed delegates from America against this step (see p. 88 above).

The validity of their objection was apparent the next day in the address of Archbishop Nikodim, who read a message from the Patriarch Alexis of Moscow. The message declared that the preservation and consolidation of world peace "is the basic problem of our times," and that "all Christians must resolutely call upon and induce all leaders of States to agree on universal and complete disarmament, with effective international control."

The theme of the next Assembly, convened in Uppsala in 1968, was: "Behold, I make all things new." The responsibility of the churches for the situation in state and society was emphasized, along with the importance of cooperation with non-Christians. It was decreed that "the churches should render a special contribution to develop effective, non-violent strategies of revolution and non-violent change." Among the actions suggested were: letters to members of congress or parliament, demonstrations, strikes, organizing the farmers, education, organizing the slum-dwellers, lecturing, preaching and singing protest songs.[19] Apparently the situation in eastern Europe was not discussed, nor were questions raised about how all of this might be implemented in *all* parts of the world.

The fifth Assembly convened in 1975 in Nairobi. The theme was: "The Good News of Salvation Today." The trend set in the earlier discussions continued, and the so-called theology of revolution was emphasized.

Quite unexpectedly, the issue of religious persecution in Russia came up for discussion. Somehow a letter from two members of the Russian Orthodox Church reached the meeting. This resulted in a genuine discussion of human rights in Russia. Dr. Potter, the secretary-general, was instructed to look into religious freedom in the countries that had signed the Treaty of Helsinki.*

In the secretary-general's report to a meeting of the World Council's Central Committee in 1976, however, nothing was said about

---

*In the expectations of many, the Helsinki Conference (1975) was supposed to usher in a new period of *détente* between Communist and non-Communist states. The declaration issued by this Conference contained the promise "to recognize and respect the freedom of man to confess and practice his religion or faith by himself or with others in agreement with the prescriptions of his conscience."

religious persecution in Soviet Russia or eastern Europe. Some delegates to Nairobi spoke of a "conspiracy of silence" to keep the Soviet issue from surfacing.[20]

The World Council and the church

After so many centuries of division, it was no wonder the establishment of the World Council was hailed with great joy by many Christians. At first there were many who talked of the Coming Great Church.[21] Earlier we saw that Dr. van der Linde hoped for the coming of the World Church of Christ. In many different ways, theologians worked on a blueprint for this ideal situation, usually including the proviso that the World Council is not and does not wish to be a super-church.*

In essence, this association of churches, which at the same time wants to be something more than an association, does not manifest the marks of the church that are mandatory according to a Reformed and orthodox understanding of the church. These marks are: the pure preaching of the gospel, the pure administration of the sacraments and the exercise of church discipline (Belgic Confession, Article 29). While the basic setup of the organization must be called *inclusive*, its belief is *universal* and its structure *oligarchic*.

Inclusive! Each and every one is included. Instead of issuing a call to personal repentance and church reformation, the Council accepted a large number of churches, afflicted with many errors, as one large congregation. Remember the slogan: "Doctrine divides, service unites." Although the Bible tells us doctrine should be preserved,[22] it was pushed to the background, while service came to the foreground.

Among the leaders and those who are to be led there are many different opinions to be found—from liberal to orthodox to neo-orthodox, from trinitarian to unitarian, from sacramentalist to anti-ritualist. According to some people who like the term *plurality*, this is the richness of the movement; according to others, it is the movement's Achilles heel.

In connection with the question of *universalism*, we should mention that the Council's able secretary-general, Dr. W. A. Visser 't Hooft, has repeatedly and urgently warned against the dangers of syncretism. There were good reasons for issuing such warnings. In the

---

*However, the secretary-general of the Dutch Reformed Church declared in 1976: "In my view the Council of Churches is more than a church. It is the beginning of con-ciliarity" (Weekly Bulletin of the Dutch Reformed Church, September 16, 1976).

decisions of the Council we are struck by a repeated appeal to God's fatherhood over all men and to the universal redemption wrought by Christ—not as a general, well-meant invitation to all to come to Him but as an actual state of affairs.

Söderblom, the father of the ecumenical movement, was an expert in comparative religions. He was convinced there is not just one Old Testament. The number of Old Testaments is proportional to the number of religions in the world.[23] In all religions we find a prelude to the gospel.

This idea was applied in the theology of dialogue or discussion. The implication is that no attempts should be made to convert unbelievers by pointing to the only way and the only name by which they will be saved (Acts 4:12). Instead, reports of religious experiences are exchanged. In this way, the Holy Spirit will mysteriously do His work.

At the instigation of the World Council, 22 Mohammedans and Christians held a meeting in March of 1969 at Cartigny, close to Geneva.

> The purpose of this dialogue is in the first place that both religions come to a better appreciation and mutual understanding. Furthermore this dialogue aims at the posing of those questions which may contrib-

The praesidium of the World Council of Churches. Front right: W.A. Visser t'Hooft, secretary general. Second from the left (standing): Otto Dibelius.

ute to the spiritual deepening and renewal of both religions. Finally the dialogue may occasion to accept practical responsibilities on a common basis.[24]

J. A. E. Vermaat, who writes about comparative religions, adds that in the Mohammedan mosque in The Hague, a service was held in which the Dutch Reformed minister J. G. Jacobs, the Roman Catholic priest J. A. A. van der Well and the imam of the mosque officiated.[25]

More than once the *oligarchic* structure of the World Council has been criticized. Essentially, the government of this global movement is in the hands of a small number of men, ecumenical experts who not only prepare the meetings but also exercise a great influence on the formulation of future decisions.

To a certain extent all of this is unavoidable. This is the way a big business should be operated. But a basic question still confronts us: Should the churches be organized as a big business? Are permanent offices and ministrations apart from those of the local churches justifiable on the basis of Scripture? Shouldn't national and international assemblies of the church be of short duration and bear a humble character?

The World Council and the Bible

At New Delhi (1961), the basis of the World Council was extended by adding the words "according to the Scriptures." But this did not mean all the members of the Council now had the same idea concerning the meaning and authority of the Bible.

After the meeting at Evanston in 1954, an inquiry concluded that "the divided church heard only dimly the Word of God through the Bible."[26] P. G. Schrotenboer points out there were "literalists, neo-orthodox, and theological liberals; later (in 1961) the Orthodox churches with their views on the teaching of the early church joined the Council."[27]

Especially after the Faith and Order Conferences* of Montreal (1963), Bristol (1967) and Louvain (1971), the significance of Scripture was widely discussed. Because of the theology of the time, it became increasingly clear that this meant talking about the *problem* of Scripture. The old slogan "Doctrine divides, service unites" seemed to require a rephrasing: "The Bible divides, service unites."

---

*Those conferences were continued even after the founding of the World Council (see L. Vischer, *A Documentary History of the Faith and Order Movement*, 1963, p. 17).

In Montreal profound differences were revealed concerning the unity of the New Testament revelation of God. In Bristol the delegates noted the confessional differences within the canonical books themselves. In Louvain, this conclusion was drawn: "Application of the method of historical criticism has brought out more clearly than ever the diversity of the biblical witness. The individual passages and traditions of the Bible are all aligned to specific historical situations and the Bible is the collection of these diverse testimonies."[28] This resulted in an unavoidable conclusion: "We should not regard the Bible as a standard to which we must conform in all the questions arising in our life. We should read the Bible in the expectation that it can disclose the truth to us. That is, we should read it in anticipation of its disclosure."[29]

Consequently, the Bible should be read—and it is read. Parts of the Bible are studied in different small study groups during the sessions of the World Council. But the idea that the whole Bible has authority over the whole of human life has been abandoned.

The World Council and social life

Increasingly, the World Council regarded its task to be the conscience of mankind when it comes to social injustice in the widest sense of the term. The words of Visser 't Hooft, spoken in Uppsala, are characteristic of this attitude: "It must become clear that church members who in fact deny their responsibility for the needy in any part of the world are just as guilty of heresy as those who deny this or that article of faith."[30]

Similarly, delegates at Evanston agreed it is not necessary to first arrive at a theological consensus in order to make judgments about specific theological issues.[31] This deed-theology was most clearly formulated at the Geneva Conference held by the World Council in 1966 to discuss "Church and Society."

Civil disobedience—or revolution, for that matter—was described at that conference:

> We recognize a scale of values: human rights, constitution and legislation. We understand that laws may be defied in defense of the constitution, and that the constitution may be defied in defense of human rights.[32]

This emphasis on human rights was finally intensified to such a degree that the representatives decided everything ought to be done to change the unjust structures of society. The reason for the evil and injustice and lack of freedom is to be found in the structures. As has been rightly observed, man's sinfulness was not denied at Nairobi—it was simply ignored.[33]

It is really quite remarkable that when this point of view is applied, it means opposing a number of non-Communist countries branded essentially as police states (e.g. South Africa, Chile, Brazil, South Korea). Financial support is given to guerrilla fighters, but almost nothing is said about the deprivation of liberty and the religious persecution in Communist lands.

> There is admittedly a strangeness here, for it means that the criticism has been most outspoken in a number of non-totalitarian societies where liberty is curtailed in some but not all areas, and has been strangely silent or soft in its references to communist totalitarian societies where the infringement upon liberty touches every life zone, even that of the family and church. Here the influence of representatives from communists in the communist countries in the Council is obvious.[34]

Other ecumenical movements and associations

The idea of an ecumenical movement is not the exclusive property of the twentieth century. In the sixteenth century, men such as Erasmus, Melanchthon and Calvin yearned for Christian unity, although they had different motivations. We could say the same with regard to Spener and Zinzendorf, who put more emphasis on personal piety than on ecclesiastical orthodoxy. The yearning for unity was likewise present in the men of the Enlightenment, who wanted to shake free of the bonds of a narrow-minded past.

In the nineteenth century the impulse toward a broadly evangelical, international and ecclesiastical cooperation gradually gained more ground. It would carry me too far afield to offer even a brief survey. I would remind readers only of the founding of the Evangelical Alliance (1846), which pleaded for religious freedom, Sabbath observance and missions; of the World Alliance of Christian Young Men's Societies (1855) and Christian Young Women's Societies (1894); and of the World Student Christian Federation (1886). Some international, confessional and ecclesiastical alliances were also established. I already referred to the Lambeth Conferences of the Anglicans. In addition there was the Presbyterian Alliance (since 1875), the Methodist World Alliance (since 1891), the Congregationalist World Alliance (since 1891) and the Baptist World Alliance (since 1905).

I don't claim to be exhaustive here. There are many organizations that could be mentioned. For the rest, I will restrict myself to three organizations founded at almost the same time as the World Council.

In 1948 the *International Council of Christian Churches* was founded in Amsterdam. It is a militant organization under the leadership of the American Bible Presbyterian minister Carl McIntire. In the United States it was preceded by a similar organization which has existed since 1941—the American Council of Christian Churches.

I called this Council militant, for it asks all participating churches for a clear rejection of the World Council, in agreement with the policy of the American Council. The American Council asked its member churches for a total repudiation of the Federal Council of Churches (which has existed in America since 1908) because of the presence of liberalism in the Federal Council.

The basis of this organization is orthodox. Its stated purpose is "to contend for the faith which was once for all delivered to the saints" (Jude, vs. 3). The members' missionary zeal is praiseworthy and their witness is clear. Meetings are often soul-stirring. However, there have been many complaints about its negativism, and not without reason. (The International Council takes a militant stand against the World Council, Modernism, Communism and Roman Catholicism.) Moreover, there are some dictatorial traits to be detected in its leadership. The Christian Reformed Church in the Netherlands *(Christelijk Gereformeerde Kerk)*, which became a member in 1950, withdrew in 1977.

The establishment of the *National Association of Evangelicals* in America in 1951, which was broadened in 1951 to become the World Evangelical Fellowship, was also the result of discontent with the Federal Council of Churches. Many of the members of the new Association had been members of the Federal Council. In contrast to the International Council, the National Association does not enroll churches as its members but individuals and organizations. Also, it is somewhat less militant in its conduct. It promotes evangelism campaigns such as those of Billy Graham. It likewise supports the work of Sunday schools, Christian day schools and missionaries. Its avowed purpose is "to represent all evangelical believers in all denominations and groups."[35]

Finally, I should mention the *Reformed Ecumenical Synod*, which is described by its secretary, Paul Schrotenboer, as both an "ecumenical venture" and "a call to authentic ecumenism."[36] This group, which convened for the first time in Grand Rapids in 1946, indeed intends to be a church meeting, a synod. In 1966, some 22 churches representing all the continents participated. The combined membership of the churches was about three million people.

Schrotenboer distinguishes between authentic and non-authentic ecumenicity, stressing that the former is marked by a unity with the doctrine of the apostles and a proclamation of the whole counsel of God. He adds that the Reformed Ecumenical Synod rejects *relativism* and wishes to listen obediently to the voice of God in Holy Scripture. It is interested not in a *jumboism* or a quest for large numbers but in a real unity. External unity has all too often led to inner decay. What it seeks is not a *dialogue*, in which the act of talking together is itself considered to be the way of truth, but a continuous communal listening to the Word of God. It is opposed to any *spiritualism*, any escape into a church-behind-the-church, but is determined to maintain the three marks of the church, which it views as tasks.

The matters discussed and acted upon at the various meetings of the Reformed Ecumenical Synod include the relation of church and state, Christian education, marriage problems, the last things, the place of women in the service of the church, the boundaries of the church, race relations and other such subjects of interest. Reports can be found in the Synod's published Acts.

12

Turmoil in the United States

A world power in turmoil

In 1920 the autobiography of a successful Dutch immigrant was published in New York, *The Americanization of Edward Bok*. Bok had emigrated with his parents to the United States in 1870 at the age of six. He was a completely *self-made man*. After starting out as a window cleaner and a paper boy, Bok ended up as one of the most distinguished American journalists. The account of his life, which won a Pulitzer Prize in 1921,* was a continuous success story. "Success was Edward Bok's god; he worshiped it devoutly and served it with unflagging devotion."[1]

In the America of 1920, this way of thinking was still applauded. Actually, it never totally disappeared. Devotion to success was a source of energy, and sometimes also of presumptuousness. It occasioned grand-scale enterprises, and often naive superficiality as well.

Two presidents of that era, Theodore Roosevelt (1901-1909) and Woodrow Wilson (1913-1921), were characterized by such thinking. The robust Roosevelt championed a dynamic foreign policy and wanted to give the worker in his country a "square deal." The idealist

---

*Seven Pulitzer Prizes are awarded annually in America for the highest achievements in journalism, literature, drama, etc.

Wilson, the son of a Presbyterian minister, was the man of the Four-teen Points, which were intended to pave the way to a permanent peace. In 1918 he declared: "Why did Jesus Christ not succeed thus far in moving the world to do what He has said? . . . I come with a practical plan to perform His purposes."

It is remarkable how differently people talked during and after the 1930s, when America went through the disillusionment of the first world war and the ensuing "great depression." It was the time of the "lost generation." It was the time of the somber and accusing social novel (John Steinbeck) and the hard-boiled, amoral, anti-intellectual realistic novel (Ernest Hemingway).

> Many younger ones felt deceived by their mentors, misled by elusive principles in which they had put their trust in vain. Many were over-taken by cynicism, despair, total indifference. The best among the younger authors were very suspicious of anything that looked like senti-ment or vague mysticism; they were radically opposed to it.[2]

America was in turmoil. Twice it became involved in a world war against its own wishes, but it waged both those wars, when forced to do so, with grim determination. Twice the country was flooded by a wave of pacifism, followed each time by just as high a wave of idealism about war. The first world war was hailed as "the war which would end all wars," and the second as "the war which would signify the beginning of real democracy." In both instances a period of deep disillusionment followed, combined with signs of demoralization and degeneration, and also a vexing self-examination.

These decades were also a time of enormous population growth. In 1900 the United States had about 76 million inhabitants. In 1920 there were more than 105 million. In 1940 there were over 131 million, and in 1960 about 180 million.

It was also a time of successive revival movements and meetings, which were often called "crusades." There were crusades for peace and against war, crusades for war and against isolationism, crusades against alcohol and against abortion, crusades for the conversion of this generation (John R. Mott), for a life guided by God (Frank Buchman), for a decision for Christ (Billy Graham), and for a new Pentecost (the charismatic movement).

It was a time of both Puritans and pirates. The Puritan tradition had not yet died out. In 1918, the great Dutch historian Johan Hui-zinga found in the United States, much more than in Europe, a politics "supported by ethical humanitarian elements."[3] It would be a mistake to characterize America exclusively as "the land of the dollar." Repeatedly we are confronted with a high idealism, with a desire to realize and visualize the Kingdom of God.

But the tradition of the pirates also lived on. At the beginning of the century the big capitalists were often called "robber-barons." Gangsters and Mafia organizations infested the country. The Hollywood culture produced a style of living that conflicted with many—if not all—the commandments of God. The sexual revolution opened the gates to a virtual libertinism. America was—and is—in an unconceivable turmoil.

The foundation at stake

It was Sunday, May 22, 1922. The First Presbyterian Church of New York was crowded to capacity. One of the most famous orators of the time was about to assume the pulpit. It did not matter that he was a Baptist, for he was in the regular employ of the church. Neither did it matter that he was a pronounced liberal, for his point of view was shared by many people in the audience. What really mattered was his pronounced eloquence and his persuasive power.

As was customary, his topic had been announced beforehand. He had chosen a provocative title: "Shall the Fundamentalists Win?" His words immediately met with a response. He exclaimed:

> The present world situation smells to heaven. And now, in the presence of colossal problems, which must be solved in Christ's name and for Christ's sake, the Fundamentalists propose to drive out from the Christian Churches all the consecrated souls who do not agree with their theory of inspiration. What immeasurable folly![4]

The preacher continued, expounding his own modern ideas. Why get so excited about the doctrine of the church? The main point, after all, was Christian experience. There were those who held to the Virgin Birth as a historical fact, but others, who were "equally loyal and reverent people," looked upon it simply as a way of explaining a great personality, in line with the ancient world's way of accounting for unusual superiority. Our modern mind can no longer accept a biological miracle. And what must we understand by Christ's coming on the clouds? Some hold that He is literally coming, but others express the exhilarating insight that development is God's way of working out His will until perfection is reached.[5]

This sermon did not go unchallenged. The matter was even

brought to the attention of the General Assembly of the Presbyterian Church. It resulted in the establishment of the well-known procedure which some churches have since used to maintain the outward appearance of holding the right doctrine. The Presbytery of New York requires the teaching and preaching at the New York church to conform to the Bible and the Confession of Faith. The Presbytery largely ignored the Assembly's mandate and proceeded to license candidate H. P. Van Dusen, a young man who refused to affirm belief in the virgin birth of Christ.[6]

Who were these men whom Harry Emerson Fosdick, the preacher in that Presbyterian pulpit in New York, branded "Fundamentalists"? They might be compared to the European Christians who protested against the "spirit of the age" about a hundred years ago. They were not at all a group of narrow-minded, obscure persons, as they have often been depicted as being. According to Berkouwer's description, they were "an American religious trend reacting against the advancing Modernism in our century."[7]

Many church members were startled and alarmed. They felt taken by surprise when the central facts of salvation of the Christian faith were denied, for they regarded those facts of salvation not as secondary in importance but as the very heart of the matter. They looked for a defense and began talking and organizing. They arranged Bible conferences and founded Bible colleges, simple training schools for ministers and evangelists.

Finally a series of booklets were published under the title "The Fundamentals." The financing was provided by two rich laymen, and the project was organized by the evangelist R. A. Torrey and Rev. A. C. Dixon of the Moody Church in Chicago. In these booklets the main points of the Christian faith were expounded and defended, usually in a clear and concise manner.

Those main points have generally been summarized under five headings: the miracles of Christ, His virgin birth, the substitutionary atonement, the verbal inspiration of the Bible, and the physical return of Christ.[8] However, the booklets on "The Fundamentals" appearing between 1910 and 1915 contained much more than this bare outline. K. S. Kantzer lists no fewer than twelve fundamentals. Among the authors were such scholars as James Orr, B. B. Warfield and H. C. G. Moule. Forty-one of the collected essays were directed against negative criticism of the Bible, against evolutionism, and against the errors of the Mormons, the Spiritualists, the Christian Scientists, the Roman Catholics and the Socialists. Forty-nine essays were devoted to such topics as sin and grace, the person and work of Christ, revelation and the spread of the gospel in a positive way.

We should not underestimate the influence of these booklets. There were no fewer than three million copies of them in circulation, offering support and comfort to thousands. Fosdick's angry reaction shows us that he found it worthwhile to vent his indignation publicly.

This current of opinion was characterized as "Fundamentalism" but it later turned out to be a disappointment and did not do a great deal to improve the condition of the churches. Although there was agreement on certain essentials, and opposition to Modernism served as a unifying factor, there was certainly not agreement on everything. How could Arminians and Calvinists, Presbyterians and Baptists, millenarians and non-millenarians cooperate for long?

The problem became acute when a considerable number of the Fundamentalists overemphasized the coming of a thousand-year kingdom, perhaps in the near future, and combined speculation of all sorts with this expectation. To a certain extent this was understandable; it was in part a reaction to those who awaited a kingdom of God similar to a heaven on earth, which was to be realized by means of progressive development through the application of the social gospel.

In contrast to this ideal, these Fundamentalists pointed to Christ's imminent return. Associated with this expectation were many ideas that did not agree with the historic confessions of the Reformation, ideas manifesting the influence of nineteenth-century American *dispensationalism*. These theories had gained a great deal of ground in the twentieth century through the publication of the so-called Scofield Bible.

Several dispensations in the history of God's saving work were distinguished. J. N. Darby, the father of the Plymouth Brethren* and a visitor to America no fewer than seven times, had spoken of three dispensations: the old dispensation, the dispensation of the church, and the dispensation of the coming thousand-year kingdom in which all the promises once given to ancient Israel will be literally fulfilled. His ideas penetrated many circles and prepared the way for C. I. Scofield's reference Bible, which was published in 1909. The Scofield Bible was read eagerly and soon elevated to the status of the standard Bible for many Christians.

---

*Often simply called "the Brethren," they can in turn be divided into the "Open Brethren," who invited everyone to their celebration of the Lord's supper, and the "Exclusive Brethren," who applied a rigid discipline.

Scofield distinguished no fewer than seven dispensations. The sixth of them is the dispensation of the church; it is provisional and transitory in character. The seventh dispensation is that of the thousand-year kingdom. That coming kingdom requires the special attention of believers. A great deal of attention was devoted to the great tribulation at the end of time: the rapture of the believers, which is invisible to the eye; the coming of the Antichrist; and the future of Israel.*

The fact that the dispensationalists called attention to an often neglected part of God's revelation, namely, what the Bible says about the last things, can be appreciated. All too often, however, they went astray by quoting too quickly and too literally many different texts, especially from the book of Daniel and the Revelation to John. Moreover, they tended to overlook the far-ranging significance of the Word of God, which, in the midst of contemporary life, calls us to service even in such areas as politics and social and scientific activities. The dispensationalists had their misgivings about science and culture, for they felt they had been deceived too often by scientists. They called for separation—not reformation—as far as the churches were concerned.

Especially since 1920, neo-Fundamentalism has been a powerful force on the religious scene. It has been marked by the founding of many small churches, and also by incessant internal polemics and an individual pietism. Church members withdrew from the world in all its variety to the seclusion of the inner room, from the big visible churches to the still bigger invisible church.[9]

For the purity of the church

The man who is considered by many to be the leader of the Fundamentalists, even though he often felt ill-at-ease in their company and took exception to the term *Fundamentalist*, was the able Presbyterian theologian *John Gresham Machen* (1881-1937), whom we already met earlier as a student (see p. 33 above). Like his older contemporaries Abraham Kuyper and Herman Bavinck in the Netherlands, Machen has wrestled with the problems of modern theology. He underwent a rather lengthy crisis of faith, in which he was supported by the prayer of his mother, her Bible readings with him in his childhood and also by his daily study of Scripture. Finally

---

*In the same period we find a similar movement in the Netherlands, called the Maranatha movement, under the leadership of Johannes de Heer.

he arrived at the solid conviction that would make him a guide to many people.

Machen was a *man of the church*. One of his contemporaries sketched him in the following words:

> What is it about Dr. Machen that stands out above everything else? . . . To me the answer does not lie in his scholarship, or in his teaching ability, or in his literary skill, great as all these are. In my opinion the one feature about him that overshadows everything else is this: his burning passion to see the Lordship of Christ exercised in his church.[10]

Machen was also a *man of the Bible*. He had a profound knowledge of all the objections stemming from the modern criticism of Scripture, but he was a splendid apologist:

> What a wonderful variety there is in the Bible. There is the rough simplicity of Mark, the unconscious, yet splendid, eloquence of Paul, the conscious literary art of the author of the Epistle to the Hebrews, the matchless beauty of the Old Testament narratives, the high poetry of the Prophets and the Psalms. How much we should lose, to be sure, if the Bible were written all in one style.
>
> We believers in the full inspiration of the Bible do not merely admit that. We *insist* upon it. The doctrine of plenary inspiration does not hold that all parts of the Bible are alike; it does not hold that they are all equally beautiful or even equally valuable; but it holds only that all parts of the Bible are equally true, and that each part has its place.[11]

Gresham Machen

Finally, Machen was a *man of the confes-*

sion. When confessional allegiance was disputed in his church, in spite of solemn pledges, he wrote:

> We believe that the unity of the Presbyterian Church in the United States of America can be safeguarded, not by a liberty of interpretation on the part of the officers of the Church which allows a complete reversal of perfectly plain documents, but only by maintenance of the cooperate witness of the Church. The Church is founded not upon agnosticism but upon a common adherence to the truth of the gospel as set forth in the confession of faith on the basis of the Scriptures.[12]

It was no wonder that this man, who had been a New Testament professor at Princeton since 1915, wanted to witness against the growing Modernism in his church. He witnessed not just by his words but also by his acts.

I referred to that Modernism earlier when I talked about the appearance of Rev. Fosdick in the Presbyterian pulpit in New York. The major Presbyterian assemblies were forced to respond to Modernism. The appalling growth of the new ideas, which defied Scripture and the confession, became apparent in 1924 when the so-called Auburn Affirmation was published. This document was initially signed by 150 Presbyterian ministers—and ultimately by 1300 of them. Although the signers of the Affirmation signified their willingness to remain loyal to their ordination vows, they demanded complete freedom of doctrine with regard to the inspiration of Scripture, the incarnation, the continuing life, and the supernatural power of our Lord Jesus Christ.

At almost the same time, Machen's book *Christianity and Liberalism* was published. In his text, Machen demonstrated in masterly fashion that Modernism was not one of the many facets of Christianity but deviates from it diametrically on all essential points. Machen himself summarized the contents of the book in the following words:

> What is the difference between modern "liberal" religion and historic Christianity? An answer to this question is attempted in the present book. The author is convinced that liberalism on the one hand and the religion of the historic church on the other are not two varieties of the same religion, but two distinct religions proceeding from altogether separate roots. This conviction is supported by a brief setting forth of the teachings of historic Christianity and of the modern liberalism with regard to God and man, the Bible, Christ, salvation, the Church and Christian service. If Christianity, in its historic acceptation, is abandoned, it is at least advisable that men should know what they are giving up and what they are putting in its place.[13]

In his book Machen displayed a great reverence for the majesty of God, just as Karl Barth had done in his commentary on Romans, which had been published a few years earlier. Unlike Barth, however, Machen strongly emphasized the historicity, that is, the once and for all factuality, of the great news of salvation announced in the Bible, just as he had done in 1915 in his inaugural lecture on "History and Faith."

Machen's fearless orthodox position elicited different reactions. His book was read and praised by thousands, but at the same time Machen was personally attacked, sometimes in a rather unfair way, or disparaged.[14] The Board of Directors of Princeton Seminary appointed him professor of apologetics, but the appointment was not endorsed by the assemblies of the church. Machen was even slandered with regard to his personal life.* The General Assembly dismissed the Directors of the Seminary and placed the Seminary under a new board, with the evident intention of "modernizing" the theological school.

Because Machen was deeply convinced that theological students should not be misled with false doctrines, he joined in the founding of a new theological school—Westminster Theological Seminary in Philadelphia. Cooperating with him in this venture were a number of men, including Cornelius Van Til and N. B. Stonehouse. In the new seminary, theology was, and still is, taught in an excellent, scientifically responsible manner.

The establishment of this new theological school did not mean a secession. It was a free act on the part of those Presbyterians who wished to remain faithful to Scripture and the confession. There was another such act in 1933 when the Independent Presbyterian Board for Foreign Missions was established.

In Machen's view there was no alternative. The book *Rethinking Missions* (see p. 208 above) had opened the eyes of many people to the appalling situation in various missionary areas, including people in the Presbyterian Church. Machen wrote:

> The proclamation of the gospel is clearly the joy as well as the duty of every Christian man. But how shall the gospel be propagated? The natural answer is that it shall be propagated through the agencies of the Church—boards of missions and the like. An obvious duty, therefore, rests upon the Christian man of contributing to the agencies of

---

*Because he did not support the "prohibition" of alcoholic beverages, there were some who called him an alcoholic.

the Church. But at this point perplexity arises. The Christian man discovers to his consternation that the agencies of the Church are propagating not only the gospel as found in the Bible and in the historic creeds, but also a type of religious teaching which is at every conceivable point the diametrical opposite of the gospel.[15]

Machen and his friends found themselves forced to act as they did. The boards of the church, seeing the *status quo* in the Presbyterian Church endangered, soon took countermeasures. In 1934 the General Assembly ordered the presbyteries to discipline all church members who were associated with the Independent Board of Foreign Missions. The discipline was undertaken without delay. In 1935 Machen was suspended from the ministry. In 1936 his suspension was upheld by the General Assembly. Others were dealt with in the same way.

Cornelius Van Til

These actions had a serious consequence. At a meeting held on June 11, 1936, the following resolution was adopted and signed by a number of ministers and elders:

In order to continue what we believe to be the true spiritual succession of the Presbyterian Church in the U.S.A., which we hold to have been abandoned by the present organization of that body . . . we, a company of ministers and ruling elders, having been removed from that organization . . . do hereby associate ourselves together with all Christian people who do and will adhere to us, in a body to be known and styled as the Presbyterian Church of America.[16]

This was the beginning of the church that afterward came to be called officially the Orthodox Presbyterian Church. It is deplorable that this new name appeared to be necessary, because another split occurred before long. A number of the separated Presbyterians wanted to imprint upon their new church a pronounced Fundamentalist character. They wanted rulings against the use of alcohol and felt hurt when there was criticism of dispensationalism.[17] They finally formed the Bible Presbyterian Church, in which Rev. Carl McIntire became prominent.

In the midst of this struggle on two fronts, Machen died on New Year's Day, 1937. The day before, lying on his sickbed, he told one of his friends about a vision he had, a vision in which he found himself in heaven. He said: "Sam, it was glorious, it was glorious." And a little later: "Sam, isn't the Reformed faith grand?" The following day he dictated a telegram to his friend and colleague John Murray. The last words of the telegram were: "I'm so thankful for the active obedience of Christ.* No hope without it." Shortly afterward he died.

The influence of the Orthodox Presbyterian Church was considerably greater than its rather small membership would seem to suggest. Students from various countries studied at Westminster Seminary. Among its outstanding professors were John Murray, who taught New Testament, E. J. Young, who taught Old Testament, and the apologist Cornelius Van Til.

The new church maintained good relations with the Christian Reformed Church (see Volume VI, Chap. 7). This church was highly respected by Machen, as is apparent from his favorable comments:

> There is no trouble about Church attendance in the Christian Reformed Church. The reason is that the children do not go to the public schools, but to the "Christian schools" of the Church, where they get a real, solid education with a sturdy Calvinism at the very centre of it. There is nothing like it elsewhere in America. I wish it could leaven the whole lump.[18]

The Christian Reformed Church maintained its confessing character. In the course of time it attracted thousands of students to

---

*"All the obedience which Christ has rendered for me" (Heidelberg Catechism, Answer 60).

its schools for higher education.* It extended its missionary activities especially in Nigeria, while the dogmatics professor in its seminary, Louis Berkhof, wrote a standard book on systematic theology which was popular in other schools and universities.**

Because the origins of the Orthodox Presbyterian Church and the Bible Presbyterian Church were particularly related to the northern part of the United States (which had been separated from the South ever since the Civil War of the nineteenth century as far as the majority of the churches were concerned), a secession from the Southern Presbyterian Church† took place in 1973. In that year delegates from a number of local churches met to decide on a joint course of action. They were concerned about liberal preaching and politicized church programs. A call was issued to "Form a church faithful to Scripture, the Reformed confession, the missionary mandate of the church ordered by Christ in his great commission."

At the second general assembly of this church, in 1974, a name was chosen—the Presbyterian Church in America. The new church started with 70,000 members, 350 churches and 260 ministers. In various respects it cooperates with the Orthodox Presbyterian Church.

Baptist secessions also took place to maintain the purity of the church. In 1932 the General Association of Regular Baptist Churches was founded. In 1946 came the Baptist General Conference and in 1947 the Conservative Baptist Association.

There was an extraordinarily surprising turn of events in the Lutheran Churches (Missouri Synod). In the United States there are a large number of Lutheran churches; the total membership is about 6.8 million. The largest groups are the American Lutheran Church, the United Lutheran Church and the Missouri-Synod Lutheran Church. Since its origin in the nineteenth century, the Missouri-Synod group has always been marked by the maintenance of a strict orthodoxy.

The situation seemed to change, however, after the second world war. Just as in so many other churches where everything seemed to cry out for change and renewal, Scripture and the confession were criticized. New morals were introduced, and there was a great lessening of

---

*Calvin College and Seminary in Grand Rapids; Dordt College in Sioux Center, Iowa; and Trinity Christian College in Palos Heights, Illinois.

**His two-volume *Reformed Dogmatics*, which was revised and reprinted in 1941 as *Systematic Theology* (twelfth printing in 1972).

†Its official name was: Presbyterian Church in the United States.

interest in the fundamental Lutheran question: How do I receive a gracious God? The Missouri-Synod church also found some new leaders, especially at Concordia Seminary in St. Louis. Gradually and carefully the new leaders drifted away, deviating from Scripture and the confession.

It is not surprising that all of this resulted in feelings of uneasiness among the members of the church who did not have a formal theological education. What is more surprising, however, is that such church members managed to gain the upper hand.* They found a spokesman in J. W. Montgomery, a talented young theologian who provided excellent leadership and helped to open the eyes of many through his book *Crisis in Lutheran Theology.*

At the Missouri-Synod convention of 1973, it was decided, among other things, that it was heresy to deny the miracles of the Bible as they are written down. Also beyond denial were the historicity of Adam and Eve as real persons, their fall as a real event, the imputation of the first sin to all later generations, the reliability of what is told about Jesus in the gospels with all their details, the doctrine of angels, the story of Jonah and so forth.

As a consequence of this decision, Dr. J. H. Tietjen, the president of Concordia Seminary, was suspended at the beginning of 1974. A considerable number of the students and professors subsequently founded a new seminary, which they called "Seminex" (Seminary in Exile). But the Synod did not budge, and in these Lutheran churches, at least, liberalism was excluded.

In the other large churches, we find the entire theological spectrum of opinion represented. Although only a small number of orthodox or evangelical men are to be found among the leaders, it would be a mistake to simply characterize those churches as "liberal" or "not orthodox."

The figures have probably changed already since 1957, and the value of an opinion poll should not be overestimated. But it is striking that the result of such a poll taken among ministers of all sorts of churches in 1957 by the magazine *Christianity Today* yielded the following results. Only 12 percent called themselves "liberal," and 14 percent "neo-orthodox." There were 35 percent who chose to call themselves "Fundamentalists," and 37 percent who chose the label "conservative." The difference between the last two categories was

---

*They acquired most of their information from the weekly *Christian News.*

the response to the question whether the Bible should be called "inerrant" or not.*

From Social Gospel to secular theology

Earlier I pointed to the rise of the preaching of the so-called Social Gospel (Chapter 10 of Volume VI). Its flourishing period was the first two decades of the twentieth century.

In 1908 the Federal Council of the Churches of Christ in America promulgated a "Social Creed" in which it was stated (among other things) that the churches must stand for:

> Equal rights and complete justice for all men in all stations of life;
> the right of all men to the opportunity for self-maintenance . . . ;
> the right of workers to some protection against the hardships often resulting from the swift crises of industrial change;
> the principle of conciliation and arbitration in industrial dissensions;
> the abolition of child labor;
> the regulations of the conditions of toil for women as shall safeguard the physical and moral health of the community;
> the abatement of poverty.[19]

For too long the church had been deficient in this area and had kept silent on social problems. In a forceful way, the new creed took a new direction. In the name of a number of American churches, social justice was advocated.

Was the deficiency indeed made up for in this way? In order to answer this question, we should investigate the theological background of the "creed." In vain we look for words such as sin and grace, regeneration and conversion. Nowhere does it mention the necessity of the work of the Holy Spirit.

The theology operative was the theology of the *Social Gospel*. An author who generally sympathizes with the Federal Council of Churches expresses this theology in these words: "Such then were the religious concepts: a moral God, immanent and active in human history through the form of progress, with whom men might cooperate by processes of education, goodwill, and religious faith and service in winning the last and final victory over evil, thus establishing God's reign over a brotherly and Christlike earth."[20]

---

*Recently there have been theologians who say they accept the Bible's infallibility—but not its inerrancy. In that case the term *inerrancy* means freedom from error, while infallibility means freedom from error in what it means to say, in its message.

This kingdom-of-God theology had been developed in Europe in an earlier generation by Albrecht Ritschl. In America it found its most eloquent representative in *Walter Rauschenbusch* (1861-1918), a Baptist minister. From 1902 on, Rauschenbusch was professor of church history at the theological seminary of Rochester.

With great optimism, Rauschenbusch looked for the coming of the Kingdom of God on earth as a necessary result of the evolution of human relations and structures. He viewed the Kingdom not as a millennium behind and above this earth but as one within the horizon of this earth. He wrote:

> Our chief interest in any millennium is the desire for a social order in which the worth and freedom of every last human being will be honored and protected; in which the brotherhood of man will be expressed in the common possession of the economic resources of society.
>
> ... As to the way in which the Christian ideal of society is to come—we must shift from catastrophe to development.[21]

This almost naive optimism concerning social improvements to be expected along the future path of evolution, this neglect of the deep corruption of sin—all of this should be viewed as the background to the fervor with which the Fundamentalists preached their Chiliasm and the necessity of regeneration and conversion. It also sheds light on why this period of Social Gospel preaching was followed by years of disillusionment, when world wars and a social-economic depression swept away this naive trust in humanity's ability to reach perfection slowly but surely.

Between the two world wars, the voice of Reinhold Niebuhr was frequently heard. Niebuhr wanted to be a *realistic* theologian. He called for a renewed knowledge of God and of man himself (see p. 64 above).

But this did not mean the time of the Social Gospel was over. In a totally different yet comparable way, the Social Gospel showed its face anew in the theology of the 1960s, which has been called the "secular theology." This way of thinking was advocated by such men as T. J. J. Altizer, W. Hamilton, P. Van Buren and H. G. Cox.

Both ways of thinking were products of their respective eras. Just as the beginning of the century was marked by a strong, almost exclusive social interest, the second half of the century was characterized by a far-reaching involvement in technical and economic matters and a simultaneous estrangement from God.

Just as the Social Gospel had been tinged with humanism with respect to the central place allocated to the social welfare of man, the secular theology was consistently humanistic in its description of the human situation, for it proceeded from the absence of God. For the first time in the history of the church, a "God is dead" theology appeared.*

Just as the Social Gospel had emphasized that the church exists for the sake of the world, the secular theology consistently drew the same conclusions, and left no place for the peculiar identity of the church as existing for the sake of God. Just as the Social Gospel had proclaimed that the future of the church would be found in *this* world in the victorious emergence of the Kingdom of God, the consistent conclusion drawn by the secular theology was a strong emphasis on the revolutionary character of the gospel that was in the process of liberating the world.

The book that epitomized and popularized this theology for some time and became a best seller was *The Secular City*, by H. G. Cox, a Harvard professor. In the traditional evolutionary manner, Cox explained how primitive man had viewed life and the world in their totality in relation to man and the supernatural. What history shows us, however, is a continuing process of deliverance from all extra-natural and supernatural powers; we see an increasing emancipation resulting in a state of affairs in which we can no longer speak of a "God up there" or a "God out there" but only of a God who is present in the world wherever social justice is done. When we go on strike, for example, or take some measures to improve the human situation, we are God's active collaborators. As a matter of course, we are working not with the God of revelation but with the personified fellowship of men.

Cox linked his own ideas with those of the German theologian Dietrich Bonhoeffer, who was executed by the Hitler regime (see p. 151 above). In his *Letter from Prison*, Bonhoeffer had spoken of a "religionless Christianity." Cox quoted the words: "In Jesus God is teaching man to get along without Him, to become mature, freed from infantile dependencies, fully human."[22]

It is highly dubious, however, whether Bonhoeffer, who in his earlier writings had called for a humble discipleship of Christ, would have agreed with this so-called secular theology. It is a "so-called"

---

*The slogan "God is dead" originated with the philosopher Friedrich Nietzsche, but it had never been used in such a way by theologians. T. J. J. Altizer deliberately associated himself with Nietzsche in his book *The Gospel of Christian Atheism* (1966).

theology, for it has rightly been pointed out that this way of thinking comes into direct and final conflict with historic Christianity.[23]

Pentecostals and charismatics

The date was January 1, 1901. Agnes Ozman, a student at Bethel Bible College in Topeka, Kansas, had started the day as usual by reading from the Bible. While meditating, she was struck by the thought that the New Testament believers received the Holy Spirit after hands were laid upon them (Acts 19:6). Acting on an impulse, she stood up and went to Charles Parham, the president of the college, to ask him to lay hands upon her in Biblical fashion. Initially he refused, but when she insisted he said a short prayer and laid his hands on her head. What happened next was later described by Agnes Ozman in the following words:

> It was as his hands were laid upon my head that the Holy Spirit fell upon me and I began to speak in tongues, glorifying God. I talked several languages, and it was clearly manifest when a new dialect was spoken. I had the added joy and glory my heart longed for and a depth of the presence of the Lord within that I had never known before. It was as if rivers of living water were proceeding from my innermost being . . . I was the first one to speak in tongues in the Bible school . . . I told them not to seek for tongues but to seek for the Holy Ghost.[24]

This date, January 1, 1901, has been called the birthday of the Pentecostal movement.[25] This does not mean, however, that what we meet here is a totally new phenomenon. The experience of Finney (see Volume VI, Chap. 10) agrees with that of the students of Topeka, and Finney was in turn the heir of a Methodist tradition. Agnes had been reared as a Methodist and had contacted the Holiness movement established by Finney. Thus she was moving down a familiar road.

But her embarkation on that road was a milestone, for her experience was soon shared by many. It seemed as if the time was ripe for this emotional-ecstatic form of experiential religion.

In his well-known book about cults, Kurt Hutten draws a comparison with an earlier movement, Spiritualism, which had also tried to give an answer to "the hunger questions of souls underfed by rationalism." This rationalism, which in the nineteenth century can better be called Modernism, had diluted the message of the church and transformed that message into a cultural or social program decorated with Christian terms. A reaction simply had to follow. We find this reaction not just in Fundamentalism but also in Pentecostalism.[26]

In America many new churches and sects were founded. In general they agreed with Fundamentalism, but they parted company with Fundamentalism with regard to one central doctrine—that of the Holy Spirit. The general secretary of the largest of these groups of churches, the Assemblies of God, said of his group:

> This Council considers it a serious disagreement with the Fundamentals for any minister among us to teach contrary to our distinctive testimony, that the baptism of the Holy Spirit is regularly accompanied by the initial physical sign of speaking in other tongues as the Spirit of God gives utterance, and that we consider it inconsistent and unscriptural for any minister to hold credentials with us who attacks as error our distinctive testimony.[27]

But the Pentecostal movement did not only spread through America. It also spread through Norway, Finland and Sweden, through Germany, England and the Netherlands.[28] Influential in its spread was the Norwegian Methodist preacher T. B. Barratt who, according to his own testimony, received the baptism of the Holy Spirit in Los Angeles in 1906,[29] and Dr. R. A. Torrey of Chicago, who traveled through a number of European countries.*

Especially in Germany, there was great enthusiasm for some time in the circles of the so-called "Gemeinschaftbewegung"**—until the great disenchantment struck. In 1909, 60 leaders of this movement stated in the "Declaration of Berlin": "the so-called Pentecostal movement is not from above, but from below"; it has "much in common with Spiritualism"; it is marked by "a superficial knowledge of sin and grace, conversion and regeneration"; and it propounds the error of the "pure heart" (Perfectionism).[30]

These were words of disenchantment, of great disappointment. High expectations had been raised, but they had not been fulfilled. The question arises: What were the essential features of the Pentecostals, the people of the Pentecostal movement?

We must speak in the first place about a kind of *dualism*. The Pentecostal groups recognize a twofold gospel, two kinds of operation of the Spirit, two kinds of believers. They do not deny that the gospel is being preached in many churches, but only *they* bring the *full* gospel, the gospel that not only witnesses of the cross long ago but

---

*In Blankenburg, Germany, he said: "It is one thing to be regenerated by the Holy Spirit; it is another thing to be baptized by the Holy Spirit."

**"Community movement," groups of Pietists who had already been organizing Bible circles and revival meetings for a long time.

also of the dynamic operation of the Spirit right now. They do not deny that the gifts of faith and conversion belong to the work of the Spirit, but they consider it more important to be baptized subsequently with or in the Spirit. They do not deny there are believers outside their own circle, but the higher believers are with them. Some of them have even conquered sin completely and don't need to pray the fifth petition of the Lord's Prayer any longer.[31]

We must also speak of the introduction of *ecstasy* as a mark of faith. This is particularly evident in the emphasis on speaking in tongues, and it also comes through in how the Pentecostals praise God as if in a trance.

In addition, the Pentecostals accentuate *faith healing*. There is no need for a believer to be sick. "Stronger than all sickness is the will of God to heal."[32] Well-known faith healers are Hermann Zais, Oral Roberts, T. L. Osborn and Katharyn Kuhlman.

Finally, the Pentecostals share with many other Christians the *rejection of infant baptism*. They claim a child cannot yet give account of his faith in Christ. Even if a believer maintains his membership in the church in which he was baptized as an infant, he has himself "rebaptized" in a Pentecostal meeting if he goes along with this line of thought.

At this point we have arrived at the conspicuous matter by which

At a recent Pentecostal meeting in New York's Statler-Hilton, dozens found themselves speaking in tongues.

so-called *neo-Pentecostalism* is distinguished from the original Pentecostalism. The neo-Pentecostals favor retaining membership in one of the Protestant churches or the Roman Catholic Church while at the same time becoming part of the ever-growing *charismatic movement*.

An ever-growing movement indeed! According to one of its principal spokesmen, D. J. du Plessis, it includes a communion of more than ten million people, who are to be found in almost every country in the world.[33] Neo-Pentecostalism has been called the fastest growing wing of Protestantism in the Western hemisphere.[34] It is noteworthy that many Roman Catholics, including the Belgian cardinal L. J. Suenens, participate in this movement.

The causes are the same as the ones mentioned before, but in our time they have been intensified. Ours is a world in constant crisis. Much of the current preaching is too sterile for many people, too preoccupied with social-political questions. On the other side, streams of power are promised to each one who opens up his heart to the Holy Spirit.

How is it possible for the Roman Catholic Church, which attributes so much value to the grace given in the sacraments, to open its doors to these people who put so much emphasis on baptism with the Holy Spirit? The Dutch professor W. van't Spijker tries to answer this question by pointing to a declaration that Father Kilian McDonnell drafted for the international conference of charismatic leaders in Rome in 1973.[35] In typical Roman Catholic fashion, we find talk of baptism with the Holy Spirit replaced by such terminology as "actualizing of the Holy Spirit," "waking up of the initial sacraments," and "actualizing of the already potentially received grace." Still clearer is the reference to the "manifestation of baptism, in which the hidden grace of baptism breaks through toward personal experience."

At the third meeting of this international conference, in 1975, the pope himself addressed the meeting. He declared that "attachment to the chair of Peter is an authentic sign of the operation of the Spirit." In such a way the charismatic movement can indeed find shelter under the broad wings of the church of Rome, which is still elastic, just as the "fratricelli" or little brothers of Francis of Assisi were accepted long ago in the church of Innocent III.

We should realize, however, that in all churches the Pentecostal movement has raised the question of the significance of the Holy Spirit and has called upon all Christians to reflect on their personal participation in the gifts of the Spirit and the fruits of the Spirit. All

Christians are being reminded that they are supposed to be temples of the Holy Spirit.

Nevertheless, a major obstacle remains. The Pentecostal movement sticks to its characteristic doctrine of the "second baptism." Its "full gospel" and its demand for a sign places the cross and justification in the center no more; the congregation is split into Christians of the first rank and Christians of the second rank.

13

Recent Times

Adrift

When we try to find out what is really going on in the present age, when we try to discern the *spirit of the age*, we are immediately confronted with a problem: some people argue that it is no longer possible to speak of the spirit of an age, because the unity in the pattern of life is gone. Evidently there are many spirits at work.[1]

To demonstrate what this means, Rev. M. P. van Dijk points to a show that was televised early in 1978 by the I.K.O.N., a Dutch interdenominational association. The show was called the "Faith, Hope and Love Show."

> In this show different people get the floor. The one is faithful in his or her married life, the other is not. There are homophiles and homosexuals. A homosexual woman gets a child with the help of artificial insemination and includes this child in her homosexual partnership. A man lives with two wives: three beds.
>
> The I.K.O.N. does not judge. It neither approves nor disapproves. It gives all these people the opportunity to speak for themselves. They should know themselves what to do. Does it fit into their pattern of life? Do they become happy? . . .
>
> Looking at these broadcasts, we get the impression that anything is

permitted as long as it does not frustrate man or stand in the way of his freedom or prevent him from going the way to his own self.

Spirits of the time! What we see around us is the widest variety of permissive behavior, the most excessive licentiousness, the most unrestrained individualism. But doesn't all of this testify to the presence of *one* spirit of our time, that of *secularism*, that of the inscription in the crown of Selma Lagerlöf's antichrist, "My kingdom is of *this* world"?

In the 1930s, the Dutch poet H. Marsman wrote these prophetic words after having said goodbye to Christianity:

> Empty is heaven
> in eternity blood
> in the dome of night
> only cinders and soot.
>
> Look, the earth is red
> from the tragic wine;
> paradise is dead,
> but man becomes great.

Marsman had absorbed Nietzsche, the Nietzsche of the coming superman as well as the Nietzsche who declared that God is dead. At the same time Marsman was tormented to an increasing extent by an existential fear of death. His own death bears an almost symbolic character; he was on a ship that was torpedoed by the Germans in 1940 when he tried to escape to England.

"Empty is heaven." We now have our rockets and satellites. "Man becomes great." With our computers we can now make calculations with lightning speed. Thanks to our airplanes, we can now enjoy breakfast in Paris and lunch in New York. Thanks to our medical techniques, we can forestall the arrival of unwanted children. Thanks to progressing mechanization, we can shorten working hours more and more. The time of *homo ludens*, of man totally devoted to the joy of play, seems to be at hand. In such a time, why would we still need a God?

Here we have arrived at another characteristic of our time—the *atheism* built into secularism. Atheism is not only to be found in Russia and Communist China (where every good Communist is required to be a confessing atheist), it is increasingly permeating Western society as well. It is remarkable that the well-known Dutch author Godfried Bomans, who was of Roman Catholic origin, was apparently haunted at the end of his life by the question: Is there really a personal God?* To many people, belief in a personal God belongs to an era of the past.

God has become a projection of our human spirit. This is what Feuerbach had taught in the nineteenth century. Freud reached the same conclusion via psychoanalysis, and the Dutch author Simon Vestdijk repeated it.[2] God is a projection of our dreams and efforts, of our desires and fears. God is nothing but a specter called forth by our imagination.

It is an unprecedented feature of our time that this atheism, which has long been propounded in theory by philosophers and artists of various kinds, has been adopted by certain *theologians*, who have thereby denied and forfeited their title. We have already observed this happening in America. The same phenomenon took place in western Europe.

The idea of God, which had indeed become nothing but an idea, was manipulated. The idea of Jesus was likewise manipulated to such a degree that theology lost its character and became a branch of sociology. Characteristic is the confession of faith voiced by the theologian Dorothee Sölle, which begins:

> I believe in God
> who did not make the world prepared and ready
> as a thing that should stay as it is;
> who does not reign according to eternal laws
> which are fixed with immutability,
> neither according to natural ordinances
> in which rich and poor are found.
>
> I believe in God
> who wants the protest of all that lives
> and the change of all situations
> by our labor,
> by our politics.
>
> I believe in Jesus Christ
> who was right when he
> ("a single powerless man" as we all are)
> worked for the change of all situations
> until he perished by it.
>
> I believe in Jesus Christ
> who rises in our life
> in order to set us free . . .[3]

---

*According to an opinion poll taken in 1979, faith in a personal God has declined by 24 percent among Roman Catholics since 1966. Only one-third of those who were questioned still believed in a personal God.

Equally characteristic is a confession of faith recited at the beginning of the 1970s at a Reformed youth service in the Netherlands:

Jesus, it is said
that you can give us
life eternal,
and acts are mentioned
and words are quoted
which you never did
which you never said
because you were
a man as we are.[4]

The one true God who has revealed Himself in His Word[5] is being denied. Such a denial also comes through in the manipulation of the idea of God. We hear talk of a God-in-genesis, a God who develops with nature, with men, on the way to a better future. Thus, *evolutionism*, along with secularism and atheism, is characteristic of the spirit of our age.

In the nineteenth century there were already a number of theologians who accepted the theory of evolution as an incontrovertible fact. To some theologians it has now become the canvas on which they paint their theological systems. The "creation, fall, redemption" order has been changed into a different order: "becoming, wrestling, liberation."

The word *liberation* points to another prominent element in the spirit of the age—the promotion of evolution by way of *revolution*. The changes we await are to be brought about by violent means, if need be. We are confronted here with the same paradoxical situation we encounter in connection with Karl Marx's philosophy of history; history unavoidably develops from one historical situation to the other until the classless society finally arrives. On the other hand, people, particularly the dispossessed, are called to create revolutionary situations and to make the most of them in order to hasten the coming of the final phase.

Finally, it is clear that all these forms of the spirit of the time, i.e. secularism, atheism, evolutionism and revolutionary action, run counter to the revelation given in God's Word. Motives are repeatedly borrowed from God's Word to support or illustrate a preconceived system. But no justice is done to the unity of God's revelation, to the non-repeatable facts of salvation, to the finished work of Jesus Christ, to the constant witness of the church throughout the ages, nor to the indwelling of the Holy Spirit.

Two typical philosophies

First of all we should take account of the life and work of the Jewish scholar *Ernst Bloch* (born in 1885). Although Bloch actually belongs to the generation of Karl Barth, he has drawn the attention of large numbers of theologians only in recent decades.

Bloch taught philosophy in Leipzig until 1933. When Hitler took power, he emigrated to New York via Zurich. He returned to Leipzig in 1948 but was dismissed by the Communist authorities in 1956 because of his protest against the Russian intervention in Hungary. Since 1961 he has lived in West Germany.

Bloch is not an orthodox Marxist but a neo-Marxist. He objects to Russian totalitarianism and looks forward to the coming of a free socialist state with a human face. He quotes the Bible extensively in support of his ideas, but he states explicitly that he wants to read the Bible along the "via heretica," the road of the heretics. Those heretics were right all along, and Bloch counts among his spiritual ancestors men such as Marcion and Origen, Joachim of Fiore and Thomas Münzer, and especially Ludwig Feuerbach.[6]

It is not my intention to introduce Bloch's social and political ideas. My concern is simply to show something of the way in which he puts the horses of the Bible, both Old Testament and New, before the coach of his inexorable atheism.

Bloch is an atheist. Heaven is empty and man is God. Man is free and can renovate all things. Therefore he can establish a classless society. On the way to this society, Biblical data as interpreted by Bloch can render valuable service.

In the Old Testament we meet Baal as well as Yahweh. In Bloch's view Baal is the Creator-God, the Ruler who requires subjection, while Yahweh is the Liberator-God, the God of the exodus, the God who leads man out of the house of bondage. Similarly, we find two creation stories and two prototypes of man. According to Genesis 1, man is created in the image of God. Thus he is in principle a god himself. When the serpent said, "You will be like God," this was a statement of liberation and promise. According to Genesis 2, however, man is created from the dust of the earth, which makes him servile, a slave.

Cain was the first cultured man. He did not put up with servitude but built a city instead. Korah, Dathan and Abiram were good revolutionaries.

When the Jewish prophet Jesus appears on the historical scene in the New Testament, he brings the sword and preaches revolution. He dies a martyr's death for the liberation of man. Paul was a reactionary who transformed the gospel of Christ into the message of reconciliation with an angry God. The essence of Christianity as it bears the stamp of Paul consists in a self-humiliation unworthy of man.

This is only a small sample of Bloch's ideas. We must agree with the Dutch professor A. J. Visser when he says: "Ernst Bloch nowadays meets with a response in Christian theology which is more alarming than the capitulation of so many of the German theologians in the time of Hitler to the sweet tunes of the *Blut-und-Boden* charmer. It is more dangerous for this reason, that 'German Christians,' by definition, could only be found in Germany, while the Blochianism that falsely pretends to be Christian does not stop at any border."[7]

We should also take a look at *Herbert Marcuse* (born in 1898). Like Bloch, he was a German Jew. He taught in Germany (Frankfurt) and emigrated in 1933 to America, where he occupied the chair of philosophy at the University of California in San Diego. Marcuse has been called the "father of the students' resistance" and "the prophet and high priest of the radical opposition to present society."[8]

To a lesser extent than with Bloch, we meet Biblical themes in his work. And like Bloch, he criticizes orthodox Marxism and the Russian pseudo-Marxism that has degenerated into a totalitarian bureaucracy. The world should be totally changed. The students, in particular, are called to promote or cause that change by means of revolutionary and even anarchistic activities.

Why should the students be chosen rather than anyone else? Marcuse is convinced that not much can be expected from the masses of the people. The masses have prospered too much; they have become "one-dimensional men." According to Marcuse, in their view the real is the same as the ideal. Thus they do not see their less-than-ideal condition.

An elite will therefore have to take the lead with revolutionary elan.* The elite will have to be recruited from among the outcasts of the earth. Those outcasts are no longer to be sought among the masses of the workers but among the permanently unemployed, the dropouts, those without social responsibility—particularly the students.

First the universities should be democratized. Then the entire establishment should be overturned. Via this "dialectical route," a

---

*Here Marcuse manifests an undeniable affinity with Lenin (see p. 84 above).

new future will dawn, a future in which man will no longer be subject to the tyranny of the system.

Clearly, these ideas have met with a response. Verkuyl mentions the names of such terrorists as Cohn Bendit, Rudi Dutschke, Angela Davis, and the Black Panthers. These ideas also represent the opposite of the Christian idea of salvation, and they are irreconcilable with the best humanistic ideals as well. Zuidema therefore speaks of "a post-Christian doctrine of salvation and a pseudo-way of salvation."[9]

There are two major questions unanswered by the violent theories of Marcuse. The first one is: What do you think about man? Does Marcuse have even the slightest inkling of the dark secret of sin, in which all men share without any distinction? Verkuyl rightly says: "He forgets that we all need conversion and regeneration."

The second question is: What do you think about the future? What is the basis for Marcuse's conviction that a swift execution will be followed by a new resurrection, a fierce period of terror by a new type of man, a violent revolution by a new joyful world? At this juncture J. W. Montgomery rightly points to the historical lesson that revolutionary governments are generally more repressive and unfree than the societies they overthrew.[10]

Both Bloch and Marcuse have given expression to something of the temper of our time. Each in his own way has influenced the thinking of some theologians to whom we now turn.

Time-bound theology

The term *time-bound* is used repeatedly in current theological parlance. If this expression is used to indicate how each generation has its own character and each historical period, however delineated, bears its own stamp, then there is nothing wrong with the term. Unfortunately, this term is usually used to indicate that historical data are all of relative value. What is spoken of as "time-bound" may have some value for a certain time and may represent the thinking of a certain period or age, but that value does not carry over into our time. The ideas in question have had their day.

We know from the Bible how the Jews, perhaps in the fifth century before Christ, thought about creation. Modern man must somehow interpret that creation story. Yet the story itself is time-bound. Today we know much more, and we cannot believe such a story any longer.

We know from the Bible how the original church pictured the life of Christ. We know what stories were told about His birth, His miraculous power, and His resurrection and ascension. These matters, too, have a deep meaning, but they are worded in a time-bound way. We cannot repeat them any more as they are written. This, at least, is the viewpoint of a large number of present-day theologians.

The well-known German exegete Ernst Käsemann once said we should free ourselves from "the incredible superstition that everywhere in the canon nothing but the true faith is proclaimed."[11] In 1970 a symposium was published, edited by Käsemann. It was the result of the joint efforts of 15 professional theologians—13 Protestants and two Roman Catholics. The title was "The New Testament as Canon."

The contributions were not all exactly alike in character, but in an extensive review Gerhard Maier concluded that the following traits occur in each of them. (1) These exegetes no longer conceive of the New Testament as a unit but rather as a collection of various testimonies which contradict each other and have varying degrees of validity. (2) The canon cannot be equated with the Word of God. (3) For more than 200 years theologians have been searching for the "canon in the canon," i.e. the binding Word of divine authority, but have failed to find it thus far. (4) The result is an uncontrolled subjectivity concerning what should have divine authority. (5) The Roman Catholic theologians finally take refuge in the official teaching of the church, and the Protestants in the spiritual experience of the congregation.[12]

It is most remarkable how these theologians, who often speak in a peremptory tone, forget to mention that their thought, too, is "time-bound." Because they have not believed in the Scripture that cannot be broken (John 10:35), they are repeatedly tossed about on the waves of the spirit of the age. Their words are rendered out of date as soon as they are printed.

Think of the Dutch Roman Catholic theologian E. Schillebeekx, who goes to great lengths to show how the authors of the gospel stories spoke the language of their own time and worked within the framework of their time. We should likewise use the framework of our time, e.g. existentialism or Marxism. In Schillebeekx's opinion, Jesus did not call Himself the Christ, the Son of God. His death was the murder of a prophet, to which the words of Isaiah 53 and the curse on the one who hangs on a tree (Gal. 3:13) were applied retrospectively. Jesus Himself did not consider His death to be an atoning death. The tomb was not empty, Jesus did not appear to His disciples, and there was no resurrection. Neither was there a virgin birth in Bethlehem.

M. P. van Dijk rightly concludes that man and the thinking of the present have become the yardsticks here.[13] We will now consider the position of some other theologians who have been influential in our time.

Let us be honest (J.A.T. Robinson)

In 1963 a provocative book by the Anglican bishop of Woolwich appeared—*Honest to God*. The book was such a staggering success that within two years, some 350,000 copies of the English edition had been sold. That total was surpassed by the translations. The combined world sales of the book were close to one million.[14]

Apparently the bishop spoke the language of his time. Whether it was also the language of his office is another question. When he was installed in office in 1959, he promised "to be ready with all faithful diligence, to banish and drive away all erroneous and strange doctrines contrary to God's Word."

What were his opinions with regard to the Word of God? He was not in agreement, at any rate, with the confession of the church, but he was very much in agreement with the theologians whose ideas he had popularized in his book, namely, D. Bonhoeffer, R. Bultmann and P. Tillich.

Bonhoeffer, during the last period of his life, was the man of religionless Christianity and the anonymous Christian. We have come to know Bultmann as the existential theologian who emphasized personal encounter and removed from the Bible all "time-bound" myths. Tillich originally belonged to the circle of Barth's religious-socialist friends, but he definitively dissociated himself from Barth in 1935.[15] At that time he had already emigrated to America after having been dismissed as professor under the Hitler regime in 1933. He built up a totally new theological system, which has often been spoken of as a "theology of being," in which God is called the "Ground of being" and faith is characterized as "ultimate concern." From this choice of words it is already apparent how Tillich's terminology makes more of a philosophical or theosophical impression than a theological impression. Faith in a personal God, a historical fall into sin,* the accomplished work of Christ, the possibility of prayer—all of these elements are totally absent for him.

Robinson absorbed all these ideas, which went far beyond the

---

*In Tillich's system, creation and fall coincide, as was the case with the ancient Gnostics.

reach of the ordinary church member. His book was simply meant to be a popularization of many current schools of thought.

What does Robinson mean by this talk of being "honest to God"? He means to say that present-day man, the man of the space age, can no longer believe in a God above us ("up there") or even a God outside of us, but only in a God who is identical with the deepest ground of our being. An affirmation is called theological not because it is related to a special being called God but because it asks ultimate questions about the meaning of being.

He speaks a similar language when it comes to the atonement:

> The whole scheme of a supernatural Being coming down from heaven to "save" mankind from sin, in the way that a man might put his finger into a glass of water to rescue a struggling insect, is frankly incredible to man "come of age" . . . The "full, perfect and sufficient sacrifice, oblation and satisfaction for the sins of the whole world," supposed to have been "made" on Calvary, requires, I believe, for most men today more demythologizing even than the Resurrection.[16]

Robinson claims Jesus never called Himself God. He was not the Word Incarnate but "the Man for others." The important point is simply to follow Jesus' example by showing love to others. That love *(agapé)* is the only imperative principle of Christian action. Robinson plainly states that "nothing by itself can always be labeled as wrong." Sexual relations before marriage, for example, may perhaps be wrong or perhaps right. The important thing is the presence or absence of love.

What we find here disagrees radically with historic Christianity.[17] Nevertheless, what Robinson brought to expression was indeed to be found in a great many hearts. His countryman

John A.T. Robinson

Alasdaire MacIntyre concluded: "We can now see that Dr. Robinson's voice is not just that of an individual, that his book testifies to the existence of a whole group of theologies which have retained a basic theistic vocabulary but acquired an atheistic substance."[18]

Back to history (W. Pannenberg)

While Robinson is not in the first place a professional theologian and therefore can perhaps be credited with speaking in an intelligible way, Wolfhart Pannenberg is a German dogmatics professor who, perhaps for that reason, does not always speak in lucid terms. In fact, some have hailed his writings as coming from a man who "holds to a fully historical resurrection of Christ,"[19] while others claim that he only *seems* to believe in the resurrection.[20]

The resurrection plays an important role in Pannenberg's theology, at any rate. He disclaims Bultmann's attempt to qualify it as a myth, as well as Barth's attempt to qualify it as an event but not as history. Pannenberg wants to break away from the existential way of thinking, which in the final analysis ascribes importance only to what happens with or in man. What Pannenberg wants is real history and a real resurrection.

Does this mean that Pannenberg accepts the authority, unity and simplicity of Scripture? Nothing could be further from the truth! Pannenberg's way of thinking is completely evolutionary and critical of Scripture. In his book *Revelation as History*,[21] he argues that Jesus consistently accepted the Jewish tradition concerning God, and that this Jewish conception of God originated in seven different traditions. One of them was the tradition concerning Yahweh, the tribal God of the Kenites, whose origin is probably to be distinguished from the God of the exodus.

As far as Christ's resurrection is concerned, Pannenberg finds two traditions in the Bible. There is the tradition of the appearances as Paul sums them up in I Corinthians 15, and also the tradition of the discovery of the empty tomb, about which we read in the gospels. The latter tradition is marked by legendary features, but Paul was clearly referring to historical facts.[22] For that reason the resurrection should be considered a historical fact, a fact of general history.

In Pannenberg's view there is only one history. He does not distinguish between general and special revelation. In the entirety of history, the work of God unfolds in the direction of the future.

Is God a person? Pannenberg's language is obscure here. He writes:

> God, as the power of the future, is not a thing, not an object at hand that one would be able to consider from a distance or go beyond. He appears neither as a Being among others nor as the quiet background of all that is, but as the timeless Being opposite to the things. Yet His Being is perhaps to be conceived of as the power of the future.[23]

God is the power of the future. What this means, according to the description of M. P. van Dijk, is that "we modern men are no longer able to believe the fairy tale of a Father in heaven, of safety and security."[24] God *is* not—He *becomes*. The future is a divine way of existence. God is not above all things, ruling them, for in that case human freedom would be threatened. "As the power of the future, God must go beyond all things that are, because only then, as power of the future that goes beyond all things that are, can He guarantee our freedom, our freedom to go, like Him, beyond all things that are, to break through all existing situations, if need be by means of revolution."[25]

Clearly, what we find in this kind of argumentation is no longer theology but theosophy, no longer theism but pantheism. Historical facts are accepted because they fit into a certain framework. This will strike us even more forcefully when we investigate the next modes of thinking.

Wolfhart Pannenberg

Hope—for what . . . ? (J. Moltmann)

The subdued sound made by Pannenberg becomes a trumpet blast when Jügen Moltmann comes along. Moltmann cries out to rally all men of good will to revolutionary action.

Moltmann belongs to the same generation as Pannenberg. Between 1945 and 1948, he shared the hard lot of the German prisoners of war. Later he was appointed professor in Wuppertal, in Bonn, and finally in Tübingen, where he was influenced by Ernst Bloch, who was also teaching there.*

When Moltmann's book *Theology of Hope* appeared in 1965, the expectations of many orthodox church members ran high again. Here was a man who would give prominent attention to some long-neglected elements of divine revelation, the very elements that were of the greatest importance for the present age—hope for a better future and a concern on the part of the church of Christ to share the lot of the "outcasts of the earth."

On closer investigation, however, it became apparent that *Biblical* hope was entirely out of the picture for Moltmann. To further the cause of liberation, he was recommending revolutionary methods not in keeping with the letter and spirit of the gospel.

How did Moltmann interpret the Bible? His exegetical principle was eschatology, the doctrine of the last things. Just as Luther viewed justification by faith alone as the central theme of the Bible, hope for the future is the central theme in Moltmann's reading of the Bible.

In the Old Testament, according to Moltmann, the exodus is fundamental. Yahweh, the God of Israel's tribes at Mount Sinai, liberates the people from their bonds and guides them to a new future.

In the New Testament the resurrection of Christ opens a new future. Christ's resurrection is the beginning of the general resurrection which is to come. Properly speaking, it coincides with the general resurrection; that is to say, it is the general resurrection projected back into the past. The question of the historical character of Christ's resurrection therefore makes no sense. If we were to emphasize it as an event that happened once and for all, we would be appreciating something *static*. We would have understood nothing of the dynamics of the working of God toward the future. The word *resurrection*

---

*Bloch has been characterized by Moltmann as "a Marxist with a Bible in his hand."

should really be placed between quotation marks, just like the word *God*.

That God is the God of liberation is a commonplace in Moltmann's books, but is He really a personal God? In Moltmann's view this question again bespeaks a static way of thinking. God is immanent in history; in other words, He *is* not—He *becomes*.

This is the freedom of God, which corresponds to the freedom of man on his way to the Kingdom of God. In the vanguard is the church. In conformity with the image of Christ, the church still shares the suffering of creation, but in conformity with that same image in this world (not in a world to come), the church will rule over all things in a realm of peace.

The way to this realm must be paved by criticism of the existing situation, by agitation, revolution:

> By undermining and demolishing all barriers, whether of religion, race, education, or class, the community of Christians proves that it is the community of Christ. This could indeed become the new identifying mark of the church in our world, that it is composed, not of equal and like-minded men, but of dissimilar men, indeed of former enemies. The way toward this goal of a new humanity involving all nations and languages is, however, a revolutionary way.[26]

In one of his subsequent works Moltmann expresses himself even more clearly. To the marks of the church (i.e. holiness, apostolocity, catholicity) he adds a new one, that of witnessing to the liberation of the world. Instead of communion of the saints he calls for the communion of friends. A friend, in his definition, is any man who loves freedom, this is why he does not favor missionary activities but calls for communion with other religions instead. He even speaks of Hinduistic, Mohammedan, Shintoistic and animistic forms of Christianity and proposes to invite all men to the Lord's supper.[27]

Jürgen Moltmann

In order to realize the hope of the world, Moltmann does not shrink from recommending violent means. "The problem of violence and non-violence is an illusory problem. There is only the question of the justified and unjustified use of force and the question of whether the means are proportionate to the ends."[28]

The German theologian Dorothee Sölle calls for liberation in a similar vein. She is as eager as Moltmann for political action. This was expressed concretely in the "political evening prayers" she organized in Cologne in 1968.

In those evening prayers, which followed the order of information, meditation and action, a special topic was dealt with each time, such as the situation in Czechoslovakia, Greece, Vietnam, or Indonesia, or the housing shortage, or military service and conscientious objection, or aid to underdeveloped countries. We should note with appreciation how concrete Christian sympathy and action were stimulated. On the other hand, it should not escape us that the content of the adjective *Christian* was totally turned to the left. Sölle herself had no doubts about this: "Already the bare fact that we belong to the Northern rich world makes us collaborators in sin . . . We can learn much more from our socialist brothers than from our theological fathers."[29] Her gospel, too, is a "pseudo-Christian activism."[30]

Liberation—from what . . . ? (G. Gutierrez)

It was only a single step from Pannenberg to Moltmann. And it is only a single step from Moltmann to Gutierrez and the other Latin American theologians who think the same way he does—the so-called theologians of revolution. One of them described the differences between the European theologians and the South American Marxist theologians in this manner: in the old world, theory and dialogue come first, while in Latin America, which is much more backward in social and economic respects, action and deeds come first.[31]

Something must be done. To Castro we must offer the hand of fellowship. The name of Che Guevara, who died as a guerilla fighter in the Bolivian jungle, should be inscribed in the book of the martyrs.[32] Machine guns must be paid for and used.

How can all of this be justified, theologically speaking? It is only a single step from the resurrection of Christ to the revolution of Christ. In this theology Christ is presented as the rebel who chose the side of the poor and oppressed. In the present-day social revolution, the salvation of Christ assumes a concrete form.

In his book *Theology of Liberation* (1973), G. Gutierrez sketches the entire process of history as a great process of emancipation, as a movement toward the future that will finally be realized when the Kingdom of God has come. In Christ all of mankind has already become in principle a temple of God. With His Spirit, Christ is in all men, whether they know it or not. Essentially there are no unbelievers.

All we are waiting for is the kingdom to be realized. It will only come when the means of production fall into the hands of the community.[33]

The future is sometimes pictured in idealistic terms:

> Bad faith will at any rate be replaced by good faith. Existence will be replaced by coexistence; operation becomes co-operation. The future is a co-production, baptized in communion. False identities such as Negroes, foreign workers, Germans, and poor have been abolished. Each man is personally responsible for his neighbor, and all men are together responsible for other men. Nobody perishes from starvation anymore. Every tear will be wiped away. Even deserts will blossom like gardens of roses. Swords will be beaten into plowshares. Nations will be walled in no more and will destroy each other no longer. They live together in one humanitarian kingdom of the world.[34]

The road to the future is one of violent revolution. One theologian has spelled out a series of revolutionary procedures, beginning with presentation techniques. Those who oppose "the establishment" and "the system" should open their mouths and write letters to the editor. They should organize protest marches. All of this finally leads to illegal techniques. There is a place for burglaries, occupations, raids, sabotage and even hostage-taking.

The present-day structures of society are evil through and through; they represent sin. The clearing away of those structures is good; by such action the new world is ushered in. Salvation has become completely worldly, and the Savior has been made completely a king of this world. Therefore the criticism raised by Dr. G. de Ru is perfectly to the point:

> There is much talk nowadays of "sinful structures" and of "structural conversion." In my view these are impossible combinations of words, theologically speaking; they are instances of an inexact usage of terms that occasions considerable misunderstanding. Sin and conversion are only directly connected with the relation between man and God. Structures, economic systems and forms of government are not sinful in themselves, and they cannot repent. They certainly can and should be changed if they are unsound, unjust, cruel, products of human egoism. But what is the use of such changes if men themselves, who accomplish the change, refuse to talk about sin and repentance? With man something must first happen before structural changes will have any salutary effect. That's the reason why the Bible does not point to the changing of structures in the first place but to the changing of individuals.[35]

H. Algra has pointed out—correctly—that the theologians of revolution do indeed recognize evil, but they always blame others instead of talking about the conversion of the sinner.[36]

Infection

The "Vermittlungstheologie" (mediating theology) of the nine-teenth century tried to build a bridge between the Christian religion and modern science, between the Christian faith and the leading philosophical schools. It was a *synthesis theology*, of which Origen had been the herald centuries before. Sometimes it stayed pretty close to the Bible, and sometimes it was miles away from it.

Many instances of this double-faced theological thinking can also be pointed out in the twentieth century. Therefore we are faced with a choice. I will discuss this matter further in connection with Dutch Reformed theology, which in various respects did not escape the infection of the spirit of the age in the second half of the century.

In the first half of our century, this theology went through a flourishing period. The growth and progress became apparent first of all in *exegetical* achievements. The Bible was translated and annotated anew.[37] It had earlier been predicted that Abraham Kuyper's blunt statements concerning the authority of Scripture would not be able to stand up once scientific exegetes faced the facts of historical-critical research, but this prediction was not borne out.

The growth and progress also became manifest in the study of the history and progress of revelation, as we see from the works of F. W. Grosheide, J. Ridderbos, S. Greidanus, K. Schilder, and B. Holwer-da. It became manifest as well in the systematic labors of K. Schilder and G. C. Berkouwer. The latter exerted a far-reaching influence through his broadly composed series of *Dogmatic Studies*, which are marked by "an extreme openness and carefulness" and "a very thorough studying and choosing of position in dogmatic problems."[38]

The growth and progress became manifest in theory of ethics[39] and in theory of missions,[40] while in philosophy an international school of Calvinistic philosophy of worldwide repute was established under D. H. T. Vollenhoven and Herman Dooyeweerd. Many able men worked hard, and the order of the day was not just intellectual orthodoxy; serious attempts were made to practice the truth being confessed in all areas of life.

All these activities took place on the basis of Scripture and the confession. In various instances, however, a growing difference of opinion began to surface. Disagreements that arose in the 1930s and 1940s gave rise to a conflict which ended in a most regrettable division of the Reformed *(Gereformeerd)* Churches in 1944.

What took place that year was the so-called "Liberation," under the leadership of Prof. K. Schilder. From that point on, the Reformed Churches and the Reformed Churches (maintaining Article 31) went their separate ways.* A description of the origin and history of this conflict would carry me too far afield in this book.[41] Suffice it to say that this quarrel between brothers was related to questions concerning the confession** and the church order.† As I see it, those questions could have been resolved within the federation of churches—and should have been.

The "Liberated" churches established their own synodical federation. In Canada they have founded the Canadian Reformed Church. They are characterized by a power of conviction and determination, and also by a certain degree of exclusivity. From the start their leader, Prof. Schilder, had protested against Abraham Kuyper's doctrine of the plurifor-mity of the church. In the meantime these churches encountered some internal difficulties of their own, and a group of churches separated from them.

The Reformed Churches were damaged as a result of this struggle. The damage was all the greater because of an ecclesiastical-theological revolt that took place in their midst, beginning in the 1950s. We might speak of this revolt as a "stampede against

G.C. Berkouwer

---

*In popular parlance the former churches were sometimes called the "Synodical" churches, and the latter the "Liberated" churches. Article 31 of the Church Order of Dordt deals with the authority of a synod, and also with the limits of that authority.

**C. Veenhof, who was a professor at the seminary of the "Liberated" churches in Kampen, refers to the criticism of traditional opinions on common grace, the substantiality and immortality of the soul, the pluriformity of the church, the covenant of grace, and the sacraments. The dispute came to a head in the area of the significance of the covenant of grace for the children of the congregation.

†The issue was that of the authority of the decisions made by major assemblies (classes and synods) as compared to the authority of the local consistory.

tradition," but that would not be a complete or sufficient characterization. We might also speak of a new "Vermittlungstheologie," of a strong influence on the churches exercised by the spirit of the age.

A critical attitude toward the tradition was quite understandable during the postwar years, but arrogance was evident when parents and grandparents were arranged as a "parade of men and brethren." It was an ominous sign when both the authority of Scripture and the value of the confession were slighted.

As far as the authority of Scripture is concerned, a distinct change was observable in the attitude taken by the grand master of Dutch Reformed theology, G. C. Berkouwer, who had earlier served as an able apologist for the decisions made by the Synod of Assen in 1926. This change is indicated by H. Berkhof, his colleague at Leiden, who says that Berkouwer originally accepted the absolute authority of Scripture, then the authority of the salvation contents of Scripture, and finally only the existential import of Scripture.[42] "Berkouwer has abandoned speaking about verbal inspiration, as well as the formal application of that verbal infallible inspiration."[43] It would carry me too far afield to try to explain his new position.[44] I would point out simply that Berkouwer feels doubt has arisen in his own mind regarding the concreteness of the data in the first chapters of the Bible. His own position became clear when he confessed at the Synod of Sneek in 1970 that "he also doubted the historicity of the Adam figure in Genesis."[45]

There were others who spoke more explicitly. At that same synod, the position of Prof. H. M. Kuitert of the Free University was discussed—and not for the first time. Kuitert had denied the historicity of Adam and Eve, as a consequence of his unconditional belief in evolution as a historical fact. The Synod affirmed creation's historicity, together with the historicity of the fall into sin and the resulting imputation of sin, as confessed in the third Lord's Day of the Heidelberg Catechism. The Synod added: It has meanwhile become apparent that the opinion of Dr. Kuitert is also shared by some members of the Synod and "it therefore concludes that the unity of the confessing (church) should not be considered to be at stake to such a degree that additional decisions should be taken concerning it."[46]

The unity of the confessing church! Kuitert himself had spoken about the "landslide" that his ideas would inevitably bring about in the dogmatic expression of the Christian church. To him the whole story of creation is only a "teaching model." God is the Creator not of something in the past but of something in the present and the future. Sin is the negative power frustrating this development, and Christ "upsets" this negative element, completing the development, the history.[47]

The congeniality of the ideas with those discussed earlier in this chapter can hardly be denied. When "teaching models" are assumed in the first book of the Bible, obviously the other books are also liable to such an artificial operation.

The series entitled "Cahiers voor de gemeente" (Essays for the Congregation), in which a number of representatives of this new theology showed their colors, manifested a view of Scripture that detracted from the authority of the Word of God.* Form-criticism was applied in several ways, and it was asserted—in Lessing's vein—that something could not be taken to be true simply because it was stated in the Bible; rather, it was stated in the Bible simply because it was true.[48] The confessional standards of the church were sharply criticized. Some theologians claimed "a preacher should sometimes go directly against the contents of the Catechism in his preaching." In the same breath they said the formula of subscription can stay as it is because what really counts is not the form but the contents.[49]

But who decides what those contents really are? This question became urgent in 1971 when H. Wiersinga, a student pastor, published a book on the atonement in theological discussion. In this book, which served as his doctoral dissertation at the Free University, he denied that the suffering and death of Christ had the effect of reconciling sinful man with the holy God, and that Christ's atoning death bore a substitutionary character. Wiersinga believed Christ's suffering and death were meant to have a "shock effect." The shock would induce us to repentance and conversion. Overwhelmed by His love, we would then become new men.

The similarity with the moral theory of satisfaction propounded by the medieval theologian Abelard is obvious. It should not surprise us that Prof. Herman Ridderbos of Kampen, in a profound study, raised the question: Are we following the wrong path?[50] Sharper still was the judgment of B. Wentsel, who concluded:

---

*G. P. Hartvelt exchanged the expression "The Bible is God's Word" for the expression "The Bible is good for the Word of God" (see *Over Schrift en Inspiratie*, 1967, p. 63).

Anyone who has read the arguments of Wiersinga easily recognizes the influence of Sölle, Moltmann, Weber, and others. Generally speaking, there is strong opposition in theological quarters to the idea of retribution and atonement by satisfying the justice (requiring and punishing) of God. The conflict between the church and the views of such theologians is so sharp because the confessional standards centralize this juridical and satisfactional element of the atonement so much.[51]

The Reformed Synod of Dordrecht (1972) called Wiersinga's view "a deviation from the confession" and appointed a committee to discuss his ideas with him. The discussion took place, but Dr. Wiersinga did not change his mind. In the meantime he remained a recognized and active minister in the Reformed Churches. And the interest of many people remained directed more toward a future within the horizons of this world and the establishment of a kingdom of justice by human efforts than toward the future of the coming Christ. They forgot about the righteousness of the new heaven and the new earth, and the accompanying daily sanctification of life which exists in "a small beginning of this new obedience."[52]

Imperfect tense

How does the Kingdom come? This question has been raised repeatedly, and various answers have been proposed by the Montanists and the Donatists, the Franciscans and the Jesuits, the Puritans and the modern theologians of liberation.

When Walter Nigg adds a subtitle to his fascinating description of the long struggle for a kingdom of righteousness, he speaks of the "history of a nostalgia and a disillusion."[53] And when H. G. Leih competently describes the history of the criticism of society and revolution, he speaks of "the dream of revolution."[54] We cannot help but be reminded of the words of the Preacher, who said: "I perceive that this also is but a striving after wind" (Eccl. 1:17).

How does the Kingdom come? A 1975 issue of Christianity Today contained an interview with Dr. Byang H. Kato, the Nigerian secretary of the Association of Evangelical Christians in Africa and Madagascar. When he was asked what the evangelical Christians in Africa thought about the World Council of Churches giving money to liberation movements, he answered:

> You should be aware that even some people in the ecumenical movement would tell you that this money is being given not to buy guns but to buy food and medicine for the refugees. And from the evangelical point of view, we are of course concerned for the needs of the people

who have been displaced for political reasons or whatever. Unfortunately, there is no clear evidence that the money is not used for arms. The primary concern of the liberation movement is not relief, but war of liberation through use of force.

Now regarding political liberation I feel that Christians as individuals should be involved in their nation as citizens of both heaven and their respective countries. We should perform the duty we are called upon to do. I think individual conscience should be a guide to Christians' response to the powers that be in their different countries.

But for the Church, I don't think it is the responsibility of the Church as such to be in the forefront of political liberation. And the main reason is that the Church has the primary task of bringing about reconciliation in the world, first of all between man and God, and secondly between man and man. Both the oppressed and the oppressor are in need of the Gospel of reconciliation, the Gospel of peace. If the Church identifies itself with one sector or the other, then it is jeopardizing its right to conciliate the two parties, both of whom need the Gospel of our Lord Jesus Christ.[55]

There is a dream, a nostalgia, but there is also another way. Leih points to it when he writes:

Fortunately, there is much sincere benevolence and reformism present with many non-revolutionaries. In many countries a revolution has been avoided when a different road to improvement appeared to be open. To us this is the only road. But it should be reformation, indeed, that eliminates evil in society as much as possible.[56]

There is a world of difference between reformation and revolution. There is a large and never completed task still awaiting Christians in their thinking and doing, a task which they can tackle through organized political and social associations. Groen van Prinsterer and Abraham Kuyper took the initiative in the formation of such organizations in the Netherlands, and now they are beginning to be considered as viable options in the United States and Canada.

All the same, we live in an unfathomable crisis situation. Earlier I mentioned the powers of secularism, atheism, evolutionism and revolution. Those powers continue to press forward. P. J. Bouman wrote in 1959:

It has now come to this, that the church and faith are in difficult straits in the fringe areas of the urban-industrial society, even among the groups that take pride in their attachment to a church. The established Anglican Church, the Protestants, and the Roman Catholics are fighting a rearguard action in an environment that has been abandoned to secularism. They themselves have also been sliding backwards. Being *in* the world nowadays means that the chances are pretty slim for anyone who pretends to be able to withstand the worldly temptations.[57]

England is no exception. The future of the church there seems to be overshadowed with dark clouds.

But we are not yet at the end of time, and there are also other powers at work. Even in countries in which atheism has become the religion of the state, a thirst for higher and better values than those of a chilly materialism has become manifest, not least among the young people. In western Europe and North America we find many young people also expressing their love for Jesus, with great enthusiasm but sometimes in a very untraditional way. In various churches the interest in orthodoxy is reviving—not out of any doctrinal pride but simply because the people sense the need of the plain gospel and nothing but the gospel. The missionary activities of the churches, especially in the developing continent of Africa and in Indonesia's splendid chain of isles, are continuing faithfully and are being blessed with great results.

Time has not yet run out, and the Church of Christ may continue to build on the unchangeable promises of God. We have the promise that "this gospel of the kingdom" will be preached in the whole world (Matt. 24:14). We have the promise that the gates of Hades will not prevail against the Church (Matt. 16:18). And finally we have the promise that the believers, even when others faint with fear and foreboding because of what is coming over the world, may look up and raise their heads because their redemption is drawing near (Luke 21:28). Yes, the Kingdom will certainly come!

Notes

Introduction

1. See G. M. Trevelyan, *A Shortened History of England* (1974 edition), pp. 521-4.

2. *A History of the Church in England* (1953), pp. 390, 391.

3. See *Twentieth Century Christianity*, ed. Stephen Neill (1961), p. 30.

4. *Das Wesen des Christentums*, translated into English as *What is Christianity?* (see Volume VI).

5. See *Religion in Britain since 1900*, ed. G. S. Spikes (1952), p. 70.

6. "Idealisme," in *Christelijke Encyclopaedie*, Vol. III^2 (1958), p. 565.

7. See William Hubben, *Dostoevsky, Kierkegaard, Nietzsche, and Kafka* (1972^7), p. 104.

8. *Modern levensgevoel* (no date), p. 128.

9. Elmer T. Clark, *The Small Sects in America* (1949^2), p. 13.

10. Quoted by B. Shelley in *Evangelicalism in America* (1967), p. 78.

11. In short, Abraham Kuyper's conception of pluriformity; see my dissertation, *Abraham Kuyper als kerkhistoricus* (1945), pp. 129ff.

12. A letter from the Ecumenical Council of the Netherlands to the Reformed Ecumenical Synod, November 8, 1951.

13. Letter of Dr. Visser 't Hooft, Secretary of the World Council of Churches, to this Brotherhood.

14. One could point to Billy Graham as representative of the spirit of the National Association of Evangelicals, and Dr. Carl McIntire as representative of the International Council of Christian Churches.

15. K. D. Schmidt, in *Evangelisches Kirchenlexikon*, Vol. I (1956), p. 732.

16. See the letter of the Russian Christians published by Michael Bordeaux, in which we repeatedly read the expression "the country of antichrist" (in *Opium of the People: The Christian Religion in the U.S.S.R.*, 1966^2, pp. 217-21).

17. See *In the Shadows of Tomorrow* (1935), written by the Dutch historian Johan Huizinga.

Chapter 1

1. P. J. Bouman, *Revolutie der eenzamen* (1953), p. 56.

2. E. Troeltsch, *Zur religiösen Lage* (1913), p. 512.

3. J. R. H. Moorman, *A History of the Church in England* (1953), p. 393.

4. *Ibid.*, p. 395.

5. See Crane Brinton's Introduction to the 1962 edition of Preserved Smith's two-volume work *A History of Modern Culture*.

6. P. van Paassen, *To Number Our Days* (1964), p. 111.

7. Some ministers in the Netherlands preached in the same vein; see G. Horreus de Haas, *Godsdienst en socialisme* (1924), and *Documenta Reformatoria*, Vol. II (1960), pp. 362-4.

8. See D. B. Eerdmans, *De theologie van Dr. A. Kuyper* (1909), and C. B. Hylkema, *Oud en Nieuw Calvinisme* (1911).

9. See S. J. Ridderbos, *De theologische cultuurbeschouwing van Abraham Kuyper* (1947), pp. 272-4, and J. Douma, *Algemene genade* (1966). Douma emphasizes both the differences and points of similarity between Kuyper and Calvin (see pp. 287, 356, 360).

10. S. J. Ridderbos, *De theologische cultuurbeschouwing van Abraham Kuyper*, p. 216.

11. See Heidelberg Catechism, Answer 114.

12. A. Kuyper, *De Gemeene Gratie*, Vol. II, pp. 425-32.

13. See H. Kuiper, *Calvin on Common Grace* (1928).

14. *Institutes*, III, 7, 3.

15. W. Philipp refers to the influences of evolutionism and cultural Protestantism; see his article on "Modernismus" in *Evangelisches Kirchenlexikon*, Vol. II (1958), p. 1418.

16. Warren Sylvester Smith, *The London Heretics, 1870-1914* (1967), pp. 232-4.

17. *George Tyrrell's Letters*, ed. M. D. Petrie (1920), p. 60.

18. H. Bavinck, *Gereformeerde Dogmatiek*, Vol. I (1928), p. 93.

19. In his book *L'évangile et l'église* (The Gospel and the Church).

20. P. Althaus, "Der 'historische Jesus' und der biblische Christus," in *Theologische Aufsätze*, Vol. II (1935), p. 163.

21. O. Dibelius, *In the Service of the Lord* (1964, English translation), p. 25.

22. K. Kupisch, *Karl Barth* (1972), p. 19.

23. In *Zeitschrift für Theologie und Kirche*, 1909, ed. W. Herrmann and M. Rade, pp. 317-21.

24. See N. B. Stonehouse, *J. Gresham Machen* (1954), Chapter 5.

25. *Ibid.*, p. 125.

26. *Ibid.*, p. 127.

27. *Ibid.*, pp. 229-31.

28. O. Dibelius, *In the Service of the Lord*, pp. 80-1.

29. Stephen Neill, *Twentieth Century Christianity* (1961), p. 30.

30. W. S. Smith, *The London Heretics, 1870-1914*, p. 4.

31. K. Kupisch, *Deutsche Landeskirchen im 19. und 20. Jahrhundert*.

32. There is much literature on this subject; see, for example, S. B. Fay, *The Origins of the World War* (1930²).

33. In *Ecce Homo* (1888).

34. G. S. Spikes, ed., *Religion in Britain since 1900* (1952), p. 65.

35. See J. C. Rullmann, *Kuyper-Bibliographie*, Vol. III (1940), p. 409.

36. See Werner Kindt's article on the "Jugendbewegung" in *Evangelisches Kirchenlexikon*, Vol. II (1958).

Chapter 2

1. A. Solzhenitsyn, *August 1914* (English translation, 1972), pp. 13-14.

2. See Julien Benda, *La trahison des clercs* (1928). The quotation is from the English translation of 1955, p. 140.

3. Princess Blücher, *An English Wife in Berlin* (1920), p. 7.

4. A. Marwick, *The Deluge: British Society and the First World War* (1965), p. 31. The author also writes about labor demonstrations against the war, but soon the Labour Party and the powerful unions supported the war effort.

5. Ernest Jones, *The Life and Work of Sigmund Freud*, ed. Frilling and Marcus (1963), p. 327. According to Freud, the libido is the instinctual drive behind all human activities.

6. *Promise of Greatness: The War of 1914-1918*, ed. G. A. Panichas (1968), p. xvi.

7. H. G. Wells, *The War That Will End War* (1914), p. 14. Wells, a complete evolutionist, was deeply disappointed by the later course of events.

8. See H. E. Barnes, *A History of Historical Writing* (1963²), pp. 277, 282.

9. The historian Reinhold Kosser wrote the definitive text (see K. Kupisch, *Deutsche Landeskirchen im 19. und 20. Jahrhundert*, p. 94).

10. Moorman, *A History of the Church in England*, p. 413.

11. J. Williams, *The Home Fronts* (1972), p. 17.

12. K. Bihlmeyer, *Church History*, Vol. III (1966), p. 481.

13. S. J. Engall, *A Subaltern's Letter* (1918), pp. 119-20.

14. A. Marwick, *The Deluge*, p. 217.

15. Bishop John C. Ward, "The Effect of World War I on Religion," in *Promise of Greatness* (1968), p. 458.

16. A. Marwick, *The Deluge*, p. 109. The slogan was: "There's a girl for every soldier."

17. H. Bavinck, *Christendom, Oorlog en Volkenbond* (1920), p. 31.

18. H. Algra, *De eigen weg van het Nederlandse volk* (no date), p. 268.

19. P. J. Bouman, *Revolutie der eenzamen*, p. 230.

20. A shocking picture of the suffering of the Armenians is presented by Franz Werfel in *The Forty Days of Musa Dagh*.

21. See H. Stuart Hughes, *Oswald Spengler* (1962²), p. 89.

22. O. Spengler, *Der Untergang des Abendlandes* (1963), p. 43.

23. See Hughes, *Oswald Spengler*, p. 72, and S. J. Popma, *Modern levensgevoel*, p. 115.

24. *Der Untergang des Abendlandes*, pp. 678, 680.

25. See H. Smitskamp, "Toynbee," in *Denkers van deze tijd*, Vol. II (no date), pp. 175ff.

26. See P. Geyl, *Debates with Historians* (1955), pp. 91-178; J. Romein, *Tussen vrees en vrijheid* (1950), pp. 69-130; G. H. Clark, "Spengler and Toynbee," in *A Christian View of Men and Things* (1967 edition), pp. 53ff; H. R. Trevor-Roper, *Historical Essays* (1966), pp. 299ff.

27. J. Huizinga, *In de schaduwen van morgen*, pp. 5, 114, 168, 179.

28. J. Huizinga, *Geschonden wereld* (1945), pp. 181, 168, 242.

29. P. A. Sorokin, *The Crisis of Our Age* (1942), pp. 213ff, 190, 191, 201.

Chapter 3

1. W. Nigg, *Geschichte des religiösen Liberalismus* (1937), p. 394.

2. "Black days"—see *Scottish Journal of Theology*, No. 8 (1959), p. 57.

3. In the correspondence after Harnack's "Fifteen Questions for the Despisers of Scientific Theology Among Theologians."

4. In *The Brothers Karamazov* (1880).

5. K. Barth, *Die christliche Dogmatik im Entwurf* (1927), p. ix.

6. T. F. Torrance, in *Ten Makers of Modern Protestant Thought*, ed. G. L. Hunt (1958), p. 58.

7. K. Kupisch, *Karl Barth* (1972, Dutch translation), p. 128.

8. *Church Dogmatics*, IV, 4, p. xii.

9. W. Nigg, *Geschichte der religiösen Liberalismus*, p. 398.

10. G. W. Bromiley, "Karl Barth," in *Creative Minds in Contemporary Theology*, ed. P. E. Hughes (1966), p. 51.

11. *Ibid.*, pp. 55-7.

12. *Römerbrief* (1923), p. xxxi; see also G. C. Berkouwer, *Het probleem der Schriftkritiek* (no date), p. 29.

13. *Church Dogmatics*, I, 2, p. 529.

14. *Ibid.*, IV, 1, p. 747.

15. See K. Barth, *Die kirchliche Lehre von der Taufe* (1943); G. C. Berkouwer, *Karl Barth en de kinderdoop* (1947), and *De sacramenten* (1954), pp. 212ff.

16. K. Kupisch, *Karl Barth*, pp. 160, 161.

17. In *Natur und Genade: Zum Gespräch mit Karl Barth* (1934).

18. See P. G. Schrotenboer, "Emil Brunner," in *Creative Minds in Contemporary Theology*, p. 101.

19. K. Kupisch, *Karl Barth*, pp. 64, 65.

20. Schrotenboer, "Emil Brunner," p. 100.

21. See G. C. Berkouwer, *De algemene openbaring* (1951), Chapter 2.

22. A. Szekeres, article on Brunner in the *Christelijke Encyclopaedie*, second edition, Vol. II (1957), p. 44.

23. E. Brunner, *Der Mensch im Widerspruch* (1941), p. 102.

24. E. Brunner, *Das Ewige als Zukunft und Gegenwart* (1953), p. 164.

25. E. Brunner, *Dogmatik*, Vol. III (1960), pp. 220, 221.

26. A. Szekeres, article on Brunner.

27. See G. C. van Niftrik, *Een beroerder Israels* (1949), and H. Ridderbos, "Rudolf Bultmann," in *Denkers van deze tijd*, Vol. I (no date), p. 207.

28. K. Barth, *Rudolf Bultmann: Ein Versuch ihn zu Verstehen* (1952).

29. R. Bultmann, "New Testament and Mythology," in *Kerygma and Myth*, Vol. I, ed. H. W. Bartsch (1953), pp. 1, 2.

30. R. Bultmann, *Kerygma and Myth*, Vol. I, p. 36.

31. G. E. Ladd, *Bultmann* (1964), p. 39.

32. *Reinhold Niebuhr*, ed. C. W. Kegley and R. W. Bretall (1956), p. 36.

33. See T. Minnema, "Reinhold Niebuhr," in *Creative Minds in Contemporary Theology*, pp. 392, 394.

34. G. Brillenburg Wurth, in *Denkers van deze tijd*, Vol, I, p. 267.

Chapter 4

1. See especially Kurt Leese, *Der Protestantismus im Wandel der neueren Zeit* (1941).

2. Holl's Luther studies are to be found in his *Gesammelte Aufsätze*, Vol. I (1921). The words quoted from Harnack were spoken by him in 1926; see Harnack's *Aus der Werkstatt des Vollendeten* (1930), p. 280.

3. See especially Holl's book on the cultural significance of the Reformation (1911, English translation 1959).

4. "Was Christum treibt"—see Vol. III.

5. See G. C. Berkouwer, *Het probleem der Schriftkritiek* (no date), pp. 151ff.

6. In *Religion och Kultur* (1934), pp. 7-15.

7. G. Krüger, *Die evangelische Theologie: Ihr jetziger Stand und ihre Aufgaben* (1929), p. 27.

8. K. Schilder, *Tusschen "Ja" en "Neen"* (1929), pp. 305, 237.

9. See W. Niesel, *Die Theologie Calvins* (1938), Chapter 10; see also J. Douma, *Algemene genade* (1966), especially pp. 282ff.

10. H. Baucke, *Die Probleme der Theologie Calvins* (1922), p. 107.

11. Niesel refers to Peter Brunner's "Vom Glauben bei Calvin" (1925); A. de Quervain's masterful "Calvin" (1926); Udo Schmidt's "Calvins Bezeugung der Ehre Gottes" (1927); Peter Barth's "Calvin" (1931); and A. Göhler's "Calvins Lehre von der Heiligung" (1934).

12. See the surveys in the *Calvin Theological Journal*, started in 1971 by J. N. Tylenda and P. de Klerk. See also D. Nauta, "Stand der Calvinforschung," in *Calvinus Theologicus*, ed. W. H. Neuser (1976), pp. 71ff.

13. G. C. Berkouwer, *Het probleem der Schriftkritiek*, Chapter 8.

14. E. Doumergue, *Jean Calvin*, Vol. IV, pp. 54-84.

15. W. Niesel, *Die Theologie Calvins*, pp. 28ff.

16. J. A. Cramer, *De Heilige Schrift bij Calvijn* (1926).

17. W. Krusche, *Das Wirken des Heiligen Geistes nach Calvin* (1957); K. S. Kantzer, "Calvin and the Holy Scripture," in *Inspiration and Interpretation*, ed. J. F. Walvoord (1957).

18. J. A. Cramer, *Het bijbels onderzoek op de christelijke school* (1928).

19. G. C. Berkouwer, *Het probleem der Schriftkritiek*, pp. 271ff.

20. *Ibid.*, p. 278.

21. "Woe to me if I don't proclaim the gospel of Thomas"—quoted by J. C. Livingston, *Modern Christian Thought* (1971), p. 392.

22. J. Maritain, *The Peasant of the Garonne* (1968), p. 6.

23. J. van Heugten, Introduction to the fourth Dutch edition of 1948, p. 15.

24. Maisie Ward, *G. K. Chesterton* (1958 edition), p. 381.

25. G. K. Chesterton, *Saint Thomas Aquinas* (1960 edition), pp. 195, 196.

Chapter 5

1. F. Schwarz, *You Can't Trust the Communists* (1972[7]), p. 104.

2. H. Smith, *The Russians* (1977 edition), pp. 368, 369.

3. J. Verkuyl, *Voorbereiding voor de dialoog over het evangelie en de ideologie van het marxistisch leninisme* (no date), pp. 7, 8.

4. See S. R. Tompkins, *The Triumph of Bolshevism* (1967), pp. 282ff; L. Fisher, *The Life of Lenin* (1965), pp. 41, 42.

5. See *The Heritage of Western Civilization: Select Readings*, ed. Beatty and Johnson (1958), p. 637.

6. V. I. Lenin, *State and Revolution* (1932 edition), p. 35.

7. See H. Smith, *The Russians*, p. 664.

8. *From Under the Rubble*, ed. A. Solzhenitsyn (1976 edition), pp. 8, 9.

9. Hannah Arendt, *The Origins of Totalitarianism* (1951), p. 414.

10. J. Verkuyl, *Voorbereiding voor de dialoog*, p. 138.

11. *Ibid.*, p. 138.

12. See N. Berdyaev, *The Origin of Russian Communism* (1937), p. 195.

13. *Ibid.*, p. 202.

14. N. Struve, *Christians in Contemporary Russia* (1967), p. 113.

Chapter 6

1. C. Garbett, Archbishop of York, *In an Age of Revolution* (1952), p. 156.
2. H. J. Gamm, *Der braune Kult*, pp. 55, 56.
3. F. L. Carsten, *The Rise of Fascism* (1967), p. 9.
4. "Will, lust, pride, instinct: imperial four-in-hand." See H. G. Leih, *De droom der revolutie* (no date), p. 107.
5. R. Cecil, *The Myth of a Master-race* (1972), p. 87.
6. C. van Liere, *Algemeen Weekblad voor Christendom en Cultuur*, June 9, 1933; see also G. van Roon, *Protestants Nederland en Duitsland, 1933-41* (1973), p. 217.
7. J. Hastings Nichols, *History of Christianity, 1650-1950* (1956), pp. 382-4.
8. See E. Jäckel, *Hitler's Weltanschauung* (1969). Jäckel refers to *Die Revolution des Nihilismus*, a book by Herman Rauschning.
9. J. Romein, *In opdracht van de tijd* (1946), pp. 298-321.
10. E. Haeckel, *Die Welträtsel* (1900), pp. 121, 311-14.
11. *The Nazi Years*, ed. J. Remak (1969), p. 3.
12. In a speech of April 13, 1923 (in *Weltkriege und Revolutionen*, ed. G. Schönbrunn, 1961, p. 285).
13. In Chapter 11, entitled "Nation and Race."
14. In an article on the doctrine of Fascism, which he wrote jointly with the Italian philosopher Gentile and published in the *Enciclopedia Italiana* (1932).
15. See R. Cecil, *The Myth of a Master-race* pp. 88-93.
16. H. G. Leih, *De droom der revolutie*, p. 94.
17. A. Polonsky, in *History of the 20th Century*, ed. A. J. P. Taylor, p. 48.
18. F. L. Carsten, *The Rise of Fascism*, p. 24.
19. E. Jäckel, *Hitler's Weltanschauung*, p. 54.
20. Trial of War Criminals, Nuremberg 1947-1949. Document 075, XXXV, 7-13 (see *The Nazi Years*, ed. Remak, p. 104).
21. K. Bihlmeyer, *Church History*, Vol. III (1966), pp. 491, 492.
22. F. W. Kantzenbach, *Christentum in der Gesellschaft*, Vol. II (1976), p. 397.
23. G. van Roon, *Protestants Nederland en Duitsland*, pp. 234-5.
24. *Ibid.*, p. 222.
25. J. Neuhäusler, *Kreuz and Hakenkreuz* (1946), p. 251.
26. G. L. Mosse, *Nazi Culture* (1968), p. 238.
27. L. de Jong, *Het koninkrijk der Nederlanden in de tweede Wereldoorlog*, 5, II (1974), p. 652.

Chapter 7

1. K. D. Schmidt, *Grundriss der Kirchengeschichte* (1954), pp. 564, 566.
2. W. C. Fletcher, *A Study in Survival* (the church in Russia, 1927-43) (1965), p. 49.
3. B. R. Bociurkiw, in *Religion in the Soviet State: A Dilemma of Power*, ed. M. Hayward and W. C. Fletcher (1969), p. 19.
4. R. Valkenburg, *Rumoer rondom Wurmbrand* (1972), p. 19.
5. M. Muggeridge, *Tread Softly, for You Tread on My Jokes* (1972 edition), p. 23.
6. A. Solzhenitsyn, *The First Circle* (1968), pp. 337, 579, 580.
7. F. Schwarz, *You Can Trust the Communists (To Be Communists)* (1972 edition), pp. 123, 124.
8. W. C. Fletcher, *Nikolai: Portrait of a Dilemma* (1968), p. 152.
9. M. Bourdeaux, *Opium of the People* (1966²), p. 41.
10. J. H. Nichols, *History of Christianity, 1650-1950*, p. 356.

11. *Izvestia*, April 24, 1929.

12. B. R. Bociurkiw, in *Religion in the Soviet State*, p. 74.

13. M. Bourdeaux, *Patriarchs and Prophets* (1969), p. 16.

14. Struve, *Christians in Contemporary Russia*, p. 28.

15. O. Schabert, *Slachtoffers van het Communisme* (no date), pp. 3, 4.

16. *Ibid.*, pp. 19, 29, 30.

17. *Novoye Russkoyo Slovo* (Russian Daily), New York, September 27, 1974.

18. Bourdeaux, *Opium of the People*, p. 50.

19. Struve, *Christians in Contemporary Russia*, p. 38.

20. W. C. Fletcher, *A Study in Survival*, p. 20.

21. Struve, *Christians in Contemporary Russia*, p. 39.

22. *Ibid.*, p. 46.

23. A summary of the relevant part of the *Gulag Archipelago*, prepared by N. C. Nielson, Jr., in *Solzhenitsyn's Religion* (1975).

24. Bulletin of the Local Council of the Russian Orthodox Church of 1923, p. 12 (see Bociurkiw, in *Religion in the Soviet State*, p. 85).

25. W. Kolarz, *Religion in the Soviet Union* (1962²), p. 287.

26. J. A. Hebly, *Protestanten in Rusland* (1973), p. 93.

27. G. Vins, "Memories of My Father," in *Three Generations of Suffering* (1976), pp. 29-50.

28. *Anti-religioznik*, No. 3, 1930, pp. 6, 7; see J. Shelton Curtiss, *The Russian Church and the Soviet State, 1917-1950* (1953), p. 240).

29. Curtiss, *The Russian Church and the Soviet State*, p. 236.

30. *Ibid.*, pp. 234ff.

31. E. A. Walsh, "Why Pope Pius XI Asked Prayers for Russia on March 19, 1930," pp. 13, 14; see also W. C. Fletcher, *A Study in Survival*, p. 62.

32. N. Struve, *Christians in Contemporary Russia*, pp. 393-8.

33. W. J. Ciszek, *With God in Russia: My Twenty-three Years as a Priest in Soviet Prisons and Labor Camps in Siberia* (1960).

34. W. C. Fletcher, *Nikolai: Portrait of a Dilemma* (1968), p. 50.

35. N. Struve, *Christians in Contemporary Russia*, p. 175.

36. H. Smith, *The Russians*, p. 581.

37. Struve, *Christians in Contemporary Russia*, p. 215.

38. *Ibid.*, p. 192.

39. A quotation from a letter to their fellow believers in America, written in 1946 (Hebly, *Protestanten in Rusland*, pp. 103-5).

40. Bociurkiw, *Religion in the Soviet State*, p. 95.

41. Struve, *Christians in Contemporary Russia*, p. 91.

42. W. C. Fletcher, *Nikolai*, p. 53.

43. See Struve, *Christians in Contemporary Russia*, p. 180; Kolarz, *Religion in the Soviet Union*, p. 37.

44. Hebly, *Protestanten in Rusland*, p. 210.

45. Nielsen, *Solzhenitsyn's Religion*, p. 133; Bourdeaux, *Patriarchs and Prophets*, p. 31; Hebly, *Protestanten in Rusland*, p. 210.

46. Bourdeaux, *Opium of the People*, p. 213.

47. See *Religion and the Soviet State*, ed. M. Hayward and W. C. Fletcher, pp. 105-57, especially p. 127.

48. Bourdeaux, *Opium of the People*, p. 213.

49. Hebly, *Protestanten in Rusland*, p. 124.

50. N. C. Nielsen, Jr., *Solzhenitsyn's Religion*, p. 93.

51. Hebly, *Protestanten in Rusland*, p. 153.

52. H. Smith, *The Russians*, pp. 583, 584.

53. G. N. Shuster, *Religion Behind the Iron Curtain* (1954), pp. 32, 33.

54. R. W. Solberg, *God and Caesar in East Germany* (1961), p. 53.

55. *Ibid.*, p. 120.

56. Data in Shuster, *Religion Behind the Iron Curtain*, pp. 270, 156, 261.

57. O. Dibelius, *In the Service of the Lord* (1964), p. 184.

58. Solberg, *God and Caesar in East Germany*, pp. 145, 146.

59. Scott Latourette, *Christianity in a Revolutionary Age*, IV (1969 edition), p. 286).

60. Solberg, *God and Caesar in East Germany*, p. 195.

61. See G. C. Berkouwer, *Op de Tweesprong* (no date), pp. 23-5. Berkouwer points to the danger that Barth's position weakens the resistance.

62. See K. Kupisch, *Karl Barth* (1972), pp. 136-8; R. W. Solberg, *God and Caesar in East Germany*, pp. 278ff.

63. H. Gollwitzer, *Und führen wohin du nicht willst* (1954), p. 113.

64. See "The China Watch," in *Christianity Today*, November 21, 1975 (a conversation with David Adney, who was a missionary for that year with the China Inland Mission).

65. W. Kolarz, *Religion in the Soviet Union*, p. 258.

66. Shuster, *Religion Behind the Iron Curtain*, p. 213.

67. Scott Latourette, *Christianity in a Revolutionary Age*, pp. 201ff; K. Bihlmeyer, *Church History*, Vol. III (1966), pp. 527, 528.

68. "The Evangel in Eastern Europe," in *Christianity Today*, February 2, 1973, p. 34.

69. Scott Latourette, *Christianity in a Revolutionary Age*, pp. 352, 353.

70. Shuster, *Religion Behind the Iron Curtain*, p. 92.

71. *Ibid.*, p. 186.

72. See R. Wurmbrand, *Tortured for Christ* and *Sermons in Solitary Confinement*.

73. See R. Valkenburg, *Rumoer rondom Wurmbrand* (1972).

74. John B. Wang, "Where Have All the Churches Gone?" in *Christianity Today*, November 18, 1977, pp. 280, 281.

75. L. M. Outerbridge, *The Lost Churches of China* (1952), p. 156.

76. Quoted in the letter from Mao Tse-tung, *New Democracy*, 1949, p. 53 (see Outerbridge, *The Lost Churches of China*, pp. 175, 176).

77. Outerbridge, *The Lost Churches of China*, p. 187.

78. A. I. Kinnear, *Against the Tide* (1976³).

79. D. E. MacInnes, *Religious Policy and Practice in Communist China: A Documentary History* (1972), pp. 335, 336.

80. *Ibid.*, p. 155.

81. Outerbridge, *The Lost Churches of China*, p. 155.

82. *Ibid.*, pp. 159-67.

83. Scott Latourette, *Christianity in a Revolutionary Age*, pp. 407, 408.

Chapter 8

1. O. Dibelius, *In the Service of the Lord* (1964), p. 136.

2. P. J. Bouman, *Revolutie der eenzamen* (1953), p. 275.

3. J. Wallmann, *Kirchengeschichte Deutschlands*, Vol. II (1973), p. 276.

4. P. E. Lapide, *De laatste drie pausen en de joden* (1967), p. 104.

5. The text of all decisions is in Bihlmeyer's *Church History*, Vol. III (1966), pp. 514, 516.

6. Lapide, *De laatste drie pausen en de joden*, p. 112.

7. K. Barth and G. Kittel, *Ein theologischer Briefwechsel* (1934); see also G. C. Berkouwer, *De voorzienigheid Gods* (1950), pp. 192-4.

8. W. Nigg, *Geschichte des religiösen Liberalismus* (1937), p. 400.

9. In his introduction to the English translation of Arthur Frey's book *Der Kampf der evangelischen Kirche in Deutschland und seine allgemeine Bedeutung*, published in 1937 (pp. 9-26 of the English translation of 1938, published as *Cross and Swastika*).

10. K. Kupisch, *Die deutschen Landeskirchen im 19. und 20. Jahrhundert* (1972[2]), p. 142.

11. G. Niemöller, *Die 1. BK-Synode der DEK zu Barmen*, Vol. II (1959), p. 56.

12. Translation by A. C. Cochrane in *Reformed Confessions of the 16th Century* (1966), Appendix IV, pp. 332-6.

13. A. Frey, *Cross and Swastika*, p. 198.

14. K. Kupisch, *Die deutschen Landeskirchen im 19. und 20. Jahrhundert*, p. 156.

15. The entire sermon has been printed in A. S. Duncan-Jones, *The Struggle for Religious Freedom in Germany* (1938), pp. 271-6.

16. H. Gollwitzer in *Du hast mich heimgesucht bei Nacht* (1955). In this book, several letters by the victims of Hitler's terrorism have been collected.

17. *The Nazi Years: A Documentary History*, ed. J. Remak (1969), pp. 103, 104.

18. K. Barth, *Eine Schweizer Stimme* (1945), pp. 58, 59.

19. K. Kupisch, *Karl Barth* (1972), p. 117.

20. Dibelius, *In the Service of the Lord*, p. 163; T. Wurm, *Erinnerungen aus mein Leben* (1953), p. 145.

21. Kantzenbach, *Christentum in der Gesellschaft*, Vol. II, p. 409.

22. *The Nazi Years*, ed. J. Remak, p. 168.

23. Dibelius, *In the Service of the Lord*, p. 165.

24. *Dying We Live: The Final Messages and Records of Some Germans Who Defied Hitler*, ed. H. Gollwitzer and others (1965[4]), p. 13.

25. *Ibid.*, p. 183.

26. Goerdeler was executed on February 5, 1945 (see *Dying We Live*, pp. 85-8; see also G. Ritter, *Carl Goerdeler und die deutsche Widerstandsbewegung*, 1954).

27. Dibelius, *In the Service of the Lord*, p. 148; H. Thielicke, *Between Heaven and Earth: Conversations with American Christians* (1965).

28. Dibelius, *In the Service of the Lord*, p. 259.

29. E. Berggrav, *With God in the Darkness* (1943); Latourette, *Christianity in a Revolutionary Age*, pp. 317-21.

30. *Opdat wij niet vergeten*, ed. T. Delleman (no date), pp. 481ff.

31. *De Reformatie*, June 14 and 21, August 16, 1940.

32. K. H. Miskotte, *In de gecroonde allemansgading* (1946[2]), pp. 287ff.

33. B. van Kaam, *Opstand der gezagsgetrouwen* (1966), p. 148.

34. *Ibid.*, p. 163.

35. *Opdat wij niet vergeten*, ed. T. Delleman, p. 202.

36. De Jong, *Het koninkrijk der Nederlanden in de 2e Wereldoorlog*, Vol. V, p. 657.

37. *Opdat wij niet vergeten*, ed. T. Delleman, p. 83.

38. J. Overduin, *Faith and Victory in Dachau* (English translation, 1978), pp. 23-5.

39. Van Kaam, *Opstand der gezagsgetrouwen*, p. 128.

40. De Jong, *Het koninkrijk der Nederlanden*, Vol. V, pp. 712-24.

41. K. G. Idema, in *Opdat wij niet vergeten*, Chapter 7.

Chapter 9

1. P. Lapide, *De laatste drie pausen en de joden*, p. 111.
2. De Jong, *Het koninkrijk der Nederlanden in de 2e Wereldoorlog*, p. 689.
3. C. Zentner, *Deutschland 1870 bis heute: Bilder und Dokumente* (1970), pp. 398, 399 (from R. Hösz, *Kommandant in Auschwitz*, 1958).
4. In his *Der Sieg des Judentums über das Germanentum.*
5. Acts 18:2. On the persecution of the Jews in that time, see A. Sizoo, *Uit het wereld van het Nieuwe Testament* (1948²), pp. 122-4.
6. The so-called *Birkarth ha-minim*; see A. W. Kac, *The Rebirth of the State of Israel* (1958), pp. 175, 176; J. Jocz, *The Jewish People and Jesus Christ* (1954), p. 53.
7. *Von den Juden und ihre Lügen* (1543).
8. K. Marx, *A World Without Jews* (New York: Philosophical Library, 1959), pp. 37, 45.
9. Solomon Schwarz, *The Jews in the Soviet Union* (1951), p. 53. We find a consistent exposition of opposition against Judaism in *The Non-Jewish Jew* (1968), a book by the radical-leftist Jew, Isaac Deutscher.
10. E. H. Flannery, *Twenty-three Ages of Anti-Semitism* (1965), p. 241; Hanna Vogt, *The Jews* (1967), p. 137.
11. Flannery, *Twenty-three Ages of Anti-Semitism*, p. 243.
12. Hans Habe, *Wie einst David* (1971), p. 34.
13. H. Vogt, *The Jews*, p. 103.
14. See P. J. Bouman, *Revolutie der eenzamen*, pp. 376, 377, who writes about the childhood and education of the camp commandant Rudolf Hösz.
15. K. Barth, *Church Dogmatics*, III (1961), pp. 210-24.
16. See, for example, P. Lapide, *De laatste drie pausen en de joden*, pp. 15ff; M. I. Dumont, *Jews, God and History* (1962), pp. 138, 139.
17. A. W. Kac, *The Rebirth of the State of Israel*, p. 88.

Chapter 10

1. Bihlmeyer, *Church History*, Vol. III, p. 492.
2. J. H. Nichols, *History of Christianity* (1956), p. 368.
3. "In the Fortieth Year."
4. Especially by R. Hochhuth in his play *Der Stellvertreter* (1963).
5. P. Lapide, *De laatste drie pausen en de joden* (The Last Three Popes and the Jews).
6. O. Cullmann, "The Bible in the Council," in *Dialogue on the Way*, ed. G. A. Lindbeck (1965), p. 130.
7. R. Aubert, *Geschiedenis van de kerk*, Xb (ed. Rogier-Aubert-Knowles, 1974), p. 335.
8. G. C. Berkouwer, *The Second Vatican Council and the New Catholicism* (1965), pp. 113ff.
9. Pope John XXIII, *Journal of a Soul* (1965), pp. 365, 366.
10. R. Aubert, *Geschiedenis van de kerk*, Xb, p. 349.
11. *Journal of a Soul*, pp. 436ff.
12. *Ibid.*, p. 455.
13. On the devotion to the sacred heart of Jesus, see Volume V above. The devotion to the sacred heart of Mary had been added to it, already sanctioned by the pope in 1765.
14. E. Dhanis, S.J., *Bij de verschijningen van het geheim van Fatima* (1949), pp. 19, 20. Dhanis takes a cautiously critical attitude when he tells the story of Fatima.

15. An interesting comment is made by Dhanis: "One is inclined to include the visions of Fatima among the imagination visions . . . theologians do not object to the thesis that God can grant imagination visions" (*ibid.*, p. 31).

16. *Religion in Great Britain since 1900*, ed. G. S. Spikes (1952), p. 236.

17. L. J. Rogier, *Vandaag en morgen* (1974), p. 6.

18. See J. M. Domenach and R. de Montvalon, *The Catholic Avant-Garde: French Catholicism since World War II*, pp. 48ff.

19. See C. J. de Vogel, *De grondslag van onze zekerheid* (1977), pp. 160ff; C. Van Til, *The Great Debate Today* (1970), pp. 207ff.

20. Y. Congar, *A History of Theology* (1968), p. 9.

21. In *Forts dans la Foi*, No. 4, May-June 1968.

22. Rogier, *Vandaag en morgen*, pp. 52-6.

23. J. Hitchcock, *The Decline and Fall of Radical Catholicism* (1971), p. 55.

24. Hans Küng, *Infallibility and Inquiry* (1971); see also *Tensions in Contemporary Theology*, ed. S. N. Gundry and A. F. Johnson (1976), p. 293.

25. D. F. Wells raises a proper question here: "Where, one must ask, is the offense of the cross?" (in *Tensions in Contemporary Theology*, p. 320).

26. *Témoinage Chrétien*—quoted by J. Eppstein, *Has the Catholic Church Gone Mad?* (1971), p. 17.

27. P. E. Hughes, *Christianity Today*, March 27, 1961. A fundamental criticism of Teilhard de Chardin has been delivered by J. J. Duyvené de Wit in *Creative Minds in Contemporary Theology*, ed. P. E. Hughes (1966), pp. 407-50.

28. In *Quatember: Evangelische Jahresbrief* (Ostern 1963), p. 78.

29. *The Documents of Vaticanum II*, ed. W. M. Abbott, S.J. (1966), pp. 712, 713.

30. Quoted in *Dialogue on the Way*, ed. G. A. Lindbeck (1965), p. 94.

31. Eppstein, *Has the Catholic Church Gone Mad?*, p. 23.

32. *Documents of Vaticanum II*, pp. 27-9.

33. *Ibid.*, p. 40.

34. *Ibid.*, p. 43.

35. *Ibid.*, p. 96.

36. J. C. Livingston, *Modern Christian Thought* (1971), p. 495; C. Trimp, *Betwist Schriftgezag* (1979), p. 205.

37. *Documents of Vaticanum II*, p. 117.

38. *Ibid.*, p. 120.

39. J. W. Montgomery, *Ecumenicity, Evangelicals and Rome* (1969), p. 87.

40. *Dialogue on the Way*, pp. 142, 143.

41. J. Gijsen, *Huis op rots, huis op zand* (1977).

42. *The Crucial Questions*, by Y. Congar, J. Daniélou, E. Schillebeekx, P. Schoonenberg, J. Metz, K. Rahner (1969).

43. *The Crucial Questions*, pp. 9, 64.

44. See David F. Wells, in *Tensions in Contemporary Theology* (1976), p. 293.

45. Rogier, *Vandaag en morgen*, p. 36.

46. "Of Human Life." The encyclical dealt with the problems of marriage and birth control.

47. *Tensions in Contemporary Theology*, ed. Gundry and Johnson (1976), pp. 302, 304.

48. C. J. de Vogel, *De grondslag van onze zekerheid*, pp. 173, 174, 212, 247.

Chapter 11

1. P. G. Macy, *If It Be of God: The Story of the W.C.C.* (1960), pp. 102-4.

2. H. van der Linde, *De Wereldraad van Kerken* (1948), p. 62.

278   *THE CHURCH IN THE TWENTIETH CENTURY*

3. H. P. Van Dusen, *World Christianity* (Dutch translation, 1948), pp. 95, 96.

4. D. Hedegard, *Ecumenism and the Bible* (1954), p. 173.

5. See his *Das Werden des Gottesglaubens* (1926²).

6. See J. W. Montgomery, *Ecumenicity, Evangelicals and Rome* (1969), pp. 105-7.

7. N. Söderblom, *De ware broederschap* (no date), pp. 58, 59, 141.

8. J. H. Nichols, *History of Christianity, 1650-1950*, p. 439.

9. H. P. Van Dusen, *World Christianity* (1948), pp. 199-200.

10. In *Harper's Magazine*, January 1933.

11. Quoted by J. DeForest Murch, *The World Council of Churches* (1961), p. 20.

12. H. van der Linde, *De Wereldraad van Kerken*, p. 36.

13. See C. Vanderwaal, *Antithese of Synthese?* (1951), pp. 90, 91.

14. H. van der Linde, *De Wereldraad van Kerken*, p. 43.

15. Official Report of the First Assembly of the World Council of Churches, ed. W. A. Visser 't Hooft (1949), p. 32.

16. Macy, *If It Be of God*, p. 135; C. McIntire, *Servants of Apostasy* (1955), pp. 16ff.

17. J. H. Nichols, *Evanston: An Interpretation* (1954), pp. 92, 93. Nichols was not a negative critic. In his Introduction he wrote: "This is a history of the working of the Holy Spirit among us" (p. 7).

18. C. F. F. Henry, "W.C.C. Approves a Christian Basis," in *Christianity Today*, December 22, 1961, p. 22.

19. *Uppsala 1968* (Dutch edition), pp. 63, 106.

20. W. A. Detzler, *The Changing Church in Europe* (1979), p. 37; E. Smith, *The Fraudulent Gospel* (1977), p. 46.

21. The title of the last chapter of *The Coming Age of Christianity*, ed. J. Marchant (1950), pp. 169ff.

22. I Timothy 4:16; 6:1, 3; II Timothy 4:3; Titus 2:1, 7; II John, vs. 7-11.

23. N. Söderblom, *De ware broederschap*, p. 134.

24. *The Ecumenical Review*, Vol. XXI, p. 270.

25. J. A. E. Vermaat, *Kerk en tegenkerk* (1972), p. 72.

26. D. P. Gaines, *The World Council of Churches* (1964), p. 837.

27. P. G. Schrotenboer, *The Bible and the World Council of Churches* (1976), p. 2.

28. *Faith and Order, Louvain* (1971), p. 11; see also P. G. Schrotenboer, *The Bible and the World Council of Churches*, p. 8.

29. *Ibid.*, pp. 21, 22.

30. *Uppsala 1968*, p. 25.

31. Evanston Speaks, pp. 42, 43.

32. Official Report Geneva, p. 115.

33. P. G. Schrotenboer, *The Social Teachings of the World Council of Churches* (1977), p. 24.

34. *Ibid.*, p. 22.

35. See C. M. McIntire, *Twentieth Century Reformation* (1946³) and *The Modern Tower of Babel* (1949); see also D. Hedegard, *Ecumenism and the Bible* (1954). On the National Association of Evangelicals, see B. Shelley, *Evangelicalism in America* (1967); D. F. Wells and J. D. Woodbridge, *The Evangelicals* (1975).

36. P. G. Schrotenboer, *The Reformed Ecumenical Synod: A Venture in Confessional Ecumenism* (1965) and *The R.E.S.: A Call to Authentic Ecumenism* (1966).

Chapter 12

1. *A Treasury of Literary Masterpieces*, ed. A. H. Morehead (1969⁶), p. 28.

2. A. G. van Kranendonk, *Geschiedenis van de Amerikaanse literatuur*, Vol. II (1947), p. 214.

3. J. Huizinga, *Mensch en menigte in Amerika* (1928³), p. 170.

4. Quoted by B. Shelley, *Evangelicalism in America* (1967), pp. 59, 60.

5. N. B. Stonehouse, *J. Gresham Machen* (1954), pp. 351-3.

6. *Ibid.*, p. 355.

7. G. C. Berkouwer, *Op de tweesprong* (no date), p. 216.

8. See J. H. Gerstner in *The Evangelicals*, ed. Wells and Woodbridge (1975), p. 30. For a slightly different summary, see B. Shelley, *Evangelicalism in America*, p. 62.

9. See C. G. Aalders, "Het Dispensationalism in Amerika," G.T.T. (1947), pp. 2-16; H. M. Conn, *Contemporary World Theology* (1973), pp. 106-24; J. I. Packer, *Fundamentalism and the Word of God* (1964).

10. Dr. G. A. McLennan, quoted by H. W. Coray, in *The Outlook*, November 1977, p. 11.

11. J. G. Machen, *The Christian Faith in the Modern World* (1936), pp. 52, 53.

12. Stonehouse, *J. Gresham Machen*, pp. 367, 368.

13. *Ibid.*, p. 342.

14. *Ibid.*, pp. 357, 375.

15. *Ibid.*, pp. 345, 346.

16. P. Woolley, *The Significance of J. Gresham Machen Today* (1977), p. 41.

17. *Ibid.*, p. 42; Stonehouse, *J. Gresham Machen*, pp. 503ff.

18. Stonehouse, *J. Gresham Machen*, p. 438.

19. The whole "Social Creed" is in J. A. Hutchinson, *We Are Not Divided* (1941), pp. 46, 47.

20. *Ibid.*, p. 44.

21. W. Rauschenbusch, *A Theology for the Social Gospel* (1918), p. 224.

22. H. G. Cox, *The Secular City* (1965), p. 258.

23. H. B. Kuhn, in *Tensions in Contemporary Theology*, ed. Gundry and Johnson (1976), p. 184.

24. F. D. Bruner, *A Theology of the Holy Spirit* (1970), p. 120.

25. A. A. Hoekema, *Holy Spirit Baptism* (1972), p. 9.

26. Kurt Hutten, *Seher, Grübler, Enthusiasten* (1958⁵), p. 515.

27. E. T. Clark, *The Small Sects in America* (1949), p. 107.

28. The Dutch leader was G. R. Polman; see A. B. W. M. Kok, *Waarheid en Dwaling* (no date), pp. 297, 298.

29. His detailed personal description of this experience is to be found in Bruner, *A Theology of the Holy Spirit*, pp. 121-4.

30. E. von Eicken, *Heiliger Geist, Menschengeist, Schwarmgeist* (1964), pp. 31, 32.

31. Kok, *Waarheid en Dwaling*, p. 301.

32. L. Steiner, *Mit folgenden Zeichen: Eine Darstellung der Pfingstbewegung* (1954), p. 173.

33. P. J. du Plessis, "The World Wide Pentecostal Movement," in *Pentecost*, August 1960, p. 22.

34. *Christianity Today*, September 13, 1963.

35. W. van 't Spijker, *De charismatische beweging* (1977), pp. 12ff.

Chapter 13

1. M. P. van Dijk, in *Credo*, March 1978, p. 3.
2. S. Vestdijk, *De toekomst der religie* (1947).
3. *Politisches Nachtgebet*, quoted in J. Sperna Weiland, *Voortgezette Orientatie* (1971), pp. 80, 81.
4. *De Waarheidsvriend*, February 17, 1972.
5. Heidelberg Catechism, Answer 117.
6. Especially in his three-volume work *Das Prinzip Hoffnung* (1959); also in *Thomas Münzer als Theologe der Revolution* and *Atheismus im Christentum* (1968).
7. J. A. Visser, *Karl Marx en Lenin als kerkvaders* (1975), p. 40; see also M. P. van Dijk, *De uitdaging van het neo-marxisme* (1974), pp. 17ff; J. Sperna Weiland, *Voortgezette Orientatie*, pp. 24ff; R. Gosker, *Dialoog zonder dreiging* (1976), pp. 89ff.
8. M. P. van Dijk, *De uitdaging van het neo-marxisme*, pp. 22ff; J. Verkuyl, *Voorbereiding voor de dialoog over het evangelie en de ideologie van het marxistisch leninisme*, second printing (no date), pp. 60ff.
9. S. U. Zuidema, *De revolutionaire maatschappijkritiek van Herbert Marcuse* (1970).
10. J. W. Montgomery, *The Suicide of Christian Theology* (1975³), p. 212.
11. E. Käsemann, *Das neue Testament als Kanon* (1970), p. 407.
12. G. Maier, *The End of the Historical-Critical Method* (1977), pp. 26-49.
13. E. Schillebeekx, *Jezus van Nazareth en het heil der wereld* (1975); M. P. van Dijk, *Theologie tussen gisteren en morgen* (1977), p. 115.
14. H. M. Conn, *Contemporary World Theology* (1973), p. 54.
15. In his article entitled "What is Wrong with 'Dialectic' Theology?"
16. J. A. T. Robinson, *Honest to God* (1963), pp. 78, 79.
17. Harold B. Kuhn, in *Tensions in Contemporary Theology* (1976), p. 178.
18. *Encounter*, September 1963; see also J. W. Montgomery, *The Suicide of Christian Theology*, p. 51.
19. Montgomery, *The Suicide of Christian Theology*, p. 199.
20. D. F. Freeman, in the *Westminster Theological Journal*, Vol. I (1973), p. 112.
21. *Offenbarung als Geschichte* (1963; English edition, 1968).
22. W. Pannenberg, *Jesus—God and Man* (1968), pp. 88, 89.
23. W. Pannenberg, *Grundfragen systematischer Theologie* (1967), p. 393.
24. M. P. van Dijk, *Afscheid van de polarisatie* (1972), p. 30.
25. *Ibid.*, p. 32.
26. J. Moltmann, *Religion, Revolution and the Future* (1969), p. 141.
27. J. Moltmann, *The Church in the Power of the Spirit* (1977).
28. J. Moltmann, *Religion, Revolution and the Future*, p. 143.
29. J. Sperna Weiland, *Voortgezette Orientatie*, p. 77.
30. Visser, *Karl Marx en Lenin als kerkvaders*, p. 58.
31. J. M. Bonino, *Christians and Marxists* (1976), pp. 29, 30.
32. *Ibid.*, p. 135.
33. See M. P. van Dijk, *Theologie tussen gisteren en morgen*, p. 102.
34. P. Reckman, "Naar een strategie en metodiek voor sociale aktie," quoted by H. Algra in *De revolutie permanent* (1974). Algra compares this position with that of Rousseau (pp. 19ff).
35. G. de Ru, *De verleiding der revolutie* (1976²), p. 125.
36. H. Algra, *De revolutie permanent*, p. 23.
37. In the series "Korte Verklaring der Heilige Schrift met Nieuwe Vertaling" and "Kommentaren op de Heilige Schrift" (both since 1922).

38. G. W. de Jong, *De theologie van dr. G. C. Berkouwer* (1971), p. 2.

39. Also noteworthy were the works of W. Geesink, *Gereformeerde Ethiek* (1931) and of G. Brillenburg Wurth, *Het christelijk leven* (1951).

40. J. H. Bavinck wrote an excellent *Inleiding in de Zendingswetenschap* (1954).

41. In the Netherlands much has been written about this topic. A helpful survey on both sides is presented in the article on "Vrijmaking" in the *Christelijke Encyclopaedie*, Vol. VI (1961²). I have written about the situation at some length in Chapter 11 of *Het Dwaze Gods* (1950).

42. H. Berkhof, "De methode van Berkouwers theologie," in *Ex Auditu Verbi* (1965), pp. 37ff.

43. G. W. de Jong, *De theologie van dr. G. C. Berkouwer*, p. 46.

44. Especially in *De Heilige Schrift*, two volumes (1966-67). See the criticism of C. Van Til in *The New Synthesis Theology in the Netherlands* (1975), pp. 62ff.

45. G. C. Berkouwer, *De Heilige Schrift*, Vol. II, pp. 314, 315; De Jong, *De theologie van dr. G. C. Berkouwer*, p. 215.

46. Quoted by M. J. Antzen, *Ootmoed of hoogmoed* (1973), p. 126.

47. In his lecture on "Schepping en evolutie" (Report of the Conference on Questions of Evolution, 1966, pp. 25-38).

48. H. M. Kuitert, *Verstaat gij wat gij leest?* (1968), p. 60.

49. C. Augustijn, *Kerk en belijdenis* (1969), pp. 72, 73.

50. H. Ridderbos, *Zijn wij op de verkeerde weg?* (1972).

51. B. Wentsel, *Hij voor ons, wij voor Hem* (1973), p. 142.

52. Heidelberg Catechism, Answer 114.

53. W. Nigg, *Das ewige Reich: Geschichte einer Sehnsucht und einer Enttäuschung* (1944).

54. H. G. Leih, *De droom der revolutie* (no date).

55. *Christianity Today*, September 26, 1975.

56. Leih, *De droom der revolutie*, p. 191.

57. P. J. Bouman, *Vijfstromenland* (1959), pp. 66, 67.

Index of Names

Index of Principal Subjects